THE
———

BAR TLE TT

**SCHOOL
OF
ARCHITECTURE
UCL**

BARTLETT SCHOOL OF ARCHITECTURE 2012

In the 1990s the Bartlett, already an established institution, transformed itself into arguably the most influential School of Architecture on the British architectural scene. It accomplished this through experimentation: With new ideas and relentless invention staff and students dared to push the boundaries of architecture, creating a sense of exploring the unknown that re-energized the School. This encouraged a culture of individuality, promoting diversity and a great range of design positions that was exceptional at the time.

This new ethos continued into the first decade of the new millennium, informing the School's work from the ground up. The production of the School became more grounded and better known, and many units became established in their own right. Public appearances, new publications, and a flood of awards, confirmed the School's reputation. Ideas of the 90s became manifest and elaborated, challenged by changing tendencies in the wider international scene. But while so many other schools became obsessed with a rather orthodox interpretation of the digital, in which topological (surface-led) and parametric discourses became dominant, the Bartlett resisted this trend by pursuing a more culturally engaged approach that allowed for the impact of advanced technology to be understood in a more open and critical way. Rather than radicalising into one or another orientation, the Bartlett developed a more hybrid (for some 'unclear') attitude that crossbred the analogue and the digital, as well as combined historical/theoretical and design research cultures. The School flourished without fear of being too culturally oriented or insufficiently parametric, allowing instead a holistic approach to architecture to flourish.

Both the School and the larger profession are now in the process of profound change that is forcing us architects to rethink our field of action and to question our 'gravitas' in both professional practice and education. These changes do not only effect the way in which we understand our body and the natural and built environment, but also how we are exposed to new technological developments, such as digital-fabrication processes, intelligent and bio-materials, advances in a microscopic and nanoscopic scales, etc. The Bartlett is an interdisciplinary School of Architecture within a world-leading Faculty of the Built Environment, where staff and students are engaged in critical research. New ideas and solutions are uniquely found at the intersection of various disciplines. This is fostered by the School's tradition over the last 20 years of challenging prevailing dogmas that threaten the creative and critical contribution of architectural academia. An inherent diversity of positions, skills and methodologies, and a diverse range of media and subjects thrive throughout the School's studios and programmes.

The Bartlett today is not only a School known for its sophisticated design and theory; it is also a 'School of many schools' of thought and practice. The

Bartlett understands architecture as integrally connected to a cluster of other disciplines, and encourages each individual to find a path through this network to develop innovative approaches to architecture. In times of change, staff and students know how much there is at stake and that the Bartlett should be as a place for activism and agency rather than mere competency and accomplishment. It is a place that avoids a strictly vocational response to a shifting context by stimulating risk-taking people who aim to contribute to the world through true experimentation.

Key to this are the Bartlett's students, who continue to have a relentless drive for creation and invention. They are famous for their dexterity and ingenuity, their critical minds, their hard work and their outstanding achievement. Just look behind the drawings and models and you will recognise a body of lateral thinkers and designers who delve into prospective and original thinking. It is work that is inspired by history, but questions traditional models and aesthetics. It looks critically for innovation. It puts forward new realities and materialities, and probes with new social and political agendas. The Bartlett is, and will continue to be, ultimately irreverent in its architectural production.

Let us now thank you all for your tremendous efforts and dedication, which have again made this an extraordinary year. The School owes its success to all of you — our staff and students, our consultants, critics and examiners, as well as our sponsors and friends. It has been a great privilege to work with you all once again.

Frédéric Migayrou
Bartlett Professor of Architecture

Marcos Cruz
Director of the Bartlett School of Architecture

PART 3

PGCAAR

GRAD. ARCHITECTURAL DESIGN

URBAN DESIGN

MA ARCHITECTURAL HISTORY

PhD BY DESIGN

PhD HISTORY AND THEORY

SUMMER SCHOOL

SUMMER FOUNDATION

**The Bartlett School of Architecture
would like to thank Allford Hall
Monaghan Morris for their generous
support of this year's catalogue.**

**ALLFORD
HALL
MONAGHAN
MORRIS**

Morelands
5-23 Old Street
London EC1V 9HL
T 020 7251 5261
info@ahmm.co.uk
www.ahmm.co.uk

Project: Dagenham Park Church of England School
Client: Thames Partnership for Learning and
         London Borough of Barking & Dagenham

fletcher priest architects
london + kōln + rıga

Rogers Stirk Harbour + Partners

Foster + Partners

**ALLFORD
HALL
MONAGHAN
MORRIS**

VAa
Vidal y Asociados arquitectos

JOHN M^cASLAN + PARTNERS

The Bartlett School of Architecture would like to thank our sponsors for their generous support

—

**The Bartlett School of Architecture
would like to thank Foster + Partners
for their generous support of this
year's Summer Show.**

Foster + Partners
www.fosterandpartners.com

fletcher priest architects
trust

Rogers Stirk Ha

pour + Partners

Design

Professional
Studies

History & Theory

Technology

Research

DESIGN

The term 'design' derives from the Italian *disegno*, meaning drawing, and suggesting both the drawing of a line and the drawing forth of an idea. *Disegno* allowed the three visual arts — architecture, painting and sculpture — to be recognised as liberal arts concerned with ideas, a status that they had rarely been accorded previously. In 1563 Giorgio Vasari founded the first art academy, the *Accademia del Disegno* in Florence. The academy replaced workshop instruction with education in subjects such as drawing and geometry, which emphasised the visual arts' association with the intellect.

A model for art and architecture schools ever since, Vasari's academy enabled painters, sculptors and architects to converse independently of the craft guilds.

In the new division of labour, architects acquired complementary means to practice architecture that became as relevant as building, namely drawing and writing. Consequently, architects — especially influential ones — tend to talk, write and draw as well as build. Sebastiano Serlio and Andrea Palladio are notable early exponents of this tradition, and Le Corbusier and Rem Koolhaas are more recent ones.

The architect as we understand the term today was established in Italy in around 1450, in France a century later and in Britain in the following century with Inigo Jones. But the history of design from the fifteenth century to the twenty-first has not been seamless; a significant departure occurred in the nineteenth century due to industrialisation, which gave new emphasis to the architect's role in the production of artefacts as well as ideas, while the advent of CAD/CAM now aligns thinking and making in a manner that references the thirteenth century as well as the twenty-first.

From the new foundation programme to doctoral research, the Bartlett School of Architecture encourages and emphasises design experimentation that is informed by social responsibility and stimulated by the creative dialogue between writing and making, and analogue and digital drawing. The relations between the drawing, text, artefact and building are multi-directional. For example, drawing may lead to building. But writing may also lead to making, or building may lead to writing and drawing. If everyone reading this text listed all the architectural works that influence them, some would be drawings, some would be texts, and others would be buildings, artefacts and spaces either visited or described in drawings and texts. Studying the history of architecture, it is evident that researching, testing and questioning the limits of architecture occur through drawing, writing and making as well as building.

Professor Jonathan Hill
Director of Design

PRIZES

BSc Arch Year 1

Good Honours' Standard Work Prize
Robin (Ruochong) Fu
Olivia Hornby
Ellie Sampson

Herbert Batsford Prize
Emily Priest

BSc Arch Year 2

Narinder Sagoo Drawing Prize
Matthew Lyall

Grocer's Company Scholarship
Isobel Parnell

BSc Arch Year 3

Donaldson Medal
Brook (Ting Jui) Lin

Fitzroy Robinson Drawing Prize (Digital)
Fergus Knox

Fitzroy Robinson Drawing Prize (Hand drawing)
Brook (Ting Jui) Lin

Dean's List
Brook (Ting Jui) Lin
Luke Scott
Samuel Douek
Sarah Edwards
Marcus Stockton
Ashley Hinchcliffe
Fergus Knox
Matthew Lucraft
Alec Scragg
Cherry Beaumont
Christopher Worsfold
Amy Begg

MArch Arch Year 4

Rogers Stirk Harbour Bursary
Alice Brownfield

MArch Architecture Year 5

Sir Banister Fletcher Medal
Ifigeneia Liangi

Bartlett Design Research Award
Emma Flynn

Fitzroy Robinson Drawing Prize
Martin Man Fai Tang
Thomas Smith

*Rogers Stirk Harbour Bursary
(2010–2011)*
William Fisher

Dean's List
Carmelo Arancon
Janinder Bhatti
Kwan Kit Franky Chan
Jonathan Cohen
Emily Farmer
Emma Flynn
Sophie George
Mina Gospavic
Patrick Hamdy
Thomas Harvey
Katherine Hegab
Amy Hiley
Louisa Danielle Hodgson
Julian Zi Huang
Birgir Örn Jónsson
Madhav Kidao
James Kitson
Maria Knutsson-Hall
Michelle Lam
Ifigeneia Liangi
Ned Scott
Joseph Ransom Shaw
Thomas Smith
Yeung Piu So
Yi Su
Martin Tang
Gabriel Warshafsky
Sam Welham
Richard Wood

PROFESSIONAL STUDIES

From day one, architecture students are asked to question the role and function of the architect in a profession and the construction industry which are constantly in state of change through innovation in design and procurement; technological advances; economic pressures and politics.

The Professional Studies team commitment to delivering high quality education in professional matters runs throughout the school's teaching and learning at undergraduate and postgraduate level.

The teaching programmes draw on a wide range of expertise. The multi-disciplinary structure of the Faculty provides a community where preconceptions are continually challenged through encounters with fellow students, teachers (many of whom run their own practices) and numerous visiting experts.

Students' own individuality, their ambitions and career aspirations are nurtured within the framework of innovative professional studies courses, as well as through informal advice on practice and employment.

The Bartlett School of Architecture has an outstanding track record in the range of practices that graduates later join, ranging from the smaller niche specialist design practices to multi-disciplinary global conglomerates.

Susan Ware
Director of Professional Studies

PRIZES

BSc Architecture Year 3

Professional Studies Prize
Anna Lisa McSweeney

Part 3

Ross Jamieson Memorial Prize
Benjamin Ridley — Summer 2011
Alan Worn — Autumn 2011

YEAR 1 — THE PRODUCTION OF THE BUILT ENVIRONMENT

BSc architecture students work with Planning and Construction and Project Management students on the 'Production of the Built Environment' course which introduces the various professionals and organisations involved with the process of producing buildings, towns and cities. The broader social, political and economic forces are explored through project work both individually and in multidiscipline group work. A field trip in term 2 enables students to apply the analytical skills interpreting the context of the built environment taught in the first term in a European city.

YEAR 3 — PREPARING FOR PRACTICE

In preparation for the year out in practice students are introduced to the practice of architecture through research-led group presentations and lectures into selected subjects. Students gain an understanding of the construction process and the possible range of experiences available during a year working in practice. The understanding of roles and responsibility of the architect in the design, procurement and construction of projects inform the students' design work. Students are introduced to architectural practice and management, current professional issues and the processes and relationships within the construction industry, including the brief, construction team, communication, sustainability, cost and economics, contracts and professional liability.

THE YEAR OUT

The year out course continues the students' connection with the Bartlett and provides career guidance, support and monitoring of practical experience through individual tutorials and themed recall lecture and seminar days.

YEAR 4 — DESIGN REALISATION PROGRAMME

The Design Realisation course in year 1 of the two-year MArch (ARB/RIBA Part 2) programme brings together professional practice, technology and construction through a unique configuration of individual design units, practice tutors, technical consultants and visiting lecturers. The course introduces students to core knowledge that is required in the realisation of buildings in professional architectural design practice. Students consider the influence of, and develop an attitude towards, the construction, technology and the profession, which are all seen as having an integral role within the creative design process. Students are introduced to elementary matters involved in running of architectural consultancies and building projects; the progression of works from commission to completion and the broad range of strategies that influence the design and construction of buildings. Students will demonstrate through an individually authored report an advanced understanding of and significant abilities in core knowledge that is required in the realisation of buildings.

ARB/RIBA PART 3

The ARB/RIBA part 3 course and examination is open to non-Bartlett students and is truly international, attracting candidates from over 25 different countries. The course prepares candidates for registration as an architect in the UK through a comprehensive modular taught course. The Part 3 lecture course is available for architectural practices as CPD.

ARB PRESCRIBED EXAMINATION PREPARATION WORKSHOPS

The Bartlett in association with the RIBA North West and ARB provide a workshop programme to guide international students wishing to register as architects in the UK under the EU Qualifications Directive though the preparation of documentation and presentation of portfolios for the ARB Prescribed Examination.

HISTORY & THEORY

Architectural history and theory is a staging post, a provisional place of reflection, a continual project. And it is omnipresent, for every architect, every historian, every theorist, whether knowingly or not, uses some intersection of history and theory every time they design, document, discuss or speculate.

At the Bartlett, architectural history and theory interjects at all levels, from introductions to architectural analysis, from encounters with buildings to the elaboration of critical processes, from public discussions to individually focused research projects, and from factually-based empirical studies to theorised speculations and creative writing practices.

Professor Iain Borden
Director of Architectural History & Theory

Ashley Hinchcliffe
Soy Cuba — A Childish Perspective?
MArch Architecture Year 4 History & Theory
Tutor: Dr. Jan Birksted

When watching the film Soy Cuba (directed by Mikhail Kalatozov , 1964) it is not only the camera movements or the monochromatic film which represent childhood experiences – it's their combination with the details: a small flicker of light; a moving reflection on a glass surface; the rough texture on a wall; a shining piece of metal; splinters on a piece of wood; a shadow passing across a face; the cracks between paving slabs; a trouser leg rippling in the wind; and air bubbles in water.

These are only my personal observations. If someone else were to watch Soy Cuba their noticeable details would be different. These details are prominent because of the proximity to objects, the angles we are observing

from, but, significantly, we are observing the details as we would in reality traveling through the landscape, and not due to magnification or montage. This is where the dream-like, imaginary world of a child comes to life in Soy Cuba. The combination of camera movements and small details culminate in moments where the imagination of director Kalatozov merge with our perception and memory, and enhanced by high contrast black-and-white film. The infrared lens used in Soy Cuba to create this extreme contrast also emphasises the dreamlike: "In great architectural spaces there is a constant deep breathing of light, shadow inhales and illumination exhales".

PRIZES

BSc Architectural Studies

History and Theory Prize for Distinguished Work
Seth Pimlott

BSc Architecture Year 3

History and Theory Prize for Distinguished Work
Ashley Hinchcliffe

MArch Architecture Year 4

History & Theory Prize
Douglas Fenton

MArch Architecture Year 5

Ambrose Poynter Prize
Tia Randall

RIBA President's Medal for Dissertation nomination
Mathew Leung

ERA SAVVIDES
Nicosia 2012: What Culture?
Contested Identities and a Blurred Urban Agenda
BSc Year 3 Dissertation
Tutor: Professor Murray Fraser

The "question of culture" reflects on how collective intellectual and creative achievement have historically been used to legitimize certain behaviours, practices, traditions and ways of living. As the world moves closer through globalisation and an apparent tendency towards a more generic aesthetic, the role of cultural identity emerges as a central question. This essay discusses global tendencies in relation to cultural as well as ethnic distinctiveness of localised identities. In addition, to identify architecture's response, or the lack thereof, to such trends, it examines specific moments of collision where distinct local identities are in a state of reaction or mutation in the face of global tendencies. Where is the role of localised cultural identity within the global city? How do we forge creative co-existence of these apparently opposed forces? Wherein lie opportunities for architectural creativity within this complex globalisation?

The essay focuses on Cyprus, examined through two contrasting case studies: 'The Mall of Cyprus' and the competition-winning redevelopment proposal by Zaha Hadid for Eleftheria Square in the old centre of Nicosia. While the former is the first true shopping mall on the island, feeding into an identity crisis already present within the Cypriot socio-cultural fabric, the latter tries to re-establish a sense of urbanism in a decaying historic area and remains the subject of heated local debates over its de-constructivist form. By analysing complex economic, social and political centre-periphery dynamics, the essay suggests a bittersweet relationship between these seemingly independent projects.

TECHNOLOGY

Readers would expect that technology and design have an intimate and intrinsic relationship in creating the built environment. They might also know that the integration of these subjects in architectural education and practice is increasingly complex, non-linear, exciting, and daunting, and that this coupling has been the focus of heated debate for an eternity. This is a debate in which we revel, provoke and participate.

Following last summer's show, we ran a technology forum for all associated staff, and in the presence of invited guests from academia and practice, trained a spotlight on everything we and our students do, in and around the teaching and understanding of technology in architecture. It was an informed and constructive debate, and one that recognised how seriously our students commit to this field of research, and how innovative, witty, and creative their response so often is.

What is evident in their work, is that Bartlett students approach technology, environmental and computing modules as an ambitious design study. They observe, they learn, they experiment, they act, and most of all, they contribute.

This practice is nurtured by an extraordinarily dedicated and diverse staff collective in a progression of sequential steps from the deep end of Year 1, to the testing grounds of Year 2 and Year 4, and the laboratories of Years 3 and 5 (further comment on Years 4 & 5 can be found later in this volume).

On this footing, 2011-12 has been another year of progress making. All technology lectures are now open to all students, and include international guests and local pioneers. The pool of world-class support consultants has expanded and diversified, and the forum has been rescheduled to run again this summer. Next year we can look forward to a +£400k further investment in additional state of the art facilities, as the tools, techniques, and questions of how we design and make the built environment continues to evolve. In the meantime, our confidence in our students' ability to grapple with and address the grand challenges of our time with intelligence, dedication and skill is running high.

Bob Sheil
Director of Technology & Computing

PRIZES

BSc Architecture Year 3

Environmental Design Prize
Matthew Lucraft

Making Buildings Prize
Gary Edwards

BSc Architecture Year 4

Leverhulme Trust Bursary
Samantha Rive
Biten Patel

Design Technology Prize Nominees
Graham Burn
Tamsin Hanke
Joanna Pawlas
Tom Svilans
Viktor Westerdahl

BSc Architecture Year 5

Leverhulme Trust Bursary
Negin Ghorbani-Moghaddam

RESEARCH

The Bartlett School of Architecture has a world leading research profile, created by the excellent and original work produced by its staff and the considerable impact that this work has on design culture and scholarship on an international level. This position of leadership is reflected in our achievement of the highest rating among the Architecture and Built Environment submissions to the UK 2008 Research Assessment Exercise (RAE), with the highest percentage of 'world leading' (4*) staff outputs.

Our research advances five principal fields of knowledge: architectural history and theory, architectural design and the production of buildings, urban design and theory, advanced technology and computation, and design research. These fields correspond to the undergraduate and postgraduate teaching streams of the School where we attach great value to the ongoing interaction between research, teaching and learning.

Many of us work across these fields, overlapping traditional boundaries and pointing to new transdisciplinary research areas. The outcomes of our research include authored and edited books, landscape and urban proposals, buildings, prototypes, conceptual designs, exhibitions, installations, competition entries, digital archives, refereed articles and chapters.

Some of the areas we are currently working on include: the spatial, material and contextual innovation of design; advanced aesthetics; design history and criticism; sustainable communities and urbanism; proposals for new environmental strategies; historical scholarship in the area of modernism across cultures; the study of the everyday life of buildings, local sites and communities; critical spatial theory and practice; site writing; craft and digital fabrication; material knowledge and innovation; biotechnology; advanced computation and robotics; new technologies of representation, performativity and interactivity; architecture's intersection with fine art, geography, philosophy, anthropology, environmental engineering, biology and computer science.

Situated within UCL, our research culture reflects the University's position and its Grand Challenges in Sustainable Cities, Global Health, Intercultural Interaction and Human Wellbeing. The Faculty of the Built Environment and other University departments offer a wealth of expertise and we increasingly team up with colleagues across the Faculty and UCL.

Our large international student communities in the MA, MArch and PhD programmes are a key constituency in the School's research culture and so we continuously foster a variety of research exchanges between tutors, supervisors and students. These exchanges are increasingly enriched by the vibrant community of part-time staff and specialist consultants, who share their own knowledge and research questions with the School on a weekly basis.

Located within the centre of London, we are privileged to have many opportunities to collaborate on research projects with the most creative professional practices, industries and organisations, while we also work with a variety of national and international partners, research centres, and public engagement institutions.

TThe following list presents a selection of achievements by research staff during this year.

Dr Yeoryia Manolopoulou
Director of Architectural Research

PRIZES

STAFF RESEARCH AWARDS

Selected Awards and Honours

Professor Adrian Forty
RIBA Honorary Fellowship, 2012

Niall McLaughlin
'Student Accommodation, Somerville College'
AIA Excellence in Design Award, 2012

Niall McLaughlin
'C4D, Cranfield University'
RIAI Award for Best Over Seas Project, 2011, and RIBA Award, 2011

Professor Jane Rendell
'Site-Writing:
The Architecture of Art Criticism'
Commendation for University-located

Research, RIBA President's Awards for Research, 2011

Dr Tania Sengupta
'Producing the Province: Colonial governance and spatial cultures in district headquarter towns in Eastern India'
Shortlist for RIBA President's Award f or Outstanding PhD Thesis, 2011

sixteen*(makers)
'55/02'
RIBA Award, 2011

PAVILIONS FOR LONDON

The Greater London Authority has selected five design research teams to realise temporary architectural installations for the London Olympics and

Paralympics 2012:

Laura Allen and Mark Smout (SmoutAllen), Professor Iain Borden, Luke Pearson and Sandra Youkhana
'Universal Tea Machine'

Alisa Andrasek and Jose Sanchez (biothing)
'BLOOM _ Crowd Sourced Garden'

Dr Marjan Colletti and Dr Marcos Cruz (marcosandmarjan)
'The ALGA(e)zebo'

Professor cj Lim, John Chang, Samson Lau and Martin Tang
'Tr(ee)logy'

Dr Yeoryia Manolopoulou and Anthony Boulanger (AY Architects)
'House of Flags'

BSc Architecture

BSc Architectural Studies

ANNEX TO THE BARTLETT

Frosso Pimenides, Patrick Weber

Year 1 Staff: **Tim Barwell, Margaret Bursa, Johan Hybschman, Lucy Leonard, Brian O'Reilly, Sara Shafiei, Matt Springett, Nikolas Travasaros**

The Bartlett's BSc degree programme aims to develop a creative, diverse and rigorous approach to architecture and design from the outset. Year 1 is centred on the design studio and is taught to the year as a whole. Students learn to observe, draw, model and design, through a series of creative tasks before embarking on an individual small building project sited in the context of London.

The main intention of the first year at the Bartlett is to explore 'ways of seeing' - understanding and interpreting objects/events/places and learning to look beyond the visible into the unseen and 'absurd' qualities of things and places. In this way, a place can also be seen as something with its own identity, which each student can personally interpret. The importance of 'character' and 'personality' is emphasised throughout the design process whether it concerns analysis, site interpretation or architectural vision. A number of recording techniques are used as a way of clarifying the subject rather than as purely graphic representation. Through being aware of the possibilities and limitations of various techniques, each student is learning to express and then develop critically and appropriately, through their own intuition, an idea for an architectural proposition.

In the first year architecture is explored individually through cultivating ideas, exploring imagination and nurturing curiosity. Students explore, describe and communicate their ideas through a range of two- and three-dimensional techniques. The aim is to be serious, passionate and ruthlessly experimental - always pushing the boundaries of possible realities.
Being open and naïve in their working method, students are encouraged to take risks - not being afraid of making mistakes is forming the basis of the approach as they often form the basis of a new idea, a different way to see the world around them. It is the path to new possible architectures.

Students started the year by exploring ideas around the term 'Annex'. Through a series of iterations they designed a device that allowed them to annex themselves to a specific location or situation in London. After this they worked in groups on an installation project in Sir John Soane's Country House Pitzhanger Manor in Ealing. Each of the six groups explored the space through the installation of a site-specific interpretation of a piece of furniture (chair, table, wardrobe, chest, desk and bed) and a building material (brick, glass, wood, brass, lead, stone). In term 2 the whole year explored Istanbul through surveying and interpretation. A 'Section' though a very specific location was chosen as the vehicle to narrate their findings.

From February onwards each student was asked to develop and design a building sited in London Fields in East London. Interpreting the idea of a 'Library' each student developed an annex to the existing site. Students investigated the local site, history and culture; translating and incorporating these 'findings' into their ideas and building designs. A profound understanding of the 'site' and the magic of the place formed the basis for the work.

The buildings ranged from a local Herb Library, a Natural Dye Library, a Puppet Library and Theatre, a Library for Botanical Illustrations specific to the site, to a strategic building starting the reforestation of the fields over the next 100 years.

Year 1 Students: Nadira Amrani, Alexandria Anderson, Charlotte Archer, Laurence Blackwell-Thale, Matthew Bovingdon-Downe, Daryl Brown, Tom Budd, Max Butler, Amanda Campbell, Supichaya Chaisiriroj, Joyce (Xi Yao) Chen, Muzhi Chen, Yvonne Cheng, Harry Clover, Marcus Cole, Emma Colthurst, George Courtauld, Douglas Croll, John Cruwys, Clare Dallimore, Christophe Dembinski, Rufus Edmondson, Alexandra Edwards, Chloe Ellis, Katharine Feltwell, David Flook, Robin (Ruochong) Fu, Christian Georcelin, Robin (Xiang) Gu, Claire Haugh, Jamie Hignett, Konrad Holtsmark, Olivia Hornby, Casper Horton-Kitchlew, Mouna Kalia-Sacranie, Ysabel Kaye, Dina Khaki, Emma (Fong Yi) Khoo, Jaemin Kim, Min (Minkyoung) Kim, Suhee Kim, Will Kirkby, Karen Ko, Tomiris Kupzhassarova, Greg (Gregorios) Kythreotis, Paalan Lakhani, Maggie Lan, Shirley Lee Mei Ying, Perry (Wenhao) Li, Lichao Liu, Frances (Lingzhe) Lu, Lisa McDanell, Smiti Mittal, Ian Ng, Huynh Nguyen, Qianwen Ou, Nic (Cheol-Young) Park, Bethany Penman, Catherine Penn, Abigail Portus, Emily Priest, George Proud, Cassidy Reid, Louise Rymell, Ellie Sampson, Jack Sardeson, Akil Scafe-Smith, Claire Seager, Saskia Selwood, Rose Shaw, Laura Skeggs, Elin Soderberg, Sarah Stone, Chris Straessle, Carolyn Tam, Sam Tan, Benedict Tay, Ivo Tedbury, Joshua Toh, Joe Travers-Jones, Hei Man (Isabelle) Tung, Daisy Ursell, Marie Walker-Smith, Aviva (Yiren) Wang, Jessica Wang, Angus Whitehead, Timmy Whitehouse, Simon Wimble, Carolyn Wong, Max Worrell, Andrew Yap, Park Hin Yeung, Angel (Anqi) Yu

Fig. Y1.1 Small drawing room/chest/lead. Both lead, the material, and a chest, as a furnishing, have qualities that extend further than their physical presence. The installation attempted to convey the subtlety of these while manipulating the viewer into engaging with the room in a new way. Through its uses, lead conveys a strong sense of curiosity and balance — it is polished and attractive, yet toxic. The chest is an object linked with protection as you lock away your possessions in order to keep them from harm. The lock thus becomes paramount to create this security, and the piece can be seen as a device you must engage with in order to disclose the room's history that might otherwise be overlooked. Due to a natural curiosity to participate with the new, visitors interact with the piece, moving handles to attempt to align and understand its workings. Through changing the focal lines that run through the slides, the observer is influenced into appreciating the small, often mundane details of the room that although may seem insignificant actually tell the rich story of inhabitation in the space.

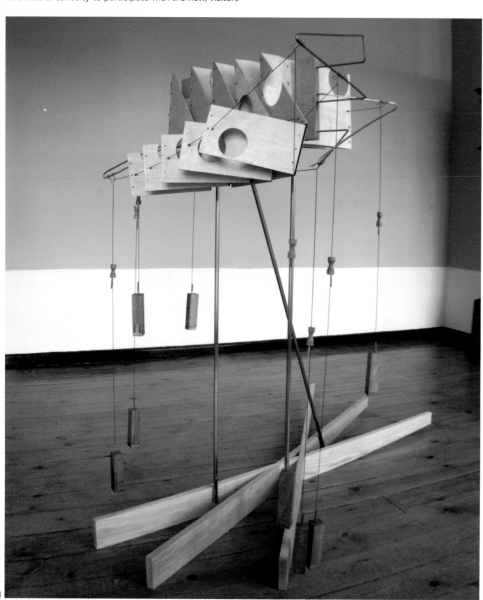

Y1.1

Fig. Y1.2 — Y1.3 While there is a sense of deliberate orientation, it is contradicted by the ability to personally navigate your view to a partial degree. The installation was fundamentally pivoted between the many interrelating halves that seem to be opposed to each other yet actually rely on their conflicting elements in order to retain balance; be it physical, theoretical or aesthetic. **Fig. Y1.4** The device is a tool to allowed the viewer to involve themselves with a room that may seem bare and lifeless at first. Having interacted with the piece, the participant is encouraged to explore the room without the limitations of the apparatus, thus directly understanding the space through personal interaction with it.

Y1.2

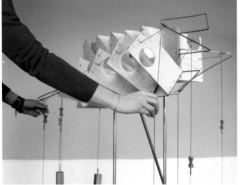

Y1.3

Y1.4

Fig. Y1.5 Upper drawing room/chair/brick. The response to the upper drawing room involved elevating the participant, allowing them to see over the recently added roof, to the landscape that Soane and his guests would have seen. Alongside these visual ties, the rising seat encouraged visitors to interact with one another, provoking social interaction within the room. The visual focus is the Cedar of Lebanon, which can be seen through the window. It is estimated to be three hundred years old, making it an unchanged feature from Soane's time in the house. Due to a series of extensions that occurred at Pitzhanger, the current roof hinders present visitors from indulging in Soane's garden and consequently this installation was tailored to raising a seated guest to a height that will enabled them to view the tree. The elevation of the person, physically allowed them to see over the roof that is indicative of the present day and the time that has passed and to see the tree that Soane would have seen, allowing the participant to experientially travel back in time. The aesthetic of the ramps refer to the repetitive nature of the brick and this was expressed through the repeated parallel planks. This slating technique, reminiscent of the positive and negative spaces linked to bricks and mortar were also referenced in the design of the seat.

Fig. Y1.6 Library/bed/brass. This installation was set in Soane's old Library, where he and his wife used to sit reading, sewing and socialising by the large window. Given the brief of a brass bed, the piece incorporated aspects of Soane's character and architectural intentions. There are similarities between dreams in a state of sleep and of losing yourself in a fictional dream whilst reading. Soane would often fantasise and create imaginary situations, drawing his architectural designs as ruins in the future. Manipulation and the turning through layers of history and book pages transports you to another world in a similar way to falling asleep. Soane believed the use of light to be a key element of architecture, and incorporated many convex, concave and large flat mirrors into his rooms to reflect and create infinite fantastical effects. There is a process of transition from awake to sleep, passing through the point of control to lack of control; the tipping point of balance to imbalance. This installation was designed to take you on this journey, from an awake state in the lit room to an enveloped dream-like space, distorting and intensifying the light directly as you fall further into the dream. This effect was achieved by standing on the two footplates, holding the handles and leaning forwards falling into the 'dream state'.

Y1.6

Fig. Y1.7 Monks dining room/desk/stone. The installation explored the moment of inspiration that can occur whilst seated at a desk. In conjunction with this it investigates the ideas of erosion and change. As the 'desk' is used, the view is altered, and specific areas are either framed or blocked from view. The process involved in this erodes the base of the installation. The piece was inspired by the story behind the Monk's Dining Room. Soane created the character of Padre Giovanni or 'Monk' the guardian of the 'ruins' in his garden. As pieces of the ruins fell into disrepair the monk would collect them and bring them into the monk's dining room in order to repair and archive them. In reality the room was used to store Soane's various artifacts, such as his fragmented casts of ruins. Inspired by its surroundings the installation was intended to archive and document it's own ruin over time. The movement of the arm and body piece wears away at the base below, and the channels are designed to collect the dust that forms. In order to study the moment of inspiration the installation focused on the window, and the idea that inspiration comes from both the exterior and the self. In this it was imagined the 'Monk' observing the ruins through the window.

Fig. Y1.8 Stairwell/wardrobe/wood. This installation was set out to capture the choreography of using a wardrobe to create a response, which would influence the views of another user of the device. This began through the research into the internal pockets of space within a wardrobe and the affect of exterior light; creating shafts and barriers within the casing. Tests were made using wood through Japanese joinery, along with hand made paper and examining the materiality of natural fragmentations. The group wanted to recreate the changing depths of a wardrobe; the transitions of light that occur within it and that were so significant to Soane's internal architecture. The device had resistance between itself and the user; creating a depth through the movement of fragments that corresponded with using a wardrobe. From below, it immersed the user through a dialogue of movements in Soane's stairwell. These subsequently influenced the path of views for the upper user; possibly even withdrawing the views from their control. This project set out to create a unique experience that highlights the features of the stairwell as Soane intended, whilst also allowing viewpoints to be manipulated from the basement of the stairwell. At this level glimpses through casted fragments revealed shafts of light from the above skylight; creating a series of views obscured by the pockets within the structured frame.

Y1.8

Y1.9

Fig. Y1.9 Breakfast room/table/glass. Described as the most sombre room in Pitzhanger Manor, the Breakfast Room can be interpreted as a space of contemplation and solitude. The group's initial experiments explored the concept of the table as a divider between the shared space above the table and the unknown space below the table. A glass table however, removes this division and effectively exposes the person who is seated in the space. In experiments glass was melted down, fused to other objects, crushed and encased to gain a more thorough understanding of it as a material. It was the property of transparency that was chosen. Experimenting and documenting different materials such as wax, glass wax, and salt crystals eventually led to soap as the material for the table. Through exploring the functions of a table, it became increasingly important that the installation made reference to the fact that Soane only ever used the space for a finite amount of time. It became the intention to re-enact this fleeting moment through the use of a fragmented surface coming together when a human interacts with it. Much like Soane's home, the surface of the table is made up of a varied collection of materials, each carefully encased in a crafted brass frame. The article that Soane blamed for his wife's death entitled 'Death Blows' forms the mapping structure for the surface of the table. The use of light in the installation was intended to amplify the object within the space, creating shadows on the walls and ceiling which moved with the surfaces distorting the viewer's perception of the space. **Fig. Y1.10** Studio Space.

THE EDGE OF LONDON
Murray Fraser, Pierre d'Avoine

The underlying aim of Unit 0 is for students to engage in a process of intensive research into contemporary architectural ideas, urban conditions, cultural relationships, practices of everyday life, and such like, and then for them to use their findings to propose innovative and challenging forms of architecture for contemporary London. Above all, students are expected to grasp the unique speculative space offered by academic study, yet combine this with a commitment to social engagement and urban improvement as if their project might actually be built. A clear understanding of the technological, environmental and developmental issues involved in their proposals is regarded as essential.

As the theme for this academic year, we asked students to think about the presence of edges and boundaries within the city. After all, buildings play vital roles as mediators and transitional zones between a wide variety of urban conditions that include:

Links between public and private spaces
Interstices between natural and man-made ecosystems
Prosthetic devices which extend the human body and senses
Connectors between areas of affluence and poverty

Boundary conditions such as walls therefore take on a double-edged existence, in that their presence can be seen as positive or negative - or even both at the same time. It was the task for students to define the terms in relation to the urban condition they had decided to engage with. Hence their design investigations were required to deal with issues of site, ground, space, form, occupation, performance and display. The designs arrived at were conceived as material forms at a scale which defined them as buildings - in other words, architectural propositions which are structural and environmental and as such engage with technology/craft and the means of production.

In order to locate these investigations, the sites for student projects were intended to be somewhere of their choosing on the north-eastern fringes of Regent's Park, close to Camden, or in the urban swathe through to Kings Cross. This area is no longer in the suburbs but 200 years ago it was literally the edge of London. Today it is an active boundary between the systems of biodiversity, economic life and social interaction which occur in Regent's Park and those in the surrounding streets. With the empty ditch that was once a spur of the Regent's Canal, or the nearby mini-city of London Zoo, or the copious bars and restaurants in Parkway, or the elegant villas of Park Village East and West, or the mainline railway that passes beneath on its way to Euston, or further to the east, the area offers a complex yet fractured borderline within the city.

Students were also expected to investigate the changing physical and social fabric of this part of London. Notably, more and more analysts are coming to the view that cities no longer have any meaningful 'physical limits'; theorists such as Henri Lefebvre long ago hinted that defined named cities would be supplanted by sprawling growth known as 'planetary urbanisation'. Therefore it seems ever more obvious that the edges that exist are within the complex fissures or folds inside urban entities such as London. In that sense, it was envisaged that the students' projects would explore the notion of edge, or boundary, to create designs that introduce different programmes and uses in an attempt to enhance the concept of urban interface.

To start off the year, the students were divided into groups of 3-4 people for the first few weeks to produce investigations and tentative designs for imaginary interstitial spaces around Regent's Park. In order to introduce a diversity of approaches, each of these groups was given a specific allocated scale: 1:1, 1:20, 1:500 or 1:10,000. Following these initial collaborative studies, each of the students pursued their own individual project for the remainder of the year, mostly in the area from Regent's Park to Kings Cross, although a couple of them chose to locate their project elsewhere in the city. As part of their research, students were also required to liaise closely with the structural engineer and environmental services designer for the unit. Out of this wide ranging investigatory process, a number of distinctive and original projects emerged.

Technical Tutors: Aran Chadwick (Atelier One), Bill Watts (Max Fordham LLC)

Visiting Critics: Ben Addy, Laura Allen, Alessandro Ayuso, Julia Backhaus, Anthony Boulanger, Mark Campbell, Rhys Cannon, Pereen d'Avoine, Jeff Day, William Firebrace, Penelope Haralambidou, Jonathan Hill, Damjan Iliev, Ben Kirk, Constance Lau, Guan Lee, Lucy Leonard, Jane McAllister, Luke Olsen, Frosso Pimenides, Laurence Pinn, Sophia Psarra, Mark Rist, Ingrid Schroder, Daniel Serafimovski, Yara Sharif, Ben Stringer, Mark Whitby

Year 2: Phoebe Nickols, Ka Yu Jamie Wong

Year 3: Ophelia Blackman, Ruthie Falconer, Roma Gadomska-Miles, Alice Haugh, David Hawkins, Elzbieta Kaleta, Kok Cin Lim, Shiue Nee Pang, Asha Pooran, Alec Scragg, Pippa Shaw Carveth, Lok Man Melody Siu

Fig. 0.1 Alec Scragg, 1:1 viewing device for looking at London from Primrose Hill (group project with Ophelia Blackman, Phoebe Nickols and Melody Siu), model. **Fig 0.2** Pippa Shaw Carveth, Pin-Wall test model with speakers. **Fig 0.3** Shiue Nee Pang, Bird's-eye perspective of new growing wall in Cumberland Street allotments (group project with Roma Gadomska-Miles and Alice Haugh). **Fig 0.4** Melody Siu, 1:1 first-person immersive perspective of voting booth for new Camden and Regents Park constituency (group project with Ophelia Blackman, Phoebe Nickols and Alec Scragg).

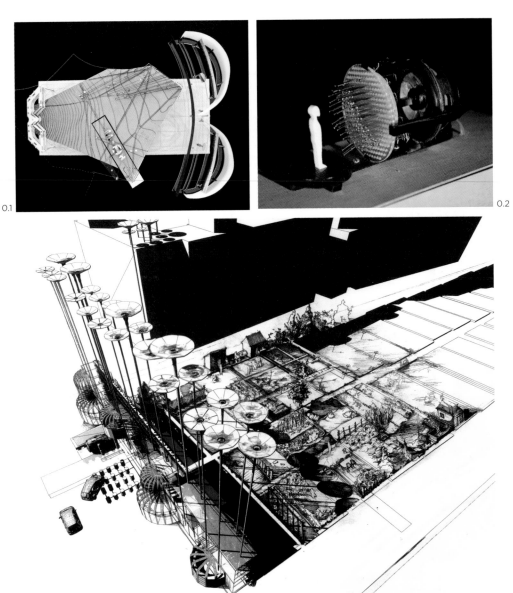

0.1

0.2

0.3

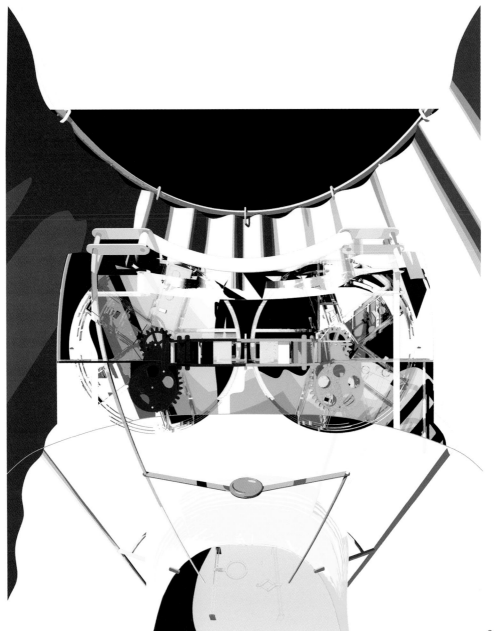

Fig. 0.5 Phoebe Nickols, Meat Market for breeding and eating exotic animals located next to Regent's Park Zoo, perspective from park. **Fig 0.6** Phoebe Nickols, Meat Market adjacent to Regent's Park Zoo, section. **Fig 0.7** David Hawkins, New inhabited structure for West Yard in Camden Market using scaffolding formwork previously used to create underground vaults, perspective.

0.5

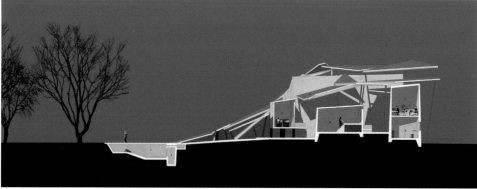

0.6

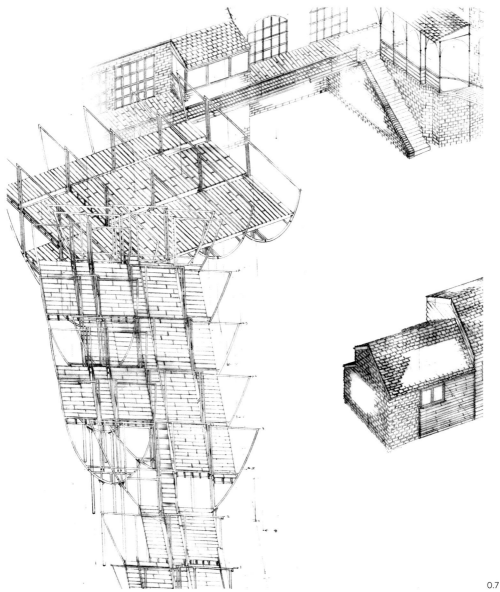

Fig 0.8 Shiue Nee Pang, Coffee growing centre and public allotments on King's Boulevard in the Kings Cross redevelopment area, perspective of street-level coffee bars. **Fig. 0.9** Roma Gadomska-Miles, Redevelopment scheme to turn the vacant Heygate Estate at Elephant and Castle into an urban farm with market building, roof plan.

0.8

0.9

Fig 0.10 David Hawkins, Study for underground vaults and above-ground scaffolding formwork in West Yard in Camden Market, model. **Fig 0.11** David Hawkins, Cast of excavation works for West Yard site, model. **Fig 0.12** Ela Kaleta, Public spa and flood control facility on Hampstead Heath, section cut through computer model. **Fig 0.13** Roma Gadomska-Miles, Redevelopment scheme for Heygate Estate, site model. **Fig 0.14** Kok Cin Lim, Floating tree market and management centre, Regents Canal, Camden, short section

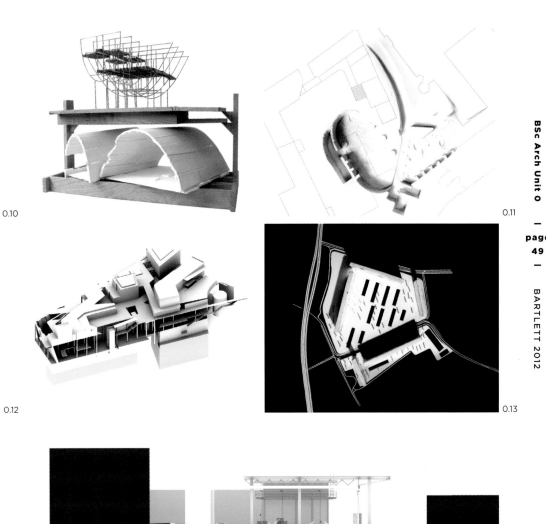

0.10

0.11

0.12

0.13

0.14

Fig 0.15 Roma Gadomska-Miles, Redevelopment scheme for Heygate Estate, bird's-eye perspective. **Fig 0.16** Kok Cin Lim, Floating tree market and management centre, Regents Canal, Camden, exploded isometric showing the components of the project. **Fig 0.17** Ruthie Falconer, Baths for weary commuters in King's Cross Station forecourt, perspective of upper-level open-air pool. **Fig 0.18** Alec Scragg, New Town Hall for Camden spanning the Euston railway cutting in Hampstead Road, perspective of computer server facility. **Fig 0.19** Alice Haugh, Naturalisation test centre and community building just off The Highway in Wapping, close-up perspective on a major festival day. **Fig 0.20** Alice Haugh, Movable pavilions inside the naturalisation test centre and

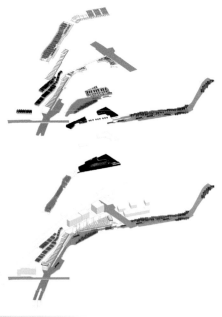

0.15

0.16

0.17

0.18

0.19

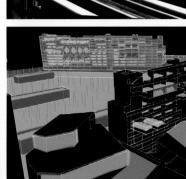

0.20

community building, study model. **Fig 0.21** Alec Scragg,
Registry Office zone within the new Camden Town Hall,
plan. **Fig. 0.22** Alec Scragg, Moss garden suspended over
new HS2 railway cutting showing illumination at night,
perspective.

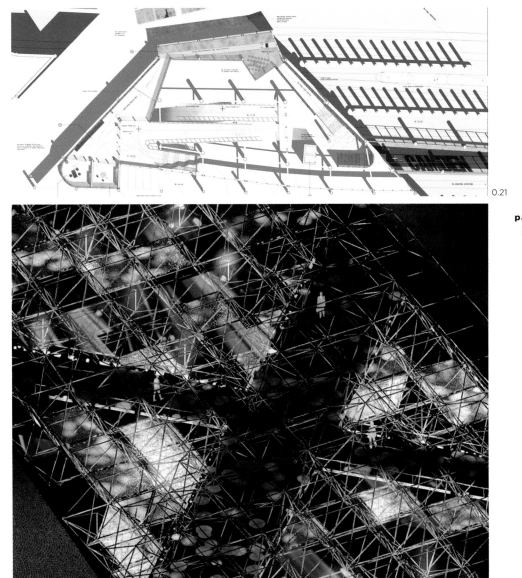

0.21

0.22

GROUNDSWELL

Penelope Haralambidou, Michael Tite, Joerg Majer

What do we mean when we talk about the 'ground', the 'earth', or the 'site'? The landscape is often seen technically, as a geothermal territory containing mineral resources, a place we clear to build upon, a biogeography where we grow food, or a spiritual realm where we bury the dead. In eighteenth century English landscape design, the manipulation of the ground represented a mastery of the environment, a harmonious nature constructed pictorially from a distance. Since the 1970's, Environmentalists have viewed the natural world deferentially as a balanced system to be preserved in equilibrium. As such we have come to idealize the landscape in a condition of controlled stasis.

Located at the edges of several interdependent worlds, Iceland sits in an unstable shifting ground, prone to unexpected swelling that is neither strictly subarctic nor Northern European. Fuelled by myth making and folklore it is also a young, volatile nature where hills are formed in a matter of weeks, a geologically active land being continually rewritten. If architecture is a reflection of the physical, cultural and social territories it occupies, then how do we respond to such lands that are in a state of 'becoming'? Can an architecture exist that is in a constant state of flux, one that is able to reflect and interpret these powerful geological transformations at a human scale? Iceland can also be seen as a microcosm of the world in 2012. Two recent traumas – the economic collapse of 2008 and the 2010 Eyjafjallajökull ash cloud – have scarred and isolated the island. Once a nation of bankers, the future of the 300,000 inhabitants hangs in delicate balance; it is unable to bail out its banks, its accession to the EU is in doubt and its arable farmlands are in ruin. The country is responding by pioneering ways in which to become self-sufficient economically and socially. It is forging new ground through the crowdsourcing of a new constitution and is developing home grown technological industries. This new frontier of invention and rebirth requires radical modes of occupancy, innovative new materialities and technologically smart methods of producing and maintaining buildings that are also carefully embedded within the identity of Iceland. This year we speculated on Iceland's future as a means of understanding and constructing our own.

In the first project entitled 'Fuel' we studied Reykjavik and Iceland from afar. Each student identified a fuel and used it as a driving force for the project. Their definition of fuel was expansive or specific but was rooted in site specific research: geothermal or seismological energy, magma, a traditional foodstuff such as Hákarl, a ceremony, a ritual, a Nordic sport or an Icelandic saga, or a strange wonder such as the northern lights, lava fields, thermal lagoons, the midnight sun, ash plumes, glaciers, turf houses, dance music, maritime mythologies, geysers, or volcanic activity.

In November we visited Iceland where students deployed their speculative devices. We immersed ourselves in Icelandic culture and developed a critical understanding of the Icelandic psyche. The second project entitled 'Phenomena' was sited in or nearby Reykjavík. Guided by the intuitive findings of the first project and personal observations in situ, students designed public buildings that respond to socioeconomic needs of Iceland's inhabitants, are fuelled by site specific phenomena and develop a critical attitude to the environment. The aim was to develop architectural prototypes that not only contemplate current economic and cultural shifts but which are also inspired by the otherworldly, such as the mythic world of the Sagas or the strange natural phenomena of the Aurora Borealis. We harnessed the latent forces from within the island and used them to conjure new atmospheres; we invented new homemade political landscapes and conceived new ways of living, a 'groundswell' of architectural ideas.

The unit is underpinned by a stimulating and nurturing studio environment where we foster a strong collaborative ethos. We encourage students to be experimental, creative and independent designers, each with their own unique architectural voice.

We would like to thank our critics: Alessandro Ayuso, Laura Allen, Kyle Buchanan, Luke Chandresinghe, Emma Cheatle, Kate Davies, Richard Difford, Professor Murray Fraser, Professor Stephen Gage, Tom Ebdon, David Garcia, Ruairi Glynn, John Goodbun, Spencer Guy, Professor Christine Hawley, Damjan Iliev, Professor Jonathan Hill, Alex Holloway, Johan Hybschmann, Luke Jones, Jan Kattein, Julian Krüger, Hugh McEwen , Will McLean, Ana Monrabal-Cook, Alexandros Mykoniatis, Tim Norman, Caireen O'Hagan-Houx, Frosso Pimenides, Dr Sophia Psarra, Charlotte Reynolds, Sarah Shafiei, Tim Sloan, Catrina Stewart, Matthias Suchert and Dr Victoria Watson.

Year 2: Chiara Barrett, Leo Boscherini, Katie Cunningham, Tom James, Daniel Scoulding, Nicholas Warner, Anthony Williams, Laura Elizabeth Young

Year 3: Nichola Czyz, Joseph Dejardin, Matthew Lucraft, Samuel Storr McGill, Anna Lisa McSweeney, Harriet Middleton-Baker, Angeline Wee

Fig. 1.1, Fig. 1.3, Fig. 1.5 Samuel McGill, Kvosin Music Technology School, interior view. An intelligent facade system utilises resonant frequencies to regulate the building's solar strategy. When frequencies are passed through free-hanging vertically stacked transparent plates, sand is made to vibrate across their surface casting dynamic shadows across the central hall. **Fig. 1.2** Nick Warner, Fishing Summer School, Lake Ellithavatn. Section cutaway interior view. The building straddles the lake's flood defence and is organised around a central conical chamber that allows the traditional Icelandic Evening Wake to occur beneath the stars. **Fig. 1.4, Fig. 1.6** Laura Young, Blooming Phytoplankton Canopy, Future Farming Research Centre, University of Iceland campus, Hàskòli Islands. 1:1 working prototype and visualisation. A tessellating roof component – based on the principle of Hooke's Law – periodically fills with phytoplankton. Green chlorophyll pigment in the fluid harnesses sunlight during the day and releases energy at night allowing the building to reduce its energy consumption.

1.1

1.2

1.3

1.4

1.5

1.6

Fig 1.7 Daniel Scoulding, Culinary Community Centre, Hafnafjordur. Perspective drawing. Influenced by the unusual Icelandic delicacies such as puffin, sheep's head and rotten shark meat, the building imagines a food production and distribution centre for traditional Icelandic foodstuff. A timber roof structure manipulates air flow to facilitate the smoking process. **Fig. 1.8** Leo Boscherini, Hafnarfjordur Thermal Baths. Ground floor plan. Located in the coastal volcanic landscape south of Reykjavik, bathers first enter elevated changing rooms above the water's edge, before returning into a sleek sunken building that merges with the strange black landscape.

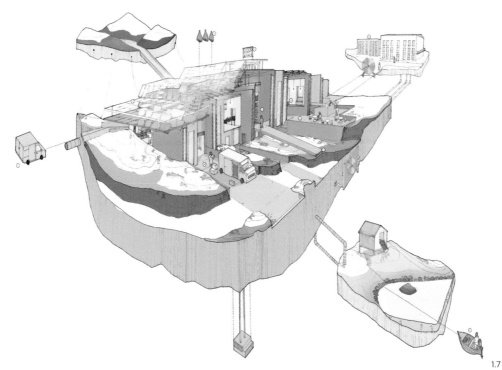

1.7

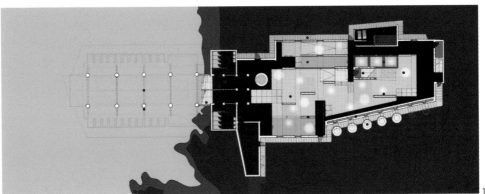

1.8

Fig. 1.9 Joseph Dejardin, HQ for the Commission for Trade and Cultural Development, Reykjavik Old Harbour, cross section through central atrium. The building is conceived as a kind of 'Cloud Palace' that will act as a catalyst to the growth of Reykjavik Harbour as a Logistical Container Port. The project interweaves three separate programmes – a Data Centre, a Government Department and a new public garden using Leonardo's double helix staircase as an organising mechanism that spirals through the building. **Fig 1.10** Tom James, Film School, Kvosin, section through cinema. A series of perforated screens that carefully control light entry, encases a complex series of interlinking interior spaces. The building acts as a vessel capable of holding light within its rock-like body.

1.9

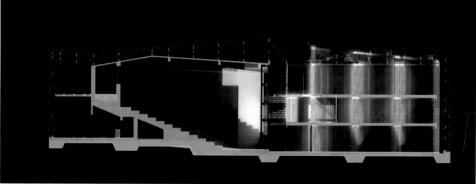

1.10

Fig. 1.11 — 1.14 Angeline Wee, Basalt Fabric Parliament, Lake Tjornin. Interior cutaway sections. Interior cutaway sections. Following the 'pots and pans revolution' of 2009, the proposal imagines a new kind of People's Parliament for Iceland. The building is constructed from an ingenious new material 'Basalt Fabric', that is imagined as a new national material symbolising Iceland's independence.
Fig. 1.15 Anthony Williams, Ossur Bionic Research Centre, Grafarvogur Lake, South bank. Site Plan. 80% of the world's prosthetics are designed and manufactured in Iceland. The building acts as a new research centre for the Ossur Corporation. A ribcage-like form winds along a single contour on the edge of the lake.

1.11

1.12

1.13

1.14

1.15

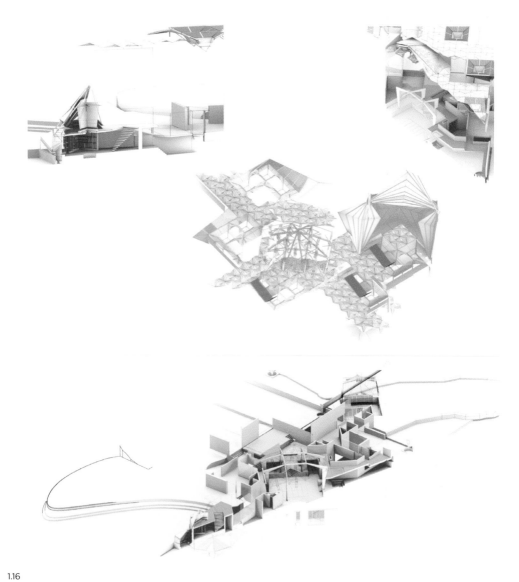

1.16

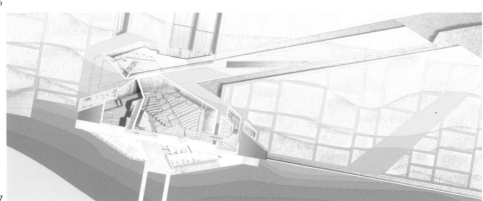

1.17

Fig 1.16 Anna Lisa McSweeney, Primary School, East Reykjavik. The school is a prototype for a new Icelandic pedagogy rooted in storytelling and the natural environment. The ground becomes the site for learning, with the dynamic roof system acting as a place for dreaming. **Fig. 1.17** Katie Cunningham, Resomation Centre, Geldinganes Island. Ground Plan. The funerary building is separated into two structures, one where the first burial ceremony is carried out and the other where the wake is observed and Funeral Ale is consumed. **Fig. 1.18** Harriet Middleton-Baker, New Co-operative Bank and Expo, Reykjavik Old Harbour. Model photograph. Responding to the Financial Crash of 2008, the Bank and Expo acts as an initiative to connect re-capitcalised Icelandic Banks to small businesses. **Fig. 1.19** Chiara Barrett, HQ for Green Activists, Kvosin. Long Section. A large space-frame holds a series of vessels, each containing one of Icelands many green activist groups. Occupy Reykjavik, Saving Iceland and the Grapevine Newspaper jostle for position with each expressing their different aims through choice of material and structural form.

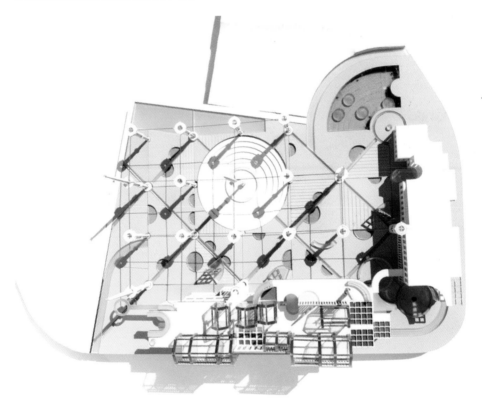

1.18

1.19

Fig. 1.20 Nichola Czyz, Digital Library and Data Centre, Seltjarnarnes. Model photographs of roof. The project imagines a future scenario where physical books within a library become redundant. The building operates at the scale of the landscape, creating its own micro-climate, and at the scale of furniture; with locally heated desks regulating the thermal environment. **Fig. 1.21** Matthew Lucraft, Icelandic Forestry Commission, Úlfarsárdalur, East Reykjavik. The Forestry Commission building imagines the beginnings of the afforestation process in Iceland. The impact of climate change has meant that Iceland's history as a barren, hostile environment is slowly reversing; with marginal temperature rises, and rising CO_2 levels creating desirable conditions for Birch tree growth. The project explores how a new self-sufficient industry might emerge and what the potential affects on the psyche of introducing forests to a sea-faring nation might be.

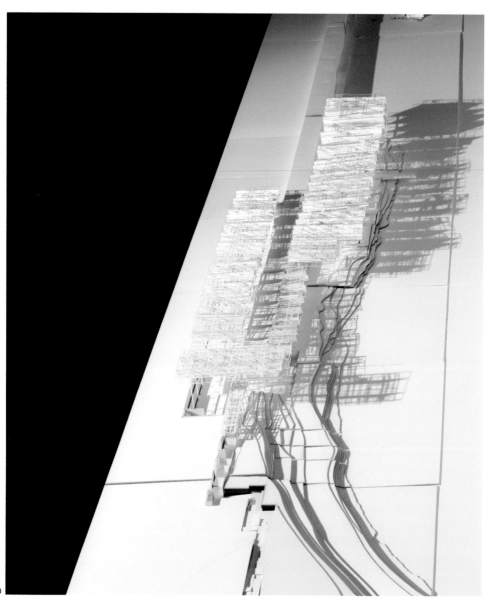

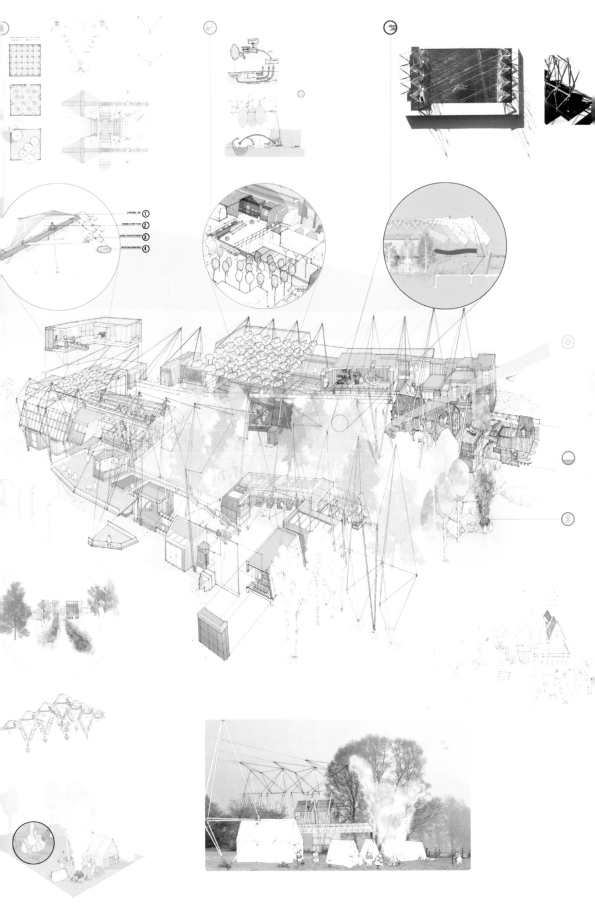

GIMME SHELTER
Julian Krüger, Damjan Iliev

We are interested in cities, their patterns, structures and the variety of spaces and boundaries that form and exist within them. This year Unit 2 explored the themes of exuberance, pragmatism and accommodation. Students were encouraged to explore, investigate and invent new building typologies in variable scales that fulfil the basic human needs from small inhabitable rooms to large complex building programmes that can generate functional and yet beautiful spaces where the individual or community can reside either permanently or temporary.

London - Urban Shelter
The year began by producing a series of experimental structures which provided micro-space living environments for specific sites in London. Students were asked to reconsider the intuitive human notion of shelter as well as its form, materiality and function. The shelter had to be comfortable and offer protection from the sun, rain, wind, cold and other climatic conditions. The concepts from the fast initial exercise culminated with the design of a small dwelling that could accommodate multiple users through shared programmatic requirements where cohabitation and socialising could take place. Its relationship to the immediate social and wider urban environment was of great significance. Methods of representation included developing 3D or physical models and a set of plans and sections to scale. Throughout the course of the whole year Unit 2 set out a series of workshops, portfolio reviews and seminars closely linked to the individual design work.

Vienna/Budapest - Building Project
In December Unit 2 visited Vienna, 'the grand dame of Europe's capitals', for architectural inspiration, unexpected conjunction and taste for the Viennese high culture, unique charm and "Lebensfreude". The city's combination of high quality architecture, impeccable urban network, well-tended cafes and diverse population has ranked it as one of the most liveable cities with the highest quality of life in the world. We embarked on an architectural pilgrimage that covered the quintessential Baroque, Art Nouveau, Wiener Moderne architectural styles and the best contemporary buildings and housing schemes that make Vienna special. We arranged special access to visit buildings by Otto Wagner, Adolf Loos, Coop Himmelb(l)au, Zaha Hadid and the Viennese Institute of Architecture and Applied Arts where we met fellow colleagues and gained vital input. We also visited Viennese architects which gave us an insight into their current work and view on architecture.

Eastern Interlude
From Vienna we took the train to visit Budapest, the capital of Hungary and second most important city of the Austria-Hungarian Empire which dissolved in 1918. We visited the great Hungarian baths, experienced the mix of derelict 19th

century bourgeois architecture, socialist housing projects and contemporary architecture and also enjoyed the famous Hungarian hospitality.

Coming back from our trip, the Unit focused on an architectural proposition at a greater scale. Students developed a building proposal for their chosen site in Vienna or Budapest. The overriding theme of accommodation was considered broadly. Students were expected to develop an architectural language and demonstrate entrepreneurial capacity to hybridise unexpected urban conditions, programmes, users, social issues and building typologies.

Thanks to all our guest critics for their wit and wisdom:
Marcos Cruz, Murray Fraser, Laura Allen, Patrick Weber, Rashid Ali, Rut Cuenca
William Firebrace, Gabby Shawcross, Krassimir Krastev, Kathy Basheva,
Juana Canet, Elena Gomez, Steven Foley, Friedrich Vitzthum, Ivana Bocina,
Justin CK Lao, Jose Sanchez Recio and Johan Voordouw.

Year 2: Julia Rutkowska, Yoana Yordanova, Miljun Celeste Wong,
Lauren Marshall, Alexia Souvaliotis, Helen Siu, Arti Braude, Saijel Taank

Year 3: Tao Wei, Nawanwaj Yudhanahas, Xin Zhan,
Stanley Hanjie Tan, Maria Goustas

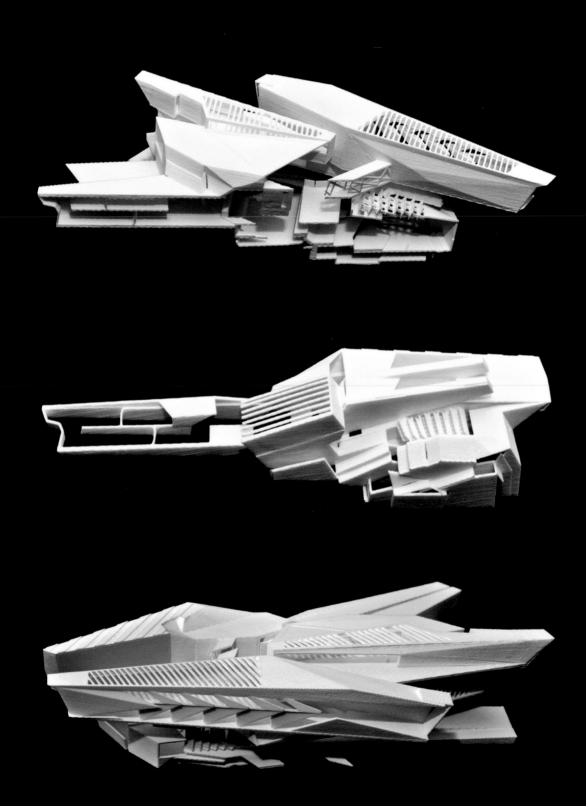

Fig. 2.1 Tao Wei, Jewish community centre located near Leopoldstad on the Danube River in Vienna. Close to the old Jewish quarter, it serves the again growing Jewish community in Vienna and offers a theatre, synagogue and various communal spaces. **Fig. 2.2** Tao Wei, View of main entrance. **Fig. 2.3** Tao Wei, Longitudinal Section.

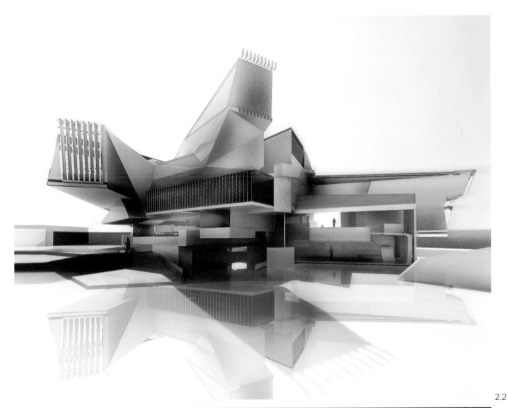

2.2

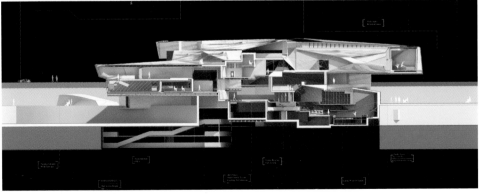

2.3

Fig. 2.4 Arti Braude, Workshop and retreat for a community craftsman in London. The small building is designed so it can be built by one person (the community craftsman) who runs a workshop which can be used by members of the Brick Lane neighbourhood. **Fig. 2.5.** Arti Braude, main building project proposes a Dervish dancing theatre and lodge accommodating annual dervish pilgrimages visiting the Gül Baba memorial in Víziváros, Budapest. **Fig. 2.6** Arti Braude, Axonometric view, Workshop, London. **Fig 2.7** Helen Siu, Tokaji-wine Headquarter in Budapest. Helen made use of the existing system of natural caves and labyrinths under the Budavári Palace. The labyrinths form part of her building which are used to store wine. Large funnels form an artificial landscape used to grow grape vines and lead natural light into the deep underground. **Fig 2.8** Alexia Souvaliotis, Axonometric view, Bike workshop in Brick Lane, London. Alexia´s building addresses the east London bike community and provides a workshop for bikes and small living unit for the owner of the shop. The building represents a large shelf structure with a construction system inspired by bikes manufacturing techniques. **Fig 2.9** Tao Wei, Extract of main building proposal showing theatre and kinetic facade envelope. **Fig 2.10** Nawan Yudhanahas, Headquarter for the International Danube River Commission, DRC in Budapest. An over sailing roof structure provides shelter for a water-landscape which reacts to the changing level of the river. The building provides an auditorium, debating chamber, offices and laboratories.

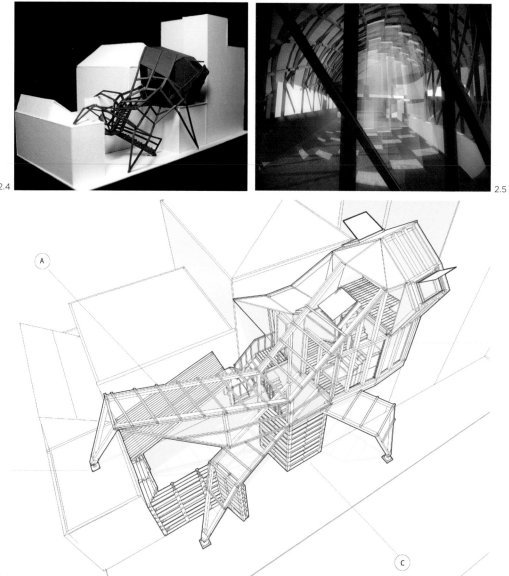

2.4

2.5

A

C

2.6

Fig 2.11 Nawan Yudhanahas, Aerial view of Danube River Commission, Budapest.

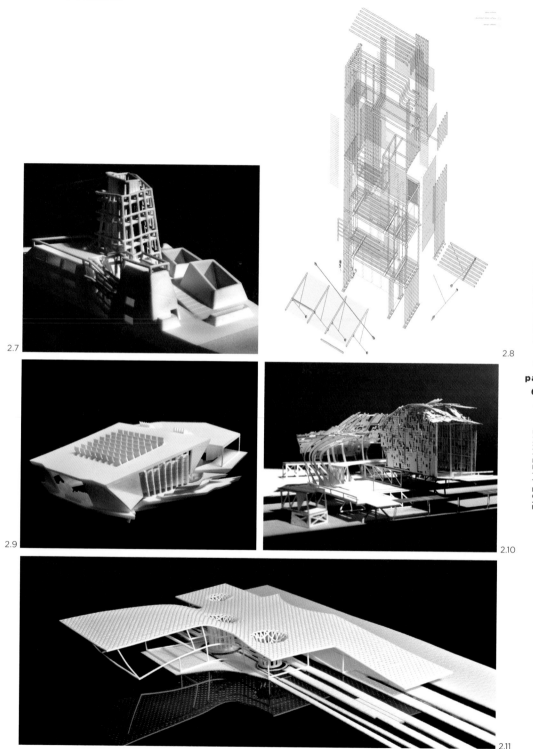

2.7

2.8

2.9

2.10

2.11

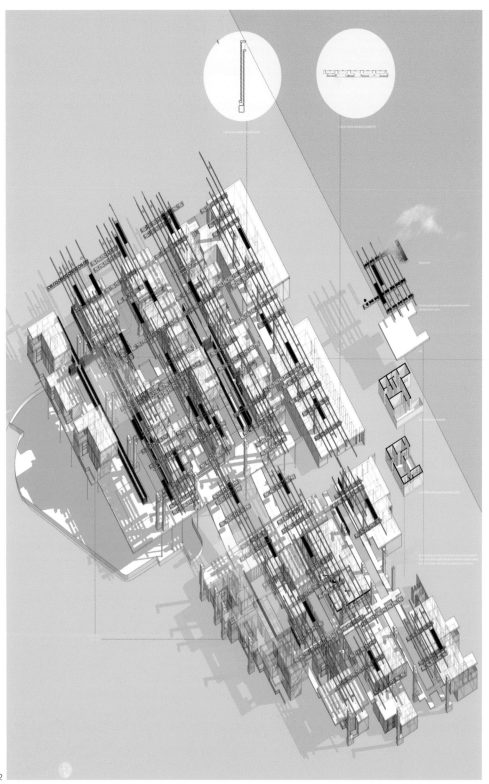

2.12

Fig 2.12 Stanley Tan, Axonometric view, Housing scheme for a self-sustainable garden community and public food market in London/ Tottenham Hale. The project studies the theme of urban-suburbanization, efficiency of urban infrastructure and rural retreat. The living units are integrated into a canopy which is used to grow vegetables and also works as a water-collection and irrigation system. **Fig 2.13** Stanley Tan, Internal perspective, Communal housing, Tottenham Hale, London. **Fig 2.14** Lauren Marshall, Aerial view, Budapest, the "World Capital of Spas", is located over a geological fault line which is the reason for the thermal activity in the ground. Lauren carried out a series of iterative landscape interventions on the slopes of Buda proposing an outdoor bathhouse with wide-ranging views of the city. **Fig 2.15** Maria Goustas, Plan, Light therapy centre in Vienna. Vienna is the home town of Siegmund Freud, the father of psychoanalysis and therapy. Light therapy is a rather new concept to treat disorders like depression. Maria's building is embedded with various embedded fibre-optic and facade envelope devices which can be exactly tuned to create different light conditions inside the centre. **Fig 2.16** Miljun Celeste Wong, Axonometric view, Dog-spa on the river Danube in Budapest. Celeste's proposition consists of a dog spa, veterinarian clinic and dog shelter for a city which has the highest population of dogs in Europe.

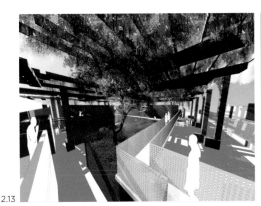

2.13

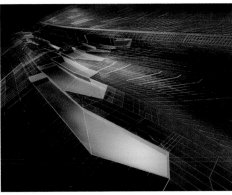

2.14

2.15

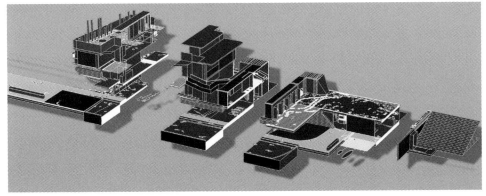

2.16

Fig. 2.17 Yoana Yordanova, Plan, Public Hammam Bath House in Vienna. Yoana´s building is a modern interpretation of a traditional Turkish bath (Hammam) and tries to integrate Turkish lifestyle into the city. A sophisticated system of routes for male and female visitors leads through the building. **Fig. 2.18** Yoana Yordanova, Aerial view of Public Hammam Bath House, Vienna. **Fig. 2.19** Saijel Taank, Plan, Fish market and fish hatchery in Vienna. The building spans across the "Wienkanal" and forms a connection between two different city quarters which are currently separated by the canal. Large tanks are used to breed fish to repopulate the river with endangered fish species. The scheme also provides a market for fish, in line with Vienna´s great tradition of food markets.

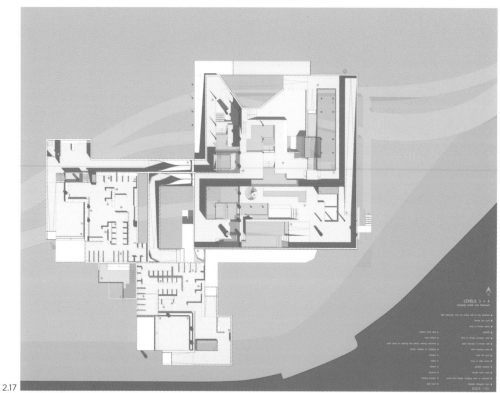

2.17

2.18

FINAL PLAN
SCALE 1:100

2.19

SUMMIT

David Garcia, Jan Kattein

Welcome to a Europe ravaged by the financial crisis. Feel the dusty wind exhale across the unfinished ghost towns of the real estate boom. Priced out of housing and marginalized by the employment market, some begin to realise the current economic system is unlikely to cope with future environmental and social challenges.

Our quest for 2012: the Pyrenees. A mountain range, 150 million years old, that has weathered a radical human transformation during the last 50. Dams and industries are re-forming the landscape to feed the ever-hungry metropolises in the lowlands. Traditional herding and rural activities are disappearing, abandoning villages and farmsteads over night to contest their own fate against the slow forces of weather, erosion and decay. All the while, extreme sports and high mountain tourism are festering. The higher, the better. Along this mountainous border, out of sight from authority and on the edge of society, a new ecology is taking hold. In tune with the local environment and responsive to the needs of the group, a movement has established itself based on the principles of fair dealing and self-organisation. Abandoned ruins, reclaimed, transform into smallholdings; micro-industries rely on the mutual exchange of goods and services ensuring self-sufficiency.

Communities are establishing a voice in how the mountains are used. Thanks to them a new architectural typology is emerging. Built structures have a certain patina inherent to the materials used for construction. Low-tech and high-tech share aims, and local materials surmount imported goods. Careful craftsmanship and a sense of purpose inform the building process. Scarcity and limited means call for ingenious solutions. Sustainability is defined by high specificity, innate to the life-style of a community whose daily routine is informed by the natural rhythms of the landscape, from valley to mountain peak.

Portable Refuge

A refuge is a place or state of safety. It can be a shelter that protects from the effects of weather, animals, or even other people. It acts as a permeable barrier between the occupant and its site, an observatory that can record the gentle or aggressive changes in weather and landscape. In section, the mountains comprise a range of climate zones with sub-tropical conditions on the Spanish Meseta to permafrost at 3000m height. How will your refuge respond to these extremes? Will it provide shelter from the heat or from the cold? Will it be sited on land or on water? Will it relate to existing communities or be home to a recluse? What will it observe and study? Project 1 will explored materials and utilised manufacturing processes that hybridised the typology of the traditional tent. It needed to allow for transformation in order to withstand extreme conditions. Its apertures needed to adjust to provide for precise observations in unknown terrain. A high degree of craftsmanship and site-specificity were given parameters. The refuge was to be constructed life-size and tested on site during our expedition to the Pyrenees and it served as an observatory, to research and localize an area of in depth study to inform Project 2.

Summit: From Valley To Peak

A landscape is commonly understood to occupy the picture plane in a horizontal direction. To fully comprehend the ecological and social complexities of the Pyrenees, a vertical reading needs to be taken. Once populated, the valley was a resourceful society, and the peaks were desolate. Climate change and the re-organisation of life-styles has reversed this trend. Ghost towns in the foothills have remained as the solemn reminders of formerly prosperous times while high altitude resorts can hardly accommodate the influx in tourism.

The term architecture is most interesting when it refers to a practise and not an object. Most buildings are built without architects. Most cities grow (and shrink) without a plan. When does architecture start and when does it end? Is a city finished when the last building is built? Is architecture an exclusive art or can it facilitate a building process that engages communities and individuals?

In project 2 we set the foundation stone for a type of architecture that can transform to accommodate the changing needs of its occupants. We explored a wide range of building methodologies appropriate for specific social and physical context in this vertical landscape. Amongst improvised survival huts, or centuries old stone villages, technology and self-made inventions have allowed communities to survive in a harsh climate. Understanding and appreciating this expertise can offer today ways of thriving.

Year 2: Melanie Cheng, Nicolas Chung, Max Friedlander, Yolanda Heng In Leung, Martyna Marciniak, Isabel Ogden, Corina Andra Tuna, Chengqi John Wan, Henrietta Watkins, Wai Yin Vivian Wong, (Tracy) Zhanshi Xiao

Year 3: Hoi Yi (Ginny) Chau, Deniz Varol, Jiatong Karen Hu

During the winter of 2011, Unit 3 embarked in an expedition to the Pyrenees, by way of 3 countries and 5 climate zones. We travelled by van and by foot to survey ecologies and visit communities in the Pyrenees. To explore a vertical landscape of ghost towns, and resurging villages, visit artificial lakes, abandoned factories, winter resorts, and extreme sport facilities from valleys at 800 meters to 3000 meters altitude snow-topped peaks. Our aim, to survey and chart, test and inhabit for several days the self built observatory/shelters and to engage at a 1:1 level with the process of design, and on site research. **Fig. 3.1** Yolanda Heng In Leung, Refuge and Floating Research Platform. **Fig. 3.2** Chengqi Wan, Tent and Undergrowth Study Unit. **Fig. 3.3** Deniz Varol, BIrd Song Relay Shelter.

3.1

3.2

3.3

Fig. 3.4 Wai Yin Vivian Wong, Mobile Hydroelectric Charging Shelter. **Fig. 3.5** Henrietta Watkins, Hydroponic Growth Tent. **Fig. 3.6** Martyna Marciniak, Squatter Shelter and Tool Kit. **Fig. 3.7** Corina Andra Tuna, Wool and Cheesecloth Hammock and Cheese Making Shelter.

3.4

3.5

3.6

3.7

Fig. 3.8 Nicolas Chung, Water Distiller Tent. **Fig. 39**Isabel Ogden, Solar Sinter Shelter. **Fig. 3.10** Jiatong Karen Hu, Portable Meteorological Suit and Shelter. **Fig. 3.11** Max Friedlander, Wind Oriented Tent with Wind Rose Generating Mechanism.

3.8

3.9

3.10

3.11

Fig. 3.12 Zhanshi Tracey Xiao, Nomad Journalist Tent
Fig. 3.13 Martyna Marciniak, Squatter Shelter and Tool
Kit. **Fig. 3.14** Melanie Cheng, Wearable Volture Spotting
Camouflage Shelter.

3.12

3.13

3.14

Fig. 3.15 Wai Yin Vivian Wong, Self Energy Supply Community Centre. **Fig. 3.16** Corina Andra Tuna, Wool Research Centre. **Fig. 3.17** Yolanda Heng In Leung, River Edge Market and RIver Rafting School.

3.15

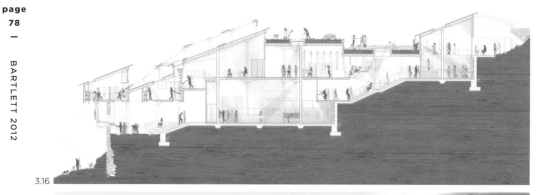

3.16

3.17

Fig. 3.18 Isabel Ogden, High Alpine Refuge. Fig. 3.19 Deniz Varol, Benedictine Monastery and Astronomic Observatory. Fig. 3.20 Chengqi Wan, Children's Agrarian Summer Camp. Fig. 3.21 Hoi Yi (Ginny) Chau, Sheep Farm and Visitor Centre. Fig. 3.22 Max Friedlander, Paragliding Centre. Fig. 3.23 Martyna Marciniak, Waste Material Recycling Factory.

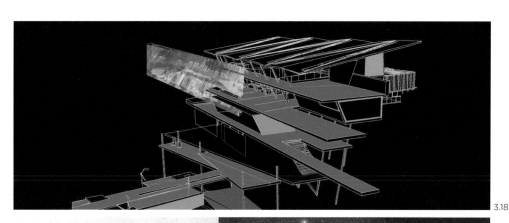

3.18

3.19

- Roofscape of Play

3.20

3.21

3.22

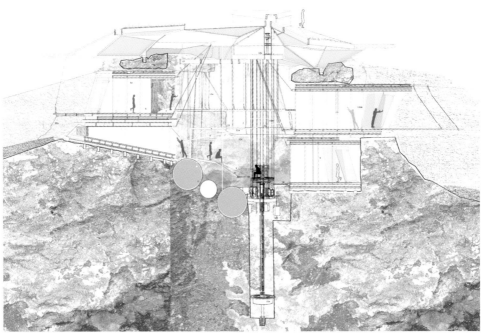

3.23

EXPO(SÉ)!

Ana Monrabal-Cook, Luke Pearson

In 2020 Silicon Valley had hoped to hold an International Exposition, which would have been the third such event in the San Francisco area's lifetime. The Bay Area is currently investigating an application for Expo 2025 despite a Government seemingly unwilling to make payment to the Bureau International des Exposition for the acceptance of the bid into a formal competition. The Exposition as an architectural construction exists in a dichotomy, at once sprawling, colourful, wilfully silly, yet carefully promoting the interests and investments of nation states and multinational corporations.

Architects have an inextricable link to those who wield power in society. Now more than ever, the production of visualisations, masterplans, sketches and films are tightly controlled to appeal to the senses of those who hold political or financial capital. It is through physical manifestations of these desires that the architects of the many follies and pavilions of International Expos have played with their audience's visual, consumerist and symbolic appetites.

The Expo provides a forum for nations to export themselves and their culture. Constructs of the power, attitude and philosophies of nations are sent across the globe for the consumption of other cultures. Crystal Palace, the Eiffel Tower, the Golden Gate Bridge, the Barcelona Pavilion and many more, have become architectures far beyond the Expo itself; becoming cultural icons that define the city they reside in.

San Francisco as a city embodies the counter-culture of the United States, yet this "free thinking" has led to it becoming the world's capital of the digital industries, where new models of control weave their way into our lives at an ever-increasing pace. But just as these Expositions paint a controlled picture of international culture - the Olympic games of the economy, science and industry - so our remote personal perception of the world is affected by information brokering. Winning the bid to host an International Expo involves a highly competitive selection process. An idealised version of the city is exported to the selection panel far in advance of the public event. The perceived benefits for a city and immediate international attention can act as catalyst for growth or as a distraction from societies real problems.

Unit Four investigated the Architectural Exposé as a counterpoint to the tightly controlled dissemination of cultural ideas in the Exposition. Exposé implies the reveal of something secret, (un)desirable, a hard truth or grotty titillation. It is the opposite to the masquerade of the World's Fair.

In approaching the Exposé as an architectural construct, we asked students to question the role of representation and communication within architectural practice. Through an initial study of the city as a remote destination, students questioned both how they might read a city from afar, but how the frameworks and systems for delivering that information to them could be harnessed as part of an architectural dialogue.

These questions resulted in novel and uniquely contextual approaches towards a 'Remote SF'. Matthew Lyall suggested an architecture occupying a spatial zone derived from the way in which Panoramio software shows geotagged photographs as locatable objects within Google Streetview. Luke Scott suggested roofscapes of buildings might become exploitable elevations for advertising or subversion, manifest through a controlled reveal mirroring the development curve of higher resolution satellite imagery. Brook Lin fabricated a hidden landscape located within the city as a reveal of the unconventional legal and social frameworks San Francisco has in place for embracing illegal immigration into the city. Other such projects spatialised political discontent, or generated infrastructures reconciling the grid system with the sinuous San Francisco Fog - students sought to derive architectural approaches that would contrast the remote city to the actual one.

Following a field trip to the SF Bay Area, these studies then became concerned with buildings that dealt both with real events and planned legacies. They engaged with the city as a dynamic body. A city that would swell with tourists swarming around the fringes of the Bay towards the proposed Expo. A city that exists on a seismic knife-edge, with near-certain knowledge of a huge quake in the next 20 years. A city that once emerged from devastation through its artistic expression, and a city where the voice of protest rings loud despite its immense economic powerbase. A city within perfect wine and crop growing country yet composed of artificial fill and contaminated land.

We would like to thank our technology tutor Toby Maclean, and our critics throughout the year: Laura Allen, Abigail Ashton, Julia Backhaus, Scott Batty, Emma Cheatle, Ming Chung, Nick Elias, Pedro Font Alba, Johan Hybschmann, Damjan Iliev, Will Jefferies, Alex Kirkwood, Guan Lee, Stefan Lengen, Luke Lowings, Frosso Pimenides, Andrew Porter, Nick Tyson, Patrick Weber, Rae Whittow-Williams. We would also like to extend our thanks to Dan Grayber for kindly showing us his studio and work in SF.

Year 2: Sonia Yuen Hin Ho, Man Lung Jackey Ip, Vanessa Lafoy, Matthew Lyall, Isobel Parnell, Carina Tran

Year 3: Kacper Chmielewski, Charles Dorrance-King, Ting Jui (Brook) Lin, Luke Scott

Fig. 4.1 Vanessa Lafoy, Telegraph Hill Community Farm – A timber framed structure allows growing components to be reconfigured depending on season and demand. The 'clip on nature' of the buildings extends to rooftop greenhouses or extra living spaces. The scheme provides an opportunity for crop growing in the cramped spaces typical of SF terraced housing. Exploded iso of housing/growing unit. **Fig. 4.2** Sonia Yuen Hin Ho, Film House – Celebrating the genesis of cinematic and photographic legacy of Alfred Hitchcock and Edward Muybridge, the building attempts to craft a paradoxical experience from the pixelated and inverted landscapes projected into the interior via optical devices, revealed progressively as you ascend the building. View into Camara obscura room. **Fig. 4.3** Man Lung Jackey Ip, Wine Bottle Protector –

Acting as a protective vessel to precious wine in areas that are prone to earthquakes, the structure detects vibrations and tremors, transforming from its normal static storing position to a tilted emergency state. Model testing spring trigger mechanism and moving components. **Fig. 4.4** Carina Tran, SF Re-use/Re-cycle – SF's recycling regime boasts 0% waste to landfills by 2020, an ambitious goal considering the existing SF Recycling Centre acts as a conduit from which rubbish bales are shipped to China. The scheme questions the integrity of the existing recycling programme and proposes a museum and plastic recycling factory incorporating heavy machinery and waste products within the building structure. View of plastic mould wall unit.

4.2

4.1

4.3

4.4

Fig. 4.5 Matthew Lyall, San Francisco Police Department Auction House – Located in an alleyway between the SFPD and a branch of the Bank of America, the design is strongly informed by the interaction of the physical and online auction process of stolen and found goods. Before having the power to sell stolen items, SFPD must hold items for at least 6 weeks in order that members of the public can claim them. A storage facility is situated on the south side of the site carefully framed by a facade of concrete batons allowing glimpses of the lots without clearly revealing them to avoid false appropriation. Objects for sale are digitised by a process of structured-light scanning techniques in order to be viewed online. Specific shadows are projected on to objects, photographed and reconstructed digitally resulting in point clouds. The specific nature of the process results in an articulated roof-scape formed of louvres designed to rotate along a horizontal axis in order to align shadows with non-vertical surfaces down below. As the objects come closer to point of sale, the digital reconstruction becomes both more accurate and of higher resolution. The breakdown in the relative scale of the stolen goods (a distortion of perceived dimensions that occurs within website frames) is simulated in real life through anamorphic arrangements of the objects within the building. Roofscape and structured light scanning louvre test models. **Fig. 4.6** Matthew Lyall, San Francisco Police Department Auction House. Roof plan of building.

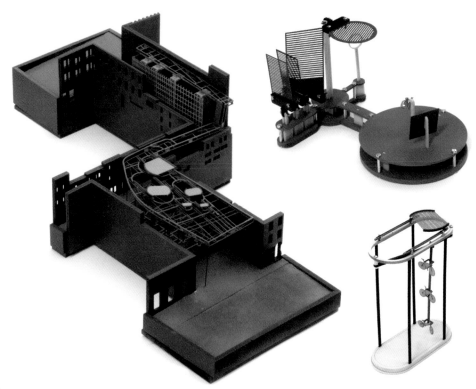

4.5

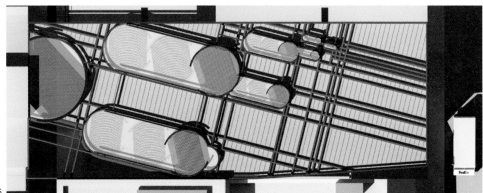

4.6

Fig. 4.7 — 4.8 Charles Dorrance-King, Occupant CA94105 – Triggered by the recent 'Occupy' movement, Occupant CA94105 is designed as an independent body to raise awareness by occupying the space above private plazas which otherwise restrict public protest and challenge public authority. The success of the occupant relies on the intensity of any online activity covering campaigns, petitions and coverage on social networks. **Fig. 4.9** Charles Dorrance-King, SF Federal Credit Union and Community Park - Just as the architecture of many of America's grand institutions was created from extraneous typologies, the proposal asserts itself as a referenced architecture. Not one of repetition or reproduction, but a deformation of existing typologies taken from the old Chamber of Commerce and other 'power buildings' around SF's Financial District. The concept of the design is a re-intepretation of old to new, re-configuring the existing building and manipulating existing decor, changing its scale, materiality and function.

4.7

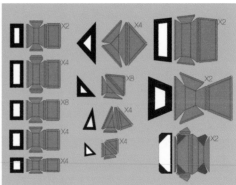

4.8

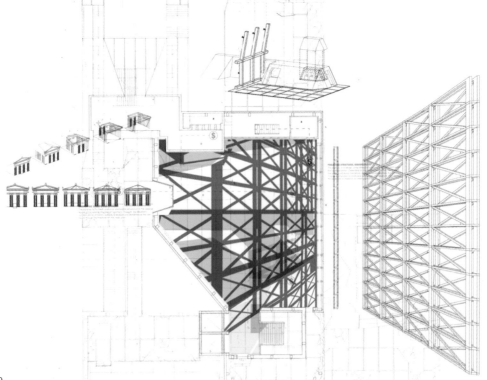

4.9

Fig. 4.10 — 4.11 Kacper Chmielewski, Bernal Hill Earthquake Rebirth Arts Centre – After the devastating earthquake in 1906, San Francisco's arts community brought the city back to life. Sited within an earthquake safe-spot, the proposal provides a private artists' residence and workspace re-engineering typical seismic structural failures to respond to specific measured trembles. The proposal manipulates the boundary between public and private, modifying the building structure to reveal artwork.
Fig. 4.12 Kacper Chmielewski, SF:FOG – investigates the irregularities of the urban grid. The fog, a landmark of the city, responds to the grid work as it meets the tops of the buildings, covering the city. Sited within streets unaccepted by the grid system, a series of proposals are developed to manipulate the fog and extrude a perfect, supertouristic-image of the orthogonal plan of San Francisco. Aerial view of SF grid with FOG Infrastructure.

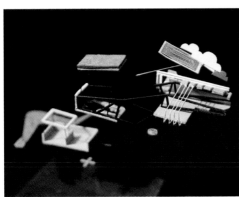

4.10

4.11

4.12

Fig. 4.13 Luke Scott, Reclaiming Hunters Poin – In response to the de-gentrification of a site previously known for it's U.S naval shipyards and 'blue-collar' demographic, the project re-appropriates traditional camouflage techniques to avoid satellite detection. By occupying gaps in the new masterplan, the roof is designed to respond to the forecasted staged upgrades of Google Earth's resolution over the next 5 years. The buildings undergo a process of 'digital weathering' in which their presence and the nature of their occupancy is gradually unveiled. Drawing of pixelated roof. **Fig. 4.14** Luke Scott, Toxic Weathering – De-contamination Facility & U.S. Navy Debriefing Centre. Treasure Island, an artificial land mass originally constructed for the 1939 Golden Gate Exposition, is threatened by resurfacing of its subterranean nuclear contamination. In a cleanup strategy the building probes the ground, drawing radioactive waste into suspended phyto-gardens, filtering and harvesting the contaminated land. Naval veterans engage in horticultural therapy to acclimatize to civilian life as contaminants trigger controlled throughout the sacrificial architecture.

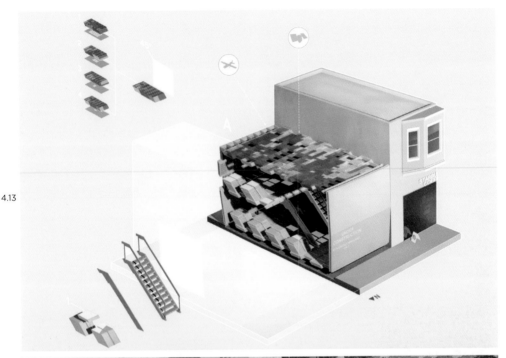

4.13

4.14

Fig. 4.15 Brook Ting Jui Lin, SF: Sanctuary City – San Francisco is known as a Sanctuary City (term used to describe practices that protect illegal immigrants). Represented through models, drawings and short animation, the project is an allegory of the current situation of undocumented immigration. Each 'moment' looks at one of the aspects, including attractive factors of the city, living situation, employment in underground business, mock citizen health care, secret methods of obtaining financial aids after migration and the economic benefits undocumented immigration brings back to the city. Collection of models. **Fig. 4.16 – 4.17, Fig. 4.18** (Overleaf) Brook Ting Jui Lin, Expo 2020 Transit Ferry Terminal – The Terminal is designed to serve Expo visitors traveling from the east coast of the Bay Area to the proposed Expo site in Moffett Federal Airfield providing temporary pavilions, a semi-permanent landscape legacy and a permanent ferry terminal that will carry on serving the city after the World Expo closes. Each temporary pavilion responds to the activities of the passengers and gradually disassembles due to construction techniques and material choices. The building also includes the Expo Human Resource Centre where, based on the Sanctuary Policy and Regulations, undocumented immigrants obtain short term working experience to begin a new life in San Francisco as the post Expo legacy of the building. Internal views through temporary structures and long section.

4.15

4.16

4.17

4.18

Unit 5

FAULT LINES
Julia Backhaus, Pedro Font Alba

"Crises are ultimately productive. They force invention. Breakdowns
incubate breakthroughs. Radical destruction gives way to new forms
of production… Architectural design is the child of crisis"

Mark Wigley, *'Space in Crisis'* Volume Magazine Issue 19 (2009)

Our world has become spectacularly unpredictable. Another year has passed where
we are continuously flooded by extraordinary stories of the unforeseen. It is not
just our social and financial models that show signs of exhaustion but the very
ground we walk on is in a state of upheaval. Between the virtual collapse of the
banking network worldwide - entire countries on the verge of bankruptcy - social
unrest not seen for decades, environmental changes like extreme rainfalls and
crippling droughts, earthquakes and tsunamis: the state of uncertainty and change
seems to be the new global paradigm. In times of upheaval comes an opportunity to
leave the familiar behind and challenge conventions with alternative propositions
and novel ideas. How can we as architects respond to environments that face
challenges of an unpredictable scale and frequency? How can Architecture become
a critical tool to remedy political, cultural or environmental conditions that
are straining our defences? How can our sophisticated production methods provide
solutions to the ever-growing social demands?

Our unit briefs set out to investigate sudden change and slow shifts as a
potential catalyst for innovation, speculation and adaption. We are interested
in finding 'ad hoc' responses to the rapid pace of our times but are equally
interested how to choreograph the slow and minute shifts in our surroundings
that can lead to large and unexpected consequences. As a unit we place
emphasis on the unique relationship between the building and its unique
immediate and wider environments and encourage our students to speculate
towards architectures that are both lyrical and relevant in their response to
our changing natural, cultural and social environments.

This year Unit 5 went on an architectural adventure beyond the familiar in
search of novel architectural tools for an increasingly uncertain world. Our
unit explored present conditions through speculation about possible futures,
considered relevance over indulgence and identified opportunities for tactical
intervention. 'What if' became the mantra for the year.

The first project was sited in London. Students were asked to identify a
fault line and explore an architectural response to the phenomenon of sudden
change. From the streets of the recent riots, extra-ordinary pressures onto
the already congested city during the Olympic games, to the bleak forecast that

London might be flooded by river water or by an overwhelmed Victorian drainage network: Project 1 was a short and intense exercise, where students were asked to speculate about present or possible future scenarios and identify sites and situations that are in demand of an immediate response. Places where rules have to be changed in order to survive. We looked at immediate and spontaneous architecture that proves that 'necessity is the mother of invention'. The approach to this project was experimental and the architectural propositions ranged from 1:1 built interventions to strategic master planning.

Our trip to Istanbul became a test bed in our search for an original and innovative architecture. Istanbul, a multifaceted and fluid city, has experienced rapid and dramatic global and local pressures. Not only is it located close to the North Anatolian fault line making it a earthquake sensitive area, it is also a city of many dualities. From its geographic location between Asia and Europe, the Golden Horn and the Bosporus, the Marmara and Black Sea to its economic divide between great wealth and poverty. The city is struggling between modernity and tradition, secularism and Islamism, democracy and repression – often in unlikely and contradictory combinations. As the city is reaching out to compete as a new global capital it faces new challenges, specifically finding ways for (re)development on the dense fabric of the historical peninsula. In the 2nd project students were asked to identify sites, spaces or economies of mounting pressures that are in need of reinvention and adaption to ensure their survival. It was our intention not to slip into nostalgia but to consider the opportunities that the current developments present for the city and to freely and fearlessly engage in conversations about the city. How can the fault lines and intersections that draw the city shape the contours of new imaginings for Istanbul? Some projects were placed between desire and knowledge; others were allegorical but perfectly meaningful.

We want to express our gratitude to our technical tutor and critic Dr Rachel Cruise. Also we want to acknowledge our guest jurors this year for their priceless advice and generosity with their time: Abigail Ashton, Bruce Irwin, Christian Parreno, Juanjo and Lola Ruiz, Sara Shafiei, Murray Fraser, Geraldine Denning, Gavin Hutchison, Francisco Gonzalez de Canales, Mark Breeze, Sam Causer, Nick Hockley, Katy Beinart, Lucy Leonard, Iain Borden, Guan Lee, Patrick Weber, Tania Sengupta and Carlos Jimenez.

Year 2: Robin Ashurst, Tik Chun Zion Chan, Joanne Chen, Him Wai Lai, Arthur Kay, Camilla Wright, Peter Simpson, Jack Sargent

Year 3: Amy Begg, Kun Bi, Samuel Dodsworth, Christopher Worsfold, Wei Zeng (Lucas) Ler, Simran Sidhu, Hui Zhen Ng

Fig. 5.1 Arthur Kay, Paranoia House. Series of architectural interventions to Terrence Fyed's Victorian house. Addressing and providing architectural solutions to specific fears derived from perceived local and global threats through the media. **Fig. 5.2** Zion Chan, Rehabilitation centre for visually impaired people in Istanbul. The road network of Istanbul itself is the evidence of the dramatic historical change of the city, which result in a complex and organic form. The mobility training for blind people requires a safe training route, which imitates the streets of Istanbul. **Fig. 5.3** Joanne Chen, Pop Up artist commune in Shoreditch. The program is a metaphor of reviving a forgotten space, providing the artists with affordable studio complexes with a strong community infrastructure as a way of self-promotion and revitalisation of the area. **Fig. 5.4** Chris Worsfold, City of London Grain reserve. Urban myth through government assurance and rumour suggest the grain reserve held on site in Canary Wharf is enough to sustain London's current population for 90 days (the figure recommended by the UN) **Fig. 5.5** Peter Simpson, Armenian Mime and Shadow Puppet Theatre. Scenery is moved into the auditorium on tracks and acrobats descend from the roof, this is all played out in front of the historic skyline of Istanbul. **Fig. 5.6** Jack Sargent, Canary Wharf due collectors. **Fig. 5.7** Robin Ashurst, Olympic Water Pavilion, an opportunity to re-instate Tower Hamlets' role in the Games, creating a theatrical event. **Fig. 5.8 — 5.9** Joanne Chen, Perfume factory, a symbol of fusing landscape and industry. The fragrance leaks out of the building through a number of chimneys, which release the steam of boiling fragrant water as a pleasant atmospheric filter. **Fig 5.10** Robin Ashurst, Golden Horn Hospital. Ambulance boats offer a pick up from the nearby Galata Bridge.

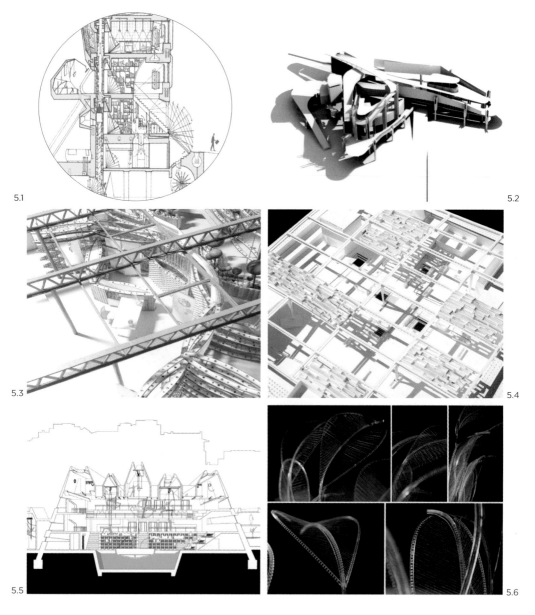

5.1

5.2

5.3

5.4

5.5

5.6

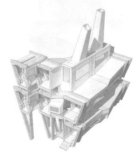

5.7

5.8

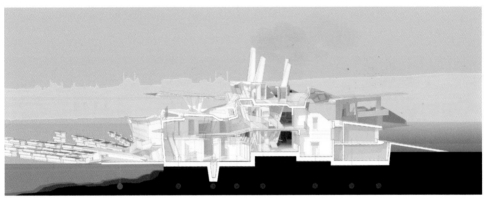

5.9

5.10

Fig. 5.11 Kun Bi, Istanbul water studios. Located on an abandoned shipyard next to the Golden Horn, this building is a combination of water related film studios and public playground. As a film shooting location, it provides water studios, diving pools, jumping pools for different types of film shooting. It also has space to simulate deep sea by using illusions. **Fig. 5.12** Lucas Ler Zeng, Feminist Coffeehouse. A recycling platform for coffee that offers a forum for discussion. At the same time exploring a robust landscape strategy for the fragile nature of the island close to Eyup.

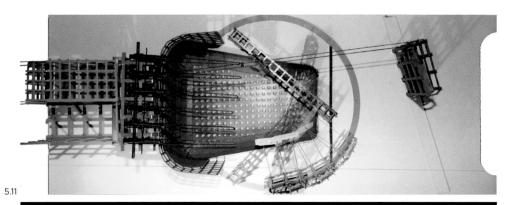

5.11

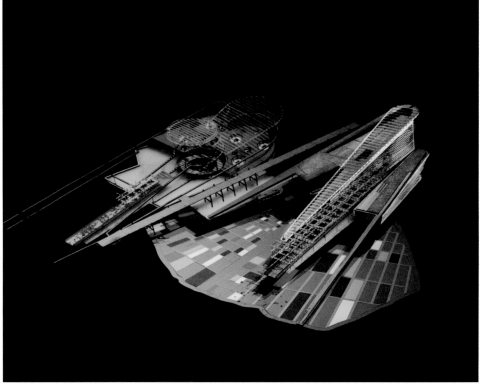

5.12

Fig. 5.13 Simran Sidhu, Timber housing village. The project investigates traditional Ottoman timber structures close to Fener and Balat, the historic home of a large Greek and Jewish population where houses are about to be eliminated in a big governmental sweep-out. **Fig 5.14** Huizhen Ng, The smoke walls walk through. Blurring the boundaries between indoor and outdoor spaces, the proposed building creates spaces in which smokers are able to smoke shisha within the comforts of interiors spaces, while complying with the Turkish Tobacco Law.

5.13

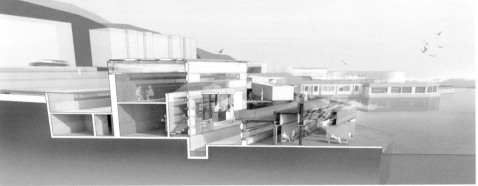

5.14

Fig. 5.15 — 5.16 Amy Begg, Stroke rehabilitation centre. The project starts by looking at the site and the therapeutic possibilities that the island can offer. The proposal attempts to return an industrial area to its original function as original pleasure gardens and addresses aspects of flooding and erosion. The centre will use music therapy in order to structure the patient's day. The public parts of the building are centred to the South West of the island so that, depending on their strength and level of recovery, patients can control how much they wish to be involved with the more public aspects of the building. Towards the East and North the building filters out into the landscape forming a tranquil setting for the patients living spaces and garden/ wildlife areas. **Fig. 5.17 — 5.19** Sam Dodsworth, traditional Turkish wedding retreat in Ortakoy. The design is a response to traditional wedding rituals and in keeping with Istanbul's history; water is used extensively via passive means of water circulation and purification. **Fig. 5.20** (Overleaf) Chris Worsfold. Locust restaurant, Schistocerca Gregaria. The project addresses food security and sustainability. Global issues with meat consumption in relation to climate change leave our diet in flux. The project seeks to investigate how the protein rich locust can both, become a sustainable food source and a product of desire.

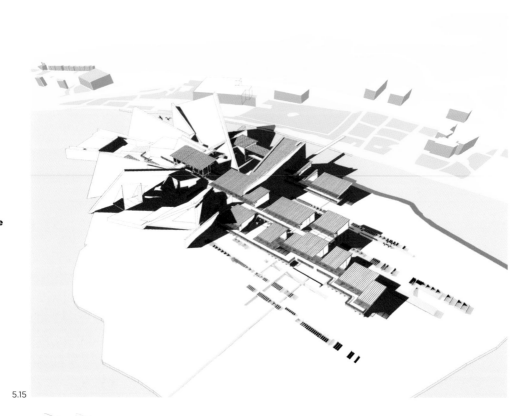

5.15

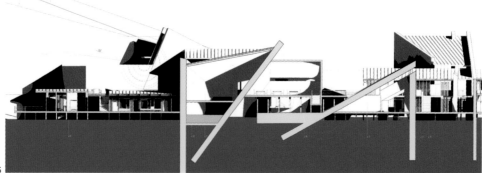

5.16

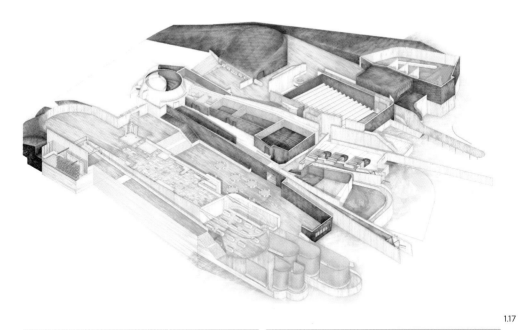

1.17

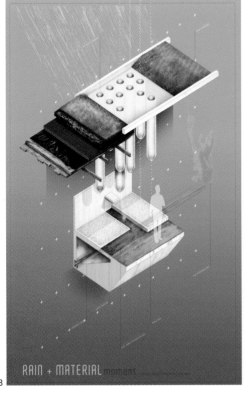

RAIN + MATERIAL moment

1.18

DECLARATION moment

1.19

5.20

SCHOOLS FOR TOMORROWLAND

Sabine Storp, Paolo Zaide

On the 18th of July, 1955, Christine Vess Watkins and Michael Schwartner were the first children to be welcomed to Disneyland. This was to be the happiest place on earth where fond memories of the past could be relived and the youth could savour the challenge and promise of the future. Tomorrowland was dedicated to the advances of Science and the Space Age, and its attractions were an invitation for the visitor to ride into the adventures of Disney's wonderful tomorrow. Participating in this dream America's larger 'forward thinking' companies used Tomorrowland to showcase their designs for the appliances and technologies to come. American Motors' Autopia exhibit represented the future of the country's multi-lane limited-access highways and Monsanto's Hall of Chemistry proposed that bio technology would benefit your life, food and health. These corporate visions came with a promise to build a new and easier way of life 'for you, your children, and generations to come'.

The rapid escalation in the development and centrality of technology is mirrored in concerns and debates about sustainability and the nature of resources which question how prepared we may really be, for an unpredictable yet extraordinary future. With more people worldwide graduating through education in the next thirty years, the systems of schooling that met the demands of industrialism need to adapt to the transformations of demography, ecology and the ways we socially interact. The unit was to explore images of the future that would provide a challenge to imagine the new schools for tomorrow.

The first term began by looking at spaces for learning, and the development of concepts, models and a proposal for the 'extension' of an existing London school. The extension was considered beyond the simplistic definition of a building addition to critically explore what 'learning' may constitute in the future, and how spaces could be created to frame this process. In consultation with the pupils and teachers of Salusbury Primary School in North London, a competition project was proposed to design an 'extension' to the school playground which reconsidered the traditional playground object or addition. In the light of Tomorrowland a range of appliances and constructs were developed that allow the children to expand their experience in 'learning to learn', discover and to imagine.

Informed by the first project, the subsequent architectural proposition sought to develop educational programmes, functions and spaces fit for the 21st Century. The field trip was to Cuba in order to study the revolutionary art schools and organopónicos, urban organic gardens off the streets of Havana. These are architectural models that favour customisation over standardisation. Students were encouraged to investigate the conditions of Havana's built and social environments; their diverse research and experience resulted in design programmes which were developed with a sense of risk, provocation and invention.

Unit 6 would like to thank our technical tutor, Matthew Springett, and critics: Samson Adjey, Abigail Ashton, Jan Birksted, Tom Brooksbank, Gonzalo Coello de Portugal, Ed Farndale, Marta Granda Nistal, Christine Hawley, William Hunter, Popi Iacovou, Tumpa Jasmin, Tim Norman, Charlotte Reynolds

Year 2: Georgina Halabi, Carl Inder, Yu-Me Maru Cheah Kashino, Huma Mohyuddin, Joshua Stevenson-Brown

Year 3: Madiha Ahmad, Samuel Douek, Geethica Gunarajah, Dean Hedman, Ashley Hinchcliffe, Emma Kitley, Nadia Wikborg, Zhang (Allen) Wen, Li (Grace) Zhou

Fig. 6.1 — 6.2 Josh Stevenson-Brown, Westbourne Community Center, Westway, London. A scheme to develop an unused stretch of land in Westbourne Park and activate the Grand Union Canal, with public, community and nursery spaces. From observations of Havana, where private spaces spill out into the street and public space is appropriated by the community, the scheme seeks to extend the use of the 'school' changing the use of the site throughout the day. **Fig. 6.3** Li (Grace) Zhou, Kindergarten / Elderly Day Care Centre, Westway, London. The spatial design facilitates a synchronised timetable of activities involving the interaction of the Kindergarten children and Elderly. The design encourages the exploration of nature and the sensorial within the building. **Fig. 6.4** Dean Hedman, Study Model of an Artificial Landscape. **Fig. 6.5** Dean Hedman, Climatotherapy Institute, Havana. Influenced by the prolific self-sufficiency of the people, culture, the rapidly aging population, and the Malecón, the programme aims to create a model of dealing with this aging population. Using the therapeutic qualities of the sea and optimised microclimates within the building, therapeutic gardens spread into the cities replacing the myth of the urban organopónicos.

6.1

6.2

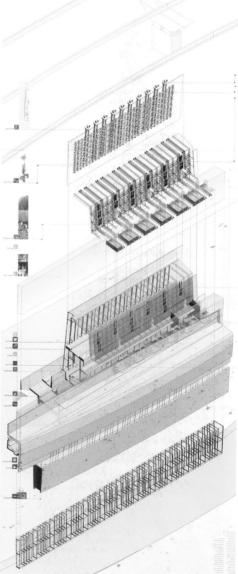

6.3

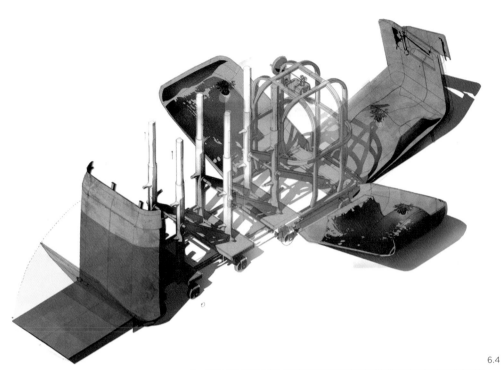

6.4

6.5

Fig. 6.6 — 6.7 Georgina Halabi, Self Sufficient Junior School and Urban Farming, Kings Cross, London. The roofs of the classrooms build an artificial landscape, which is split into zones for different outdoor uses. On the lower levels the landscape is exposed to the elements to allow for free outdoor play whilst the upper levels consist of rigid planting used to feed the school. **Fig 6.8** Carl Inder, Primary School & Cinema, Westway, London. Concepts of framing, montage and perception were developed to translate the spatial qualities of the cinematic into a spatial scheme for a school. The building aims to provide a fluid and dynamic teaching and learning environment anticipating touch-screen technology and immersive projection as the norm. The cinema auditorium is used as a key community and commercial facility. **Fig 6.9** Yu-Me Maru Kashino,Taxi Motel and Tinkering School, Kings Cross, London. A primary school set in the future, a London 'black cab' arrives and will become a classroom, furniture, or 'tinkering' workshop whilst parked in one of three taxi zones. Children engage in 'learning through play' by interacting with the various ways in which the taxis 'plug-in' to the building. **Fig. 6.10** Emma Kitley, Study for Construction School, Havana. Looking into future political changes in Cuba, the population may start to restore more buildings through a long restoration process. The school will provide young adults with the skills required to help restore their homes and cities whilst gaining independence through a new understanding in many fields of construction. The water collection and recycling principles of the building become an example for the city of Havana.

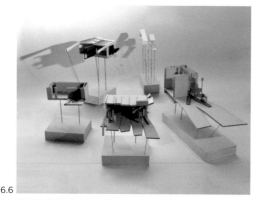

6.6

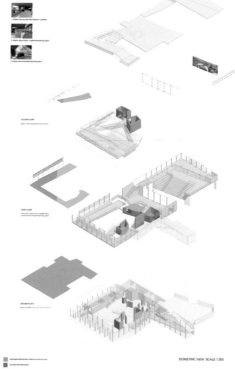

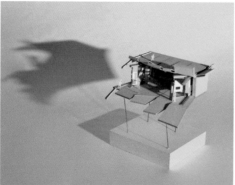

6.7

6.8

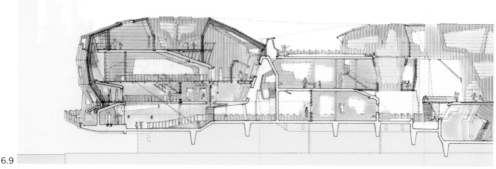

6.9

6.10>

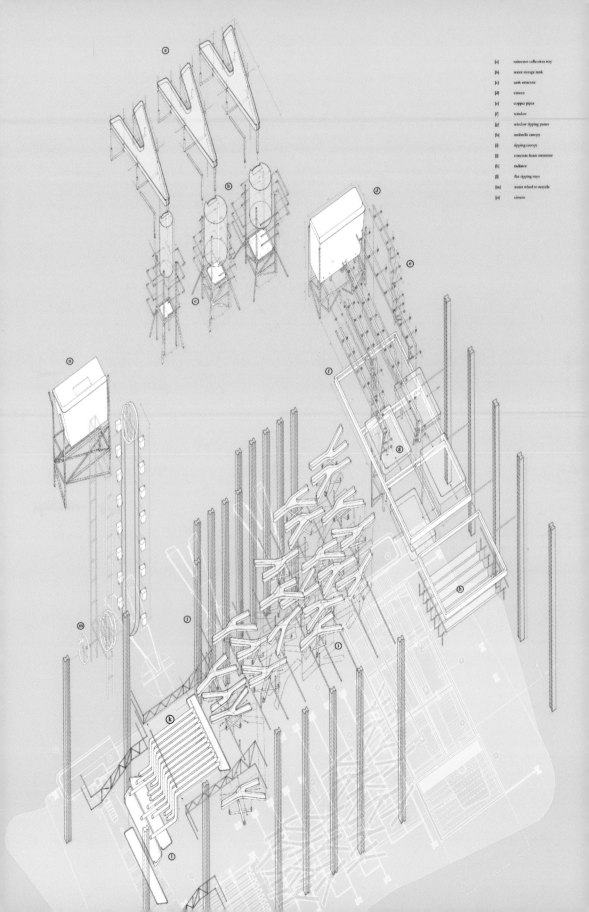

Fig. 6.11 Madiha Ahmad, Film School and Archive, Havana. The building exists in central Havana and is a response to keep the local identity alive through film. It provides an open 'groundscape', sets and spaces for 'telenovela'. These adaptable spaces for the school and an open roofscape transform into an open-air cinema at night. The building also aims to be an example of sustainable and low energy construction in Havana through the application of earth as a building material. **Fig. 6.12 – 6.13** Huma Mohyuddin, Primary School, Westway, London. The primary school is designed as an unconventional 'open classroom' experience to encourage interaction and play between pupils of different ages. The roof is a combination of various pods that are used for different purposes. Some are used to grow the children's vegetable garden, others collect water and some extrude down into the classrooms to create different learning environments. **Fig. 6.14 – 6.15** Ashley Hinchcliffe, Study for the Weather Responsive School, Havana. Located along the Malecón, the school is continuously faced with the changing weather. Built upon a system of protective layers and staggered responses, the school reacts to daily weather fluctuations through a perforated skin, which protectively wraps around the school in stages. This movement, that creates an adaptive learning environment corresponding to atmospheric conditions, dictates the interior experiences of the school. The school's ever-changing form reflects the weather, relaying the message of inclement weather as a warning beacon for the city of Havana.

6.11

6.12

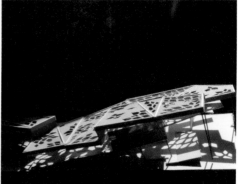

6.13

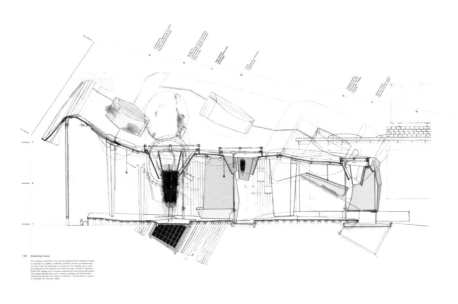

6.14

6.15

Fig. 6.16 — 6.17 Geethica Gunarajah, Casablanca Ceramics Centre, Havana. The programme facilitates the revitalisation of Cuba's architectural identity, lost since the embargo, through utilising Havana's wide local resource of Matzana red clay. The building demonstrates reinventions with modular clay construction, which consider interplay with sunlight, water and ventilation on the steep hillside site. The resulting experiential qualities appropriately accommodate the education and manufacture of clay arts and crafts. **Fig. 6.18** Yu-Me Maru Kashino, Taxi Motel and Tinkering School, Kings Cross, London. **Fig. 6.19** Nadia Wikborg, Flower Carts, Salusbury Primary School, London. The project explores how children learn about the natural world. The children are encouraged to grow and care for flowers which are brought from home to school in personal carts. **Fig. 6.20** Samuel Douek, The School of Sustainability, Havana. The culture of self-sustainability that came out of an era of challenging socio-political change is under threat. The School of Sustainability will attempt to maintain Socialist ideology in a 'post-Castro' era by educating Cubans of all ages about sustainable technologies that have been researched and developed on site. The construction and repair of the school itself will be the primary form of education, offering the opportunity for inexperienced volunteers to learn sustainable construction techniques, promoting independence from the state.

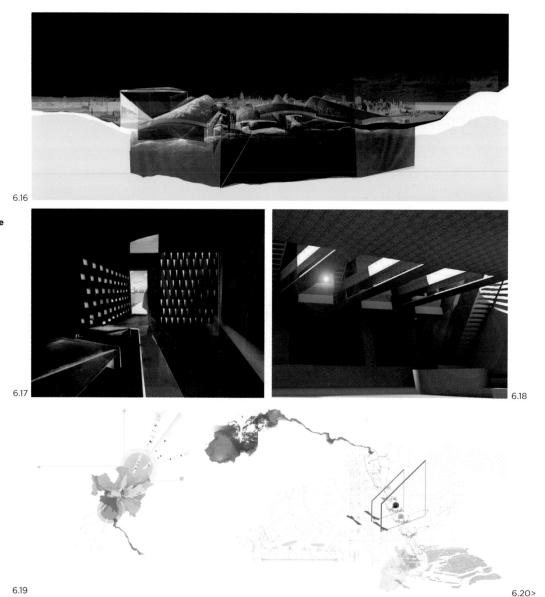

6.16

6.17

6.18

6.19

6.20>

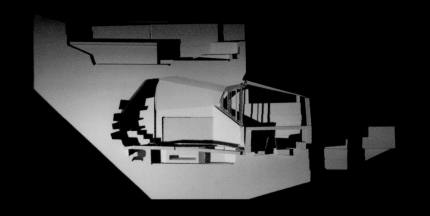
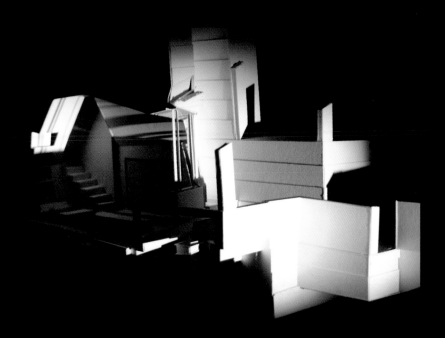
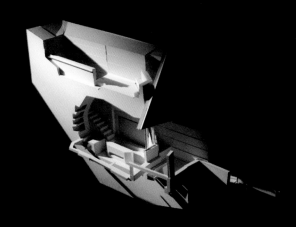

MAKING THE CITY
Ming Chung, Nick Tyson

Unit 7 investigates architecture as a material practice whereby making is intrinsic to a way of working and thinking about design.

In the 1968 seminal publication 'The Nature and Art of Workmanship', David Pye provides a definition of craftsmanship and thus sets out the role of the maker in relation to the process of production. Pye distinguishes manufacturing from craftsmanship by defining manufacturing as the 'workmanship of certainty' and craftsmanship as the 'workmanship of risk'.

Making is used as a tactic to mediate between these two modes of operation to establish a process of working that intertwines 'risk' and 'certainty'. The use of handwork as well digitally controlled tools is treated with equal importance and become mutually supportive activities within an open cycle of experimentation.

Students are encouraged to move freely between the studio and the fabrication workshop, which is regarded as an experimental laboratory and a place where design ideas are nurtured. A discipline is cultivated through the tactile contact with material and tools alongside a dialogue with specialist makers. This activity has the potential to reinvigorate a practice that employs direct material engagement to initiate alternative modes of production for making architecture.

Prototype - A Replicable Component

Term 1 began with the investigation of a single primary material, manipulated through the use of hand tools in specialist workshops and included materials such as timber, metal, plastics, ceramics, fabric and paper. Initial handwork methods involved the learning of traditional making techniques such as joinery, folding, casting, heat forming, sewing and felting.

A 1:1 scale component formed a working prototype that was determined by rudimentary jigs, templates and formwork. Digitally linked manufacturing tools were then introduced allowing the hand-made components to be reproduced as machine made or manufactured replicable components. These components were tested as physical prototypes and digitally manipulated spatial systems, which were defined by inherent material properties, logics of production and experiential qualities.

These prototypes formed an archive of material pedagogy that provided a point of departure for Project 2. The design process was recorded in the form of instruction manuals and flow charts as a way navigating the complexity of the tacit decision making process.

In November the unit made a field trip across Germany from Hannover to Berlin with building visits that included the TECTA Furniture Campus, Bauhaus Dessau, Aalvar Aalto Kulturhaus and Baupiloten Studio at Berlin Technical University.

City Jig – A Workshop Facility for Participatory Making Practices

In Term 2 the unit explored the connection between individual making practices and the fabrication of the city. Students were asked to consider hybrid building programmes to engage the public in the participatory act of making (Year 2) and to provide a manufacturing facility for the open source manipulation of machine tools (Year 3).

Post-industrial sites within Fish Island, Hackney Wick were selected to locate new prototypical architectural propositions. Host infrastructures were identified that included: Distribution & Transport, Manufacturing Facilities, Depots & Yards, Utilities, Energy & Services, Temporary Events, Public & Common Territories and Social Networks.

The idea of the jig was further explored as both a physical and conceptual tool to provide an interface with the maker as well as determining the outcomes of material production. Each student continued to investigate material detail in parallel with model making at a strategic scale.

Unit 7 would like to thank: Luis Fernandez and Christopher Matthews at Atelier One Engineers for their invaluable technical support and our guest critics Laura Allen, Abigail Ashton, Felicity Atekpe, Adam Atraktzi, Guan Lee, Anna Parker and Emmanuel Vercruysse

> Year 2: Hannah Mollie Bowers, Jessica Clements, Kate Slattery, James Tang, (Vincent) Tung Ning Yeung, (Timmy) Tae-In Yoon

> Year 3: Taimar Birthistle-Cooke, Theclalin Cheung, Carmen Lee, Allanah Hope Morrill, Lauren Shevills

Fig. 7.1 Allanah Hope Morrill, Print transfer on acrylic cast profiled concrete. **Fig. 7.2** Kate Slattery, CNC milled jigs for heat formed acrylic component. **Fig. 7.3** Jessica Clements, Cold formed mild steel flat bar lattice. **Fig. 7.4** Hannah Mollie Bowers, Wool felt non woven textile lining. **Fig. 7.5** James Tang, Papercrete cast with fibre reinforcement. **Fig. 7.6** Allanah Hope Morrill, Digital print on folded fabric-paper screen.

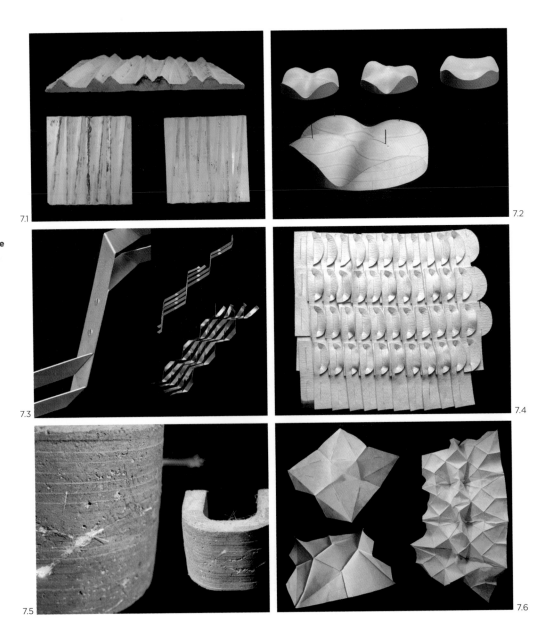

7.1

7.2

7.3

7.4

7.5

7.6

Fig. 7.7 Theclalin Cheung, CNC milled moulds and paper pulp components. **Fig. 7.8** James Tang, Cut and fold cellular cardboard units and structure. **Fig. 7.9** Carmen Lee, Slip cast interlocking ceramic envelope. **Fig. 7.10** Timmy Tae-In Yoon, Laser cut dry laminated plywood structure and detail. **Fig. 7.11** Vincent Tung Ning Yeung, Vacuum formed components for acrylic textile. **Fig. 7.12** Taimar Birthistle-Cooke, Laser cut folded aluminium skin.

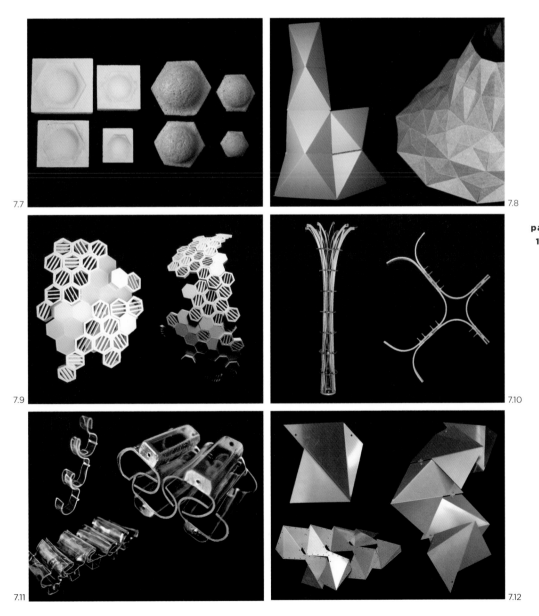

7.7

7.8

7.9

7.10

7.11

7.12

Fig. 7.13 - 7.14 Kate Slattery, Acrylic screen: CNC milled forma with heat formed laser cut acrylic component and replicable system. **Fig. 7.15 - 7.16** Lauren Shevills. Formwork jig, concrete component and rubber skin with casting residue. **Fig. 7.17 - 7.18** Vincent Tung Yeung. Glass Recycling Facility with Public Onsen, 3D printed models: Section through public baths and under-ground recycling facility.

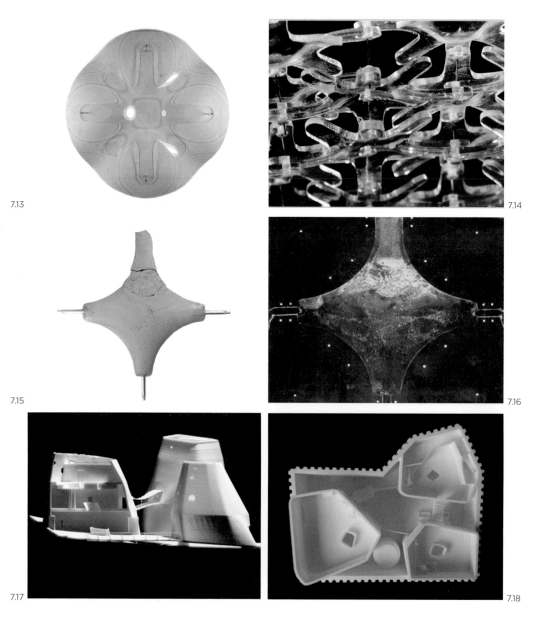

7.13

7.14

7.15

7.16

7.17

7.18

Fig. 7.19 Lauren Shevills, Furniture Manufacturing Campus. Fabric cast elements are added over time in relation to the expanding campus and the decommissioning of the existing cement works. Section through open-source workshop. **Fig. 7.20** Kate Slattery, Seed Bank and intensive growing fields. CNC milled topography with laser etched heat formed acrylic canopy. **Fig. 7.21** James Tang, Recycling Depot with Upcycling Workshop. Laser cut laminated cellular cardboard model.

7.19

7.20

7.21

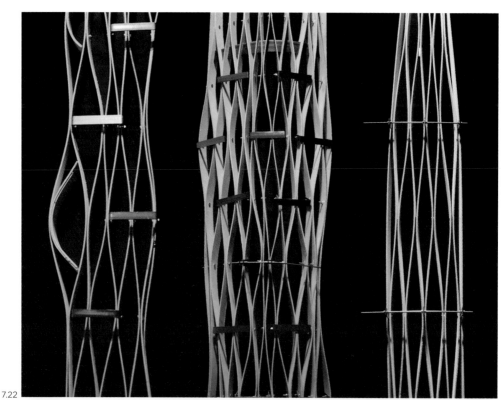

7.22

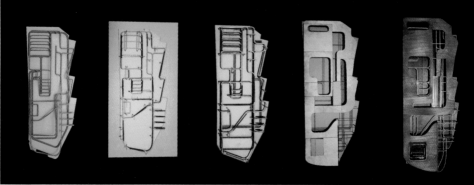

7.23

Fig. 7.24 Timmy Tae-In Yoon, Spatial studies for dry laminated plywood system. **Fig. 7.25** Allanah Hope Morrill, Open Source Print Facility. Cement board study models for suspended cast machine plinths. **Fig. 7.26** Theclalin Cheung, Speculative studies for seed embedded deployable paper pulp component.

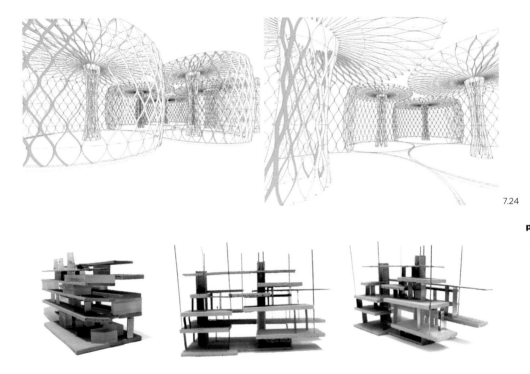

7.24

7.25

7.26

Fig. 7.27 — 7.28 Timmy Tae-In Yoon, Parasite Manufacturing Facility with Public Deck. An existing builders merchant is utilised as a host infrastructure for a timber lamination facility. Spatial studies: A continuous track provides a jig for the organisation of storage yards and implementation of sequential production processes. Open source workshops negotiate the interface between the manufacturing facility and public deck. Cold formed laminated plywood deck using CNC milled forma. **Fig. 7.29** Theclalin Cheung, Paper Recycling Facility and Public Garden. The canopy and filter pools, related to processing facility, provide the opportunity for a public garden where open access workshops for participatory activities are located. Schematic infrastructure: Canopy with bamboo grid-shell, filter pools for rainwater collection, seed embedded platforms, recycling facility, workshops and publishing house.

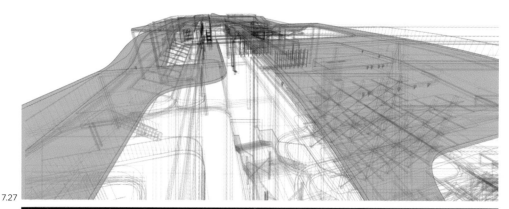

7.27

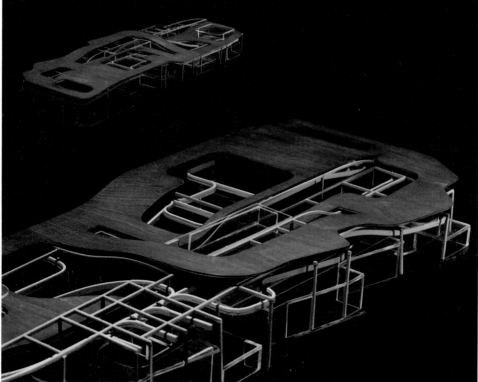

7.28

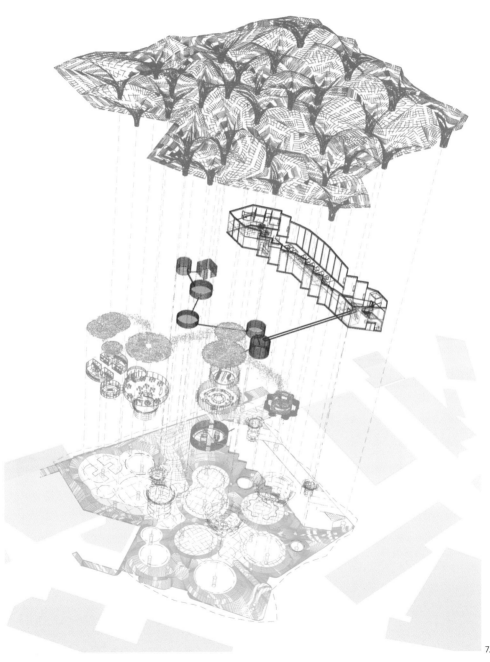

7.29

COMPOSITION

Ben Addy, Rhys Cannon

The idea of composition as a visual but also a material, programmatic and social concern has been the principle focus of our work this year. The unit's investigations initially took place in London but developed with our field trip to Morocco into detailed studies of the Medina of Fes, before culminating in accurately sited propositions specifically located in Fes el Bali, an important World Heritage Site that is currently the focus of significant economic and infrastructural investment by the Moroccan and United States governments.

The Medina of Fes is a unique city where the confluence of 9th century buildings, 15th century artisanal industry and 21st century social media and politics combine with Arab, Berber and Jewish cultures to define an intense urban scene of extraordinary but often subtly demarcated diversity. The urban form of constricted alleyways and compact squares, private courtyards and concealed service streets provides for a tight mesh of activity where the extraordinary demographic mix is held together through the use of discrete signs and the highly sophisticated composition of public and private space. Into this situation the unit proposed a diverse but contextually aware range of architectural propositions, either based on existing demands or in order to posit alternative solutions to the generally unsophisticated schemes currently under consideration by the city authorities.

Celestria Kimmins' project represents the culturally sensitive interweaving of a women's hospice and counselling service into a new market quarter, drawing on the existing materiality of the Medina as a means to code the new proposition - concealing but also on occasion subtly revealing different aspects of the scheme.

Fergus Knox has proposed a hitherto new typology for the Medina - a public park - with virtuoso technical skill and an acute consideration for simple daily interactions. The subtle interplay of public and private space that is proposed gives a suggestion as to how the proximity of artisan industry to daily life in the Medina could be maintained, and is a direct riposte to the UNESCO-backed plan to relocate much of this activity to a suburban industrial park.

The school for girls proposed by Janice Lau starts with a simple but much needed new connection between two dislocated parts of the Medina. This route is then developed into the organising element for the new school, organising different levels of accessibility around the public thoroughfare, carefully and responsibly choreographing the level of interchange between pupils and passersby.

Following an examination of service traffic in the Medina, Yin Hui Chung's wholesale market and logistics depot gives rational organising structure to the transfer of goods from van to donkey at an important entry point to the

Medina while also providing a flamboyant wholesale showroom and auction house for goods destined for the international market.

Marcus Stockton's project provides a forum for two radically different levels of commerce - an exchange for the determination and listing of the international spot price for phosphate, and the architectural support for a micro financed and micro scaled community start up initiative. The tectonic considerations of the project are supported by an extraordinary and distinctive approach to the provision of natural lighting as well as an economically and materially workable strategy for the cross financing and cross servicing of the business start up spaces.

Finally, Cherry Beaumont's masterplan for a new street on the edge of the Oued Boukhrareb channel combines an inventive environmental strategy with culturally aware compositions of public and private program. The typologies explored in detail by the project include those of madrassa, hammam and bakery as well as the private house and workspace. These typologies have been brought together into a dense architectural composition where each has been developed with an awareness of shifting politics to allow for a flexible response to the development of social attitudes, suggesting a valuable approach to development of culturally precious urban fabric.

Unit 8 would like to thank the following individuals for their invaluable criticism and advice as provided to the students during crits held over the course of the year: Andrew Abdulezer, Sarah Custance, Matthew Potter, James Llewelyn, Juliet Quintero, Simon Kennedy, James Hampton, Giles Martin, Scott Grady, Tomas Stokke, Tim Murray, Tamsie Thompson and Parvinder Marwaha.

Rhys Cannon and Ben Addy would like to extend particular thanks on behalf of the students to Andrew Best and his colleagues at Buro Happold for their continued support, design input and critical technical advice.

Year 2: Marta Dabrowska, Hao Han, Jasper Stevens, Chengcheng Peng, Qidan Chen, Tzen Chia

Year 3: Celestria Kimmins, Fergus Knox, Cherry Beaumont, Marcus Stockton, Yll Ajvazi, Tsz Yan Janice Lau, Yin Hui Chung

Fig. 8.1 Tzen Chia, Waterloo Bridge Subterranean Bathhouse, perspective diagram. Presenting London's hidden depths, a series of unique spatial experiences are explored emphasing the 'below-ground'. **Fig. 8.2** Han Hao, Centre of Craft, section. The project looks into two conditions central to the Medina: navigation and crafts. Top craftsmen live and work in the building, creating a 'crafts expo'. Visitors experience the crafts as they circulate through the building and orientate themselves within the City. **Fig. 8.3** Janice Lau, Moroccan Girl's School, model. Girl's education is currently under-provided within Fez, the building creates a public throughfare; over, in, around and balances privacy and public exposure will promoting its function. **Fig. 8.4** Jasper Stevens, The American Fondouk Donkey Hospital,

exploded axonometric. An extension to an existing veterinary charity, the building provides: stabling; treatment; educational facilities; farrier; blacksmithing and a vast rooftop pasture for the beleaguered donkeys of the Medina. Mules, horses and donkeys form the backbone of the Medina's goods distribution system and the new facilites are woven around a ramp providing direct linkage into the heart of the city.

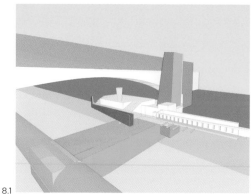

8.1

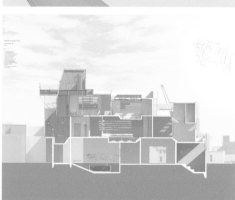

8.2

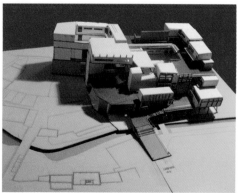

8.3

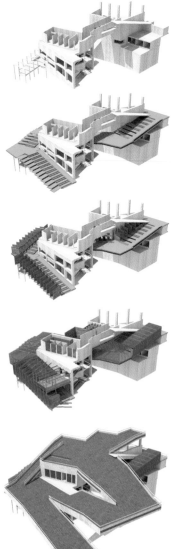

8.4

Fig. 8.5 Marta Dabrowska, 30 St Mary's Axe Registration Mark, drawing. Without directional elevation its presense is recorded through the reflections and diffraction of light permeating the streets of the City of London. **Fig. 8.6** Yin Hui Chung, Re-composable London, drawing. A framing device exploring the arrangement of views within London, deconstructing and reconstructing key spatial components. **Fig. 8.7** Celestria Kimmins, Street Market and Women's Refuge & Clinic, model. Discreetly hidden within the walls of the new Medina market and soup kitchen, reside consultancy rooms and a residential refuge and clinic.

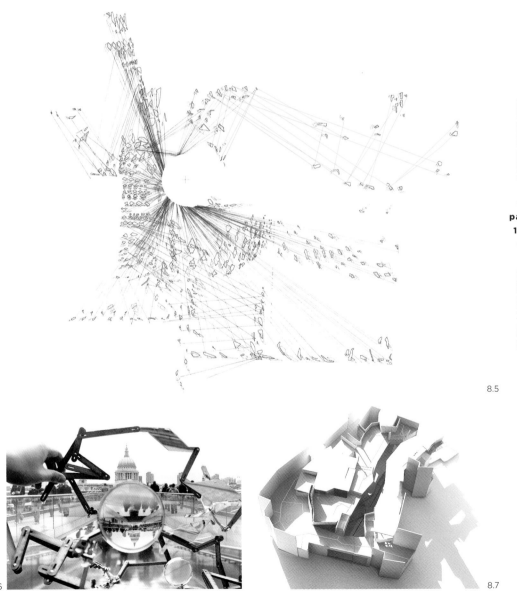

8.5

8.6

8.7

Fig. 8.8, Fig. 8.11 Marcus Stockton, Phosphate Trade Centre and Fez-al-Bali Business Regeneration Scheme - PTC-FBRS, render. Pre-emptivly addressing the demand shift of phosphate production to Morocco the Trade Building functions as a Global Hub for the Coordination and regulation of the invaluable Phosphate resource. Utilising the improved economic state of Morocco through the phosphate trade, the project speculates a business regeneration scheme within Fez-al-Bali, centred in providing the infrastructure requirements of small scale businesses. . **Fig. 8.9 — 8.10** Qidan Chen, Pattern Showcase, render. A series of cocoon like pods hover above the dense urban streetscape, their forms echoing the geometric patterns displayed within.

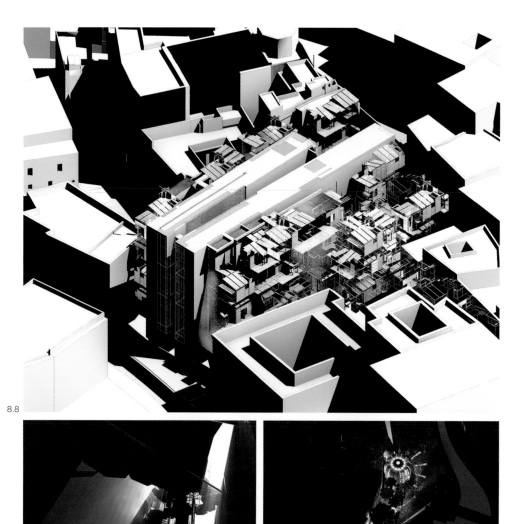

8.8

8.9

8.10

Fig. 8.12, Fig. 8.15 (Overleaf) Fergus Knox, Pearl River Gardens Regeneration Project, render & ground floor plan. Landscaped gardens and reedbeds create a new watercourse for the Wadi Boukrareb. A high-level water treatment plant cleans the river, before it is reintroduced into gardens for irrigation and public fountains. The treatment process will be made accessible to the public, educating through example, showing the benefits and the values of clean water whilst enticing people back to the river and the heart of the Medina. **Fig. 8.13** Chengcheng Peng, Rights of Light – Party Wall Speculations, model. Whilst exploring the physical limitations of UK construction legislation a series of studies evolved into the ability to distort and manipulate these 'rules' in order to produce anew and unexpected architecture. **Fig. 8.14**

Cherry Beaumont, A New Street / Fes el Bali, model. Comprising the five traditional elements of a street within the Medina: fountain; bakery; hammam; mosque and quaranic school. The new proposed arrangement elongates the traditional courtyard and public square whilst utilising passive cooling strategies exploiting the resources of the flowing river below.

8.12

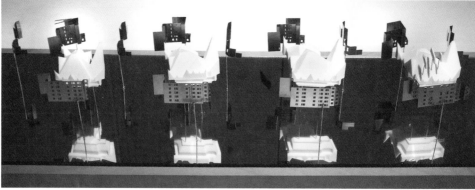

8.13

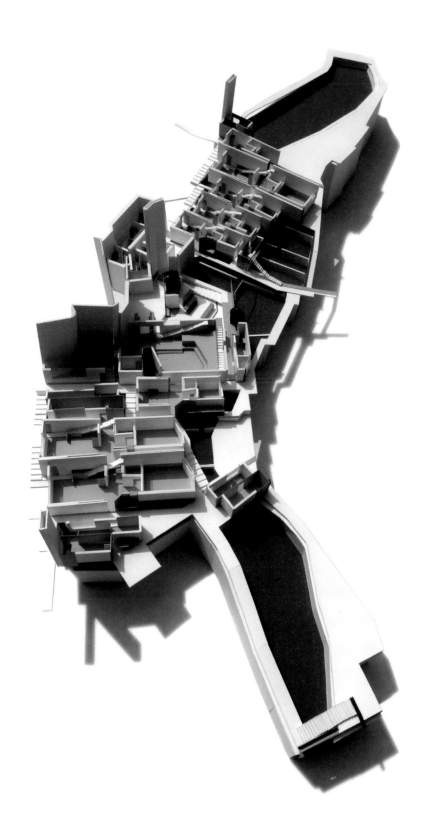

8.14

Fez Gardens and Regeneration of
Wadi Boukareb (Pearl River)

Ground Floor Plan

1. Reservoir
2. Headworks
3. Reaction Housing Platform
4. Particulate Removal by Dissolved Flotation
5. Floating Drum Barrier
6. Rear Gallery Cascade
7. Gravity Grit Aluminium Skimming Tank
8. Screening Debris Sorting and Recycling Building
9. Convey Plant
10. Primary Clarifier
11. Bioreactor Headworks
12. Aerator
13. Sludge Collection Pipe
14. Water For Treatment
15. Secondary Clarifier
16. Recirculation Room
17. Cafe Plaza
18. Cafe
19. Gallery Entrance
20. Bins
21. Pools
22. Kitchen
23. Toilet
24. Changing Lockers
25. Public Toilet H
26. Public Toilet F
27. Existing Bridge
28. Powerboat
29. Surface Run Off Gutter
30. Chlorine Contact Tank
31. Drinking Fountains
32. Pylon Bridge
33. Chromium Works
34. Chromium Baths
35. Chromium Wastewater Treatment
36. Chromium Rinsing Basins
37. Water Garden
38. Tertiary Waste Water Filter
39. Tertiary Clay Gardens
40. Lichening Climbing Horses
41. Lichening Climbing Horses
42. Deep Bed Biological Filter
43. Deep Bed Return
44. Tertiary Housing Platform
45. Bridge Penetration Building
46. Digester
47. Manufe Bins
48. Office
49. Boiler
50. Biogas Turbine
51. Water Tubing
52. Road Into Radiation Industry
53. Road Into Radiation Industry
54. Ramp Access to Subterranean Opera
55. Chrome Tannery

Scale @ 1:200

4. Bio Gas / Hydro Power Plant

E D 2. C

3. Chromium Wor

E

E

BLINDING LIGHT, SPECTACLE AT THE EDGE OF LONDON/BEIJING

Max Dewdney, Chee-Kit Lai

"The thoughtful eye must turn to the edge of the blinding light of contemporary spectacles to catch a distorted glimpse of the barely visible media that allow the intense architectural broadcasts to take place. Eventually a rich catalogue of different forms of almost nothing will come into focus. Each of these overlooked, seemingly ephemeral conditions could act as the basis for the most substantial rethinking of our field. Almost nothing will again be the substance of almost everything."

Mark Wigley, *'Toward a History of Quantity'* in Anthony Vidler (ed), Architecture Between Spectacle and Use (2008)

Spectacle has particular resonance in understanding the image of London in 2012: an incongruous mix of Olympic excitement and fears of civic disorder in the wake of fierce summer rioting. Both events are spectacular albeit in very different and extreme ways. The Olympics produce highly controlled media images whilst the riots presented a spontaneous scene of urban violence and disorder. This year we looked at the 'Architecture of Spectacle' by studying London and Beijing, both cities famous for their pomp and pageantry in epic proportions. Project 1 looked at the juxtaposition of pre-Olympic London, and its imagined legacy through the design of temporary interventions, while Project 2 proposed public buildings within the reality of Beijing post-Olympics.

Spectacle produces different kinds of representation, both live and mediated, requiring the spaces and fabric of the city to tell a story. The infrastructure required to construct a series of controlled images is often temporary and ad-hoc in nature. In society increasingly obsessed with images, rendered views of buildings circulate in the press with as much force as 'actual' architecture, therefore virtual space and physical architecture must be understood in relation to each other.

The examination of architecture's relationship to spectacle raises interesting questions of performance, time, functionality, materiality, technology, adaptability, users, viewpoints and constructions. Unit 9 is interested in architecture that has permanence and temporality, memory and loss, reality and the hyper real, fact and fiction, and in problematizing the notion that they are distinct opposites.

"Within industrial and post-industrial cultural and state formations, Spectacle implies an organization of appearances that are simultaneously enticing, deceptive, distracting and superficial."

'New Keywords: A Revised Vocabulary of Culture and Society',
by T.Bennett, L.Grossberg, M.Morris, R.Williams, p335.

This year we visited Beijing; a city of Spectacle; a vast and symmetrical metropolis whose architecture has adapted to reflect the outward image its political leaders wish to project; from Kublai Khan's rebuilding of the city in the 13th century, to the modern high-tech metropolis of today. Unit 9's fieldwork investigations established connections with a number of leading professionals within the field of architecture, urbanism and curation, in our search for sites and issues of contemporary relevance to Beijing that the student projects are set within.

Special thanks: Architecture Department at The Central Academy of Fine Arts, Beijing; Arrow Factory, Beijing; Arup Associates, Adam Smith and James Ward (Technical Consultants); Carol Lu Yinghua (Jury member Golden Lion Award at the Venice Biennale '11; British Council (Architecture, Fashion, Design); Caochangdi Workstation, Beijing; Dr Hilary Powell (AHRC Fellow in the Creative and Performing Arts); Studio X Beijing (University of Columbia); Prof Yunsheng Su (Shanghai Tongji Urban Planning & Design Institute)

Year 2: Caitlin Mary Abbott, Tahora Azizy, Benjamin Beach, Finbarr Anton Fallon, Qiuling Guan, Pavel Kosyrev, Vasilis Marcou Ilchuk, Panagiotis Tzannetakis

Year 3: Gary Edwards, Sarah Edwards, Ivie Egonmwan, Yin Sandy Lee, Jamie Lilley, Rachel Pickford, Sophie Madeleine Richards

Fig. 9.1 Benjamin Beach, Situationist Social Centre. The centre draws on the urban strategy of the Situationists to provide a community refuge with the aim to protect and preserve the urban fabric of the surrounding Hutongs through a photographic documentary process. The building provides darkrooms, cinema, exhibition space and artist residencies. Image shows site-strategy model based on Guy Debord's 'A Game of War'. **Fig. 9.2** Qiuling Guan, Peking Duck Emporium. The project explores the lost tradition of local production of livestock within the city courtyard, reinventing the typology into a contemporary urban duck farm and restaurant within downtown Beijing. Image shows perspective view at night looking north towards Tiananmen Square. **Fig. 9.3** Tahora Azizy, Urban Oasis. The hybrid programme combines water, washing and play within the city's emerging contemporary culture. It is a multilevel swimming pool, bath-house, café and restaurant sited within '798' Art and Media district in the north-east suburb of Beijing. Image shows view from entrance lobby across swimming pool to waterfall beyond. **Fig. 9.4** Rachel Pickford, Alternative Respiratory Clinic. The project addresses the city air pollution. The scheme explores the architecture of biomimicry to provide immersive environments for salt, mustard and chrysanthemum pools as a way to tackle breathing problems created by Beijing's air pollution. Image shows concept model.

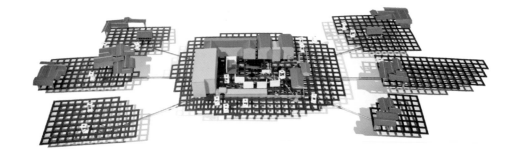

9.1

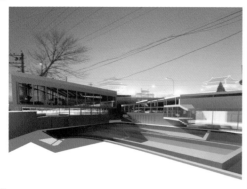

9.2

9.3

9.4

Fig. 9.5 Vasilis Marcou Ilchuk, Public Calligraphy School. See Fig. 4.9, Fig. 19 and Fig. 20 for more details. Image shows physical model. **Fig. 9.6** Sophie Richards, Inverted Tofu Temple. See Fig. 11 for more details. Image shows cutaway axonometric view. **Fig. 9.7** Sarah Edwards, Xi An Lake Institute of the Environment. See Fig.18 for more details. Image shows 1:500 masterplan model.

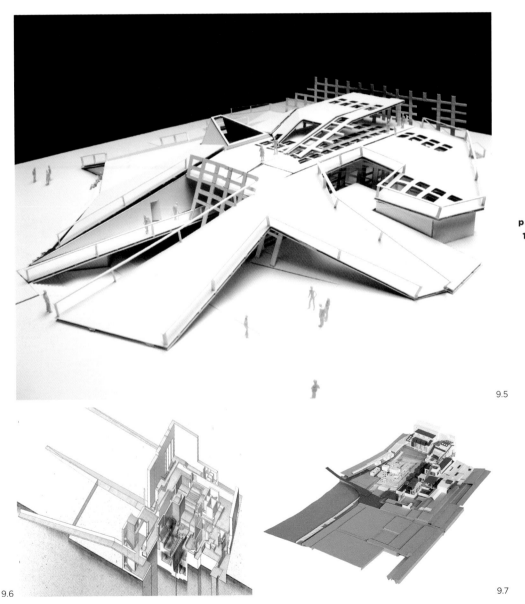

9.5

9.6

9.7

Fig. 9.8 Jamie Lilley, Sports and Social Centre for the United Kingdom Trade & Investment (UKTI) Outpost in Beijing. See Fig. 9.10 for more details. Exploded axonometric. **Fig. 9.9** Vasilis Marcou Ilchuk, Public Calligraphy School. See Fig. 19 and Fig. 20 for more details. Model basement showing circulation. **Fig. 9.10** Jamie Lilley, Sports and Social Centre for the United Kingdom Trade & Investment (UKTI) Outpost in Beijing. The building is an outpost in Beijing to act as a trade, leisure and business centre. The scheme addresses Anglo-Sino stereotypes, rituals and customs through an architecture of illusion and power. Image shows detail of 1:200 model which also functions as a 1:1 viewing device. **Fig. 9.11** Sophie Richards, Inverted Tofu Temple. The project addresses the growing return to Buddhism and vegetarianism within contemporary Chinese culture. The building provides an artificial urban well with soya allotments, tofu production and cookery school sited within '798' Art and Media district in the north-east suburb of Beijing. Image shows sectional model with light study.

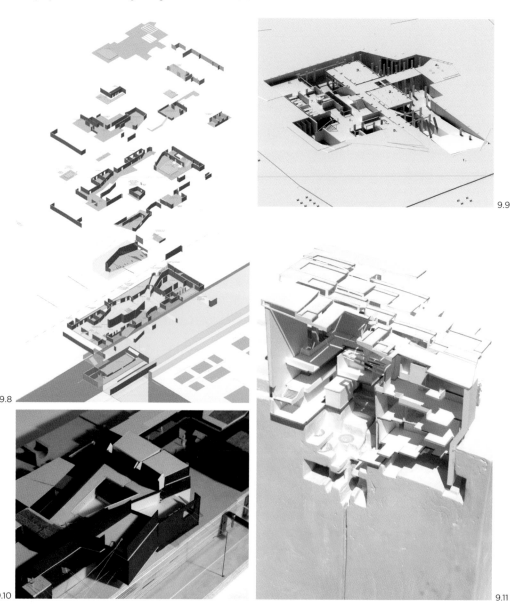

9.8

9.9

9.10

9.11

Fig. 9.12 Pavel Kosyrev, Celebration & Remembrance Centre. The project addresses the differences and similarities in the complex cultural customs and rituals of birth, death and marriage. The building provides a centre for celebration and remembrance for Weddings, Wakes and Birth Ceremonies. Sited within central Beijing the scheme provides space for families to celebrate and remember outside of the confines of their otherwise close living quarters. **Fig. 9.13** Sandy Yin Lee, Jasmine Tea House and Gardens. The building acts as self-sufficient workers' collective providing a local economy and gateway to the surrounding Hutongs. The design caters for the production of Jasmine Tea, from the growth of the Jamine flowers, to the sorting, drying and consumption of tea through collected and filtered rainwater. Image shows long section.

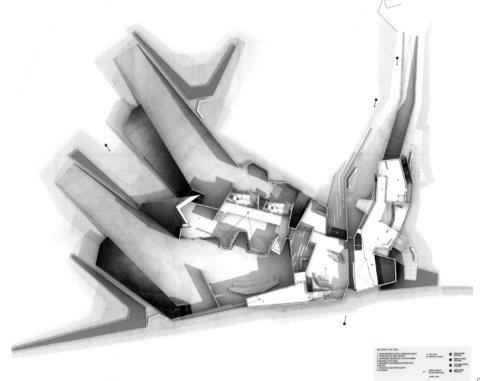

9.12

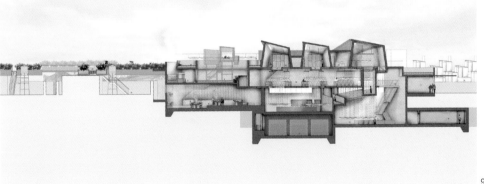

9.13

Fig. 9.14 Finbarr Fallon, Recycling Centre & Trading Cooperative. See Fig. 15 for more details. Aerial view of site and proposal. **Fig. 9.15** Finbarr Fallon, Recycling Centre & Trading Cooperative. The building addresses the valuable assets of recyclable waste (that typically occurs on the city outskirts) within downtown Beijing. The Centre provides surrounding local Hutong residents a place to recycle plastic and turn organic waste into power, serving as a model for a cooperative micro economy. Sectional view across site and proposal.

9.14

9.15

Fig. 9.16 Gary Edwards, CAFA Union. See Fig. 17 for more details. Perspective plan view. **Fig. 9.17** Gary Edwards, CAFA Union. The project proposes a student union in addressing issues of communication and democracy. Sited in the China Central Academy of Fine Arts, the building adjusts and adapts to signify and cater for a range of sporting and social events. The project addresses contemporary issues of the virtual and the real through an interactive architecture that utilises programming technology to adapt to the users' needs. Sectional perspective view.

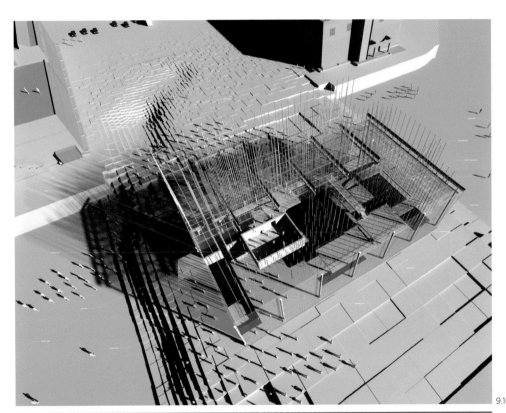

9.16

9.17

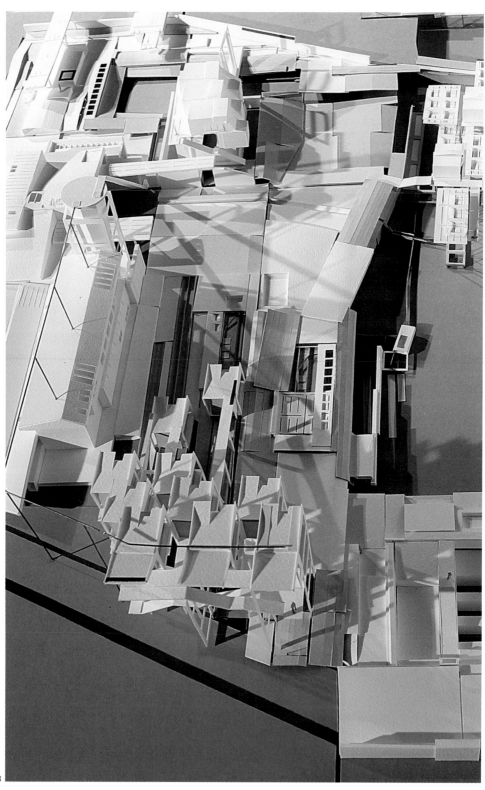

9.18

Fig. 9.18 Sarah Edwards, Xi An Lake Institute of the Environment. The project addresses Beijing's issues of water pollution and congestions by providing an urban inner city retreat. The scheme is an infrastructural landscape for the monitoring and purification of the Xi An lake, located at the outer north east boundary of Beijing's second ring road. Image shows final model looking south. **Fig. 9.19** Vasilis Marcou Ilchuk, Public Calligraphy School. See Fig. 20 for more details. Exploded axonometric model. **Fig. 9.20** Vasilis Marcou Ilchuk, Public Calligraphy School. The project celebrates the Chinese tradition of using public spaces within the city through spontaneous performance, fitness, play and learning. The building provides an open calligraphy school and student accommodation, archives, and exhibition hall, whilst the architectonics provide open platforms for more spontaneous events. Image shows detail of exploded CAD model in relation to the building's grid as a system to divide the use of individual spaces.

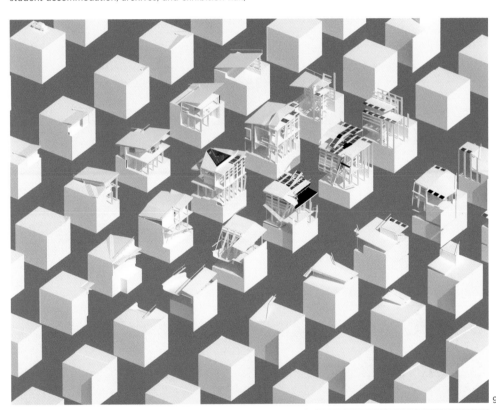

9.19

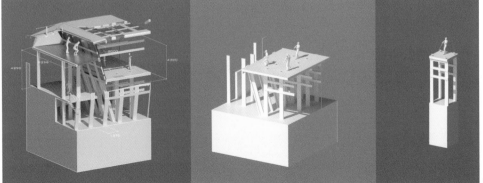

9.20

BSc ARCHITECTURAL STUDIES

Barbara Penner

The Bartlett offers a BSc (Hons) in Architectural Studies. This is a unique course that allows students to follow modules within the Bartlett in conjunction with modules in other departments of UCL. The programme has been running since 2002-3 and now has over 90 graduates and a well-established track record. Graduates have gone on to postgraduate studies and professional careers in a wide variety of fields including: journalism, landscape design, lighting design, documentary film, conservation, photography, sculpture, print-making, arts education and management, event management, planning, law, marketing and the media, property valuation, construction management, the charity sector, and heritage institutions. They have pursued further studies at places from the Royal College of Art to ETH in Zurich as well as in various UCL Masters programmes.

The great strength of the AS programme is its multidisciplinarity: students are able to tailor their own course of study to suit their particular interests and future postgraduate and career plans. It suits highly motivated, independent students who are interested in architecture and urban studies and who wish to take advantage of electives on offer elsewhere in UCL. Popular choices are Art History, Management, Languages, Economics, History, Philosophy, Mathematics, Anthropology, Law, Archaeology, and Geography.

There are two specially tailored course modules for Architectural Studies students within the Bartlett. The Dissertation is an independent written project focusing on an architectural subject of a student's choice and resulting in an investigative in-depth written report. Project X is an independent creative project in which students research an architectural idea or series of ideas through visual and other architectural media – including drawing, photography, model-making, casting, sound, film, new digital media, installation and performance – in conjunction with a short creative written piece.

Examples from both Dissertation and Project X
are reproduced on the following pages.

Yr. 2: Kate Edwards, Rebecca Li, India Smith,
Amalie White, Yixian Xie, Alexander Zyryaev

Yr. 3: Amber Fahey, Azuki Ichihashi, Lizzie Chen Nuozi,
Patrick O'Callaghan, Kawai Ho, Charlotte Moon, Seth Pimlott,
Hong Miao Shi, Leonie Walker

BSC ARCHITECTURAL STUDIES DISSERTATION

The Dissertation in Architectural Studies enables students to undertake an independent research project of 10,000 words. The emphasis is on conducting original research and producing an in-depth written report, supported by appropriate visual and textual documentation. This course is taught through individual or small group tutorials, supplemented by occasional seminars and group meetings. The aims of the Dissertation are to enable students to conduct primary research, to think critically about issues with architectural implications, and to develop and showcase practical writing and presentation skills.

Yr. 3: Amber Fahey, Patrick O'Callaghan, Kawai Ho, Charlotte Moon, Seth Pimlott, Hong Miao Shi, Leonie Walker

Extract from **SETH PIMLOTT** (3rd year)
'A Dream of Britain': Surrealism and the Everyday in the War Films of Humphrey Jennings
Supervised by Iain Borden

For several years the coming war was a nightmare to me [...] But the night before the Russo - German pact was announced I dreamed that the war had started. It was one of those dreams, which, whatever Freudian inner meaning they may have, do sometimes reveal to you the real state of your feelings. It taught me two things, first that I should be simply relieved when the long dreaded war started, secondly, that I was patriotic at heart.
– George Orwell, "My Country Right or Left", 1940

Humphrey Jennings' film Listen to Britain, made in 1942, has been seen as a singular poetic work whose power derives from its capacity to combine British life into a coordinated and harmonious symphony, at a time of intense national stress during the Second World War. However, I will show that the film's success both as art and propaganda depended on the way in which the film raised anxiety and the fear of dissolution precisely in that moment of unity. Surrealist methods and Jennings' own interpretation of them are at the heart of how he manages to hold these contradictions together, and explain how the film performs its ideological and artistic work.

Throughout his career as a poet, critic, and filmmaker, Jennings sought to describe everyday experience through surrealism – revealing the unacknowledged social and psychological phenomena within the taken-for-granted objects, images and actions of daily routine. His interest in quotidian experience developed during his involvement with Mass Observation, from 1936-1938, an organisation that attempted to document the unconscious lives of the British public. However, through looking at these mundane habits, and the effect of national events on daily life, Jennings used Mass Observation to make Surrealism something other than romanticised escapism. In turn, he used Surrealism to make Mass Observation something other than documentary usefulness. Through looking at his work with M.O. and his films Listen To Britain and A Diary for Timothy (1945), we can map his relationship to the everyday, and how he brings his own distinctive vision, influenced by surrealist techniques of collage and 'coincidence' to his subject. In these films he develops his own unorthodox surrealism.

The films are an investigation of a 'social' unconscious rather than the personal, and display a patriotism seemingly at odds with surrealist internationalism. They propose social reformation rather than revolution. Jennings' work is seen as the first example of British auteurship, a highly individual, poetic sensibility, which means that both films are instantly recognisable. Yet this artistic signature is allied to an intensely local, British, view of the world, and is intended as an instrument of social and political change. Finally, in the context of the Second World War, they are art in the service of propaganda. The work remains interesting because the films are not just historic documents; they are still alive, and remain affecting.

Extract from **HONGMIAO SHI** (3rd year)

A good piece could be written on the art audience and the educational
fallacy. We seem to have ended up with the wrong audience.
- Brian O'Doherty

For the past 300 years, there has been a tension between the aims of British exhibition creators and the responses from their viewers. Didacticism – the desire to improve minds – was the strongest rationale since the late 17th century, but it was not always achieved. Audiences were often confused by the exhibitor's method of teaching, or prioritised entertainment above learning. To ensure success in educating their viewers, exhibition organisers have often rejected visitors who did not match their ideal audience. Many exhibits originally aimed for social inclusion but withdrew that equality when organisers believed it would clash with their didactic intentions.

It is not only organisers who believe certain visitors are unsuitable: some individuals also see themselves as the wrong audience to exhibitions. In one 1990s survey conducted with ethnic minority parents living in Britain about their museum visiting habits, factors such as ethnicity, social class and education level have deterred them from visiting museums. Some perceived the space to be more suited for, in their words, "posh people", whilst others saw museums and galleries as "white people's territory". Art galleries were seen as even more "distant and elitist" than historical museums. The interviewees could not identify themselves within Britain's museums.

But despite believing these spaces would make them feel socially segregated, the same individuals thought "society needed museums" and they were "reassured by the existence of museums, even if they did not visit them". These quotes show a contradictory opinion of British museums: they are seen as both beneficial to society and culture, but also overwhelming and alien. In general, the interviewees who did not visit museums regularly believed exhibitions to be theoretically enlightening (for other people), but for themselves too difficult to understand. For them, the 'ideal' viewer already holds the perfect amount of background knowledge – they are insiders to the subject. Any other sort of visitor would be the 'wrong' audience and would not be able to understand the exhibition.

It is impossible to write a concise account through 300 years of British exhibition history in the space of this dissertation, so I will focus on what I believe to be three key examples. First, the British Museum, in particular the first decade of its establishment in 1753; second, the Great Exhibition of the Works of Industry of all Nations (or simply, the Great Exhibition) in 1851; third, the 'white cube' gallery aesthetic prominent in art exhibitions from the 1960s to present. [...]

PROJECT X

Project X aims to help students build a creative and reflective practice of their own. It enables them to undertake a mode of working that particularly interests them and an independent practice-based project in which they can research and pursue a subject of their preference. Students are asked to think of architecture in interdisciplinary ways, explore alternative approaches to design and situate their work within a broader cultural context. The work is developed in conjunction with a short written piece. A series of key questions confront students at different stages of the year concerning the nature of their practice, the contribution of their work to the broader field of architecture, the originality of their project, and the selection of appropriate media for the ideas pursued.

We started the year by researching how games, both traditional and modern, have a resonance in the design of our environment. Looking at how architects and artists have used games as a means to critique and as a tool to engage with the user. Each student designed a game of their own, working at different scales, applying a carefully composed set of rules, or regulations, that in turn were applied to a fellow student's work. Each student then followed a research path that initially stemmed from the first project, and then soon developed it's own unique direction. The resulting projects are speculative and diverse, as is the use of media, ranging from casting, hand drawing, projection, digital modelling, found sound recording and composition, caramelising, miniature installation, social media, anamorphic oil painting, to name just a few.

Yr. 2: Kate Edwards, India Smith, Amalie White,
Yixian Xie, Alexander Zyryaev

Yr. 3: Lizzie Chen Nuozi, Amber Fahey, Azuki Ichihashi,
Patrick O'Callaghan, Seth Pimlott, Leonie Walker

Fig. X.1 Nuozi Chen, Building Regulations and the Bartlett (photograph, Building Regulations, Approved Document Part M, diagram 9 & 10 applied to a standard Bartlett School of Architecture door), a series of investigations through projection and stencil that both overlay, test and tweak certain building regulations against The Bartlett School of Architecture. **Fig. X.2** Leonie Walker, Contemporary Archaeologies Conducted on Interior Domestic Spaces (archive folder), see Fig. X.7 for more details. **Fig. X.3** Alexander Zyryaev, Olympic Chess Set (model), a series of investigations and installations that observe how the general public might relate to and engage with the public environment when an everyday element is recreated and then replaced or appropriated and then reintroduced. The project culminates in the design and manufacture of an Olympic Chess board, that speculates upon the moves and game-play of two proposed opponents, the Olympic Corporate Sponsors versus the Local Activists. **Fig. X.4** Amber Fahey, Interstellar Weather Moderated for Domesticity (photograph, Interstellar Map, calculations and initial scale drawing, Somers Town Observatory), see Fig. X.8 for more details.

X.1

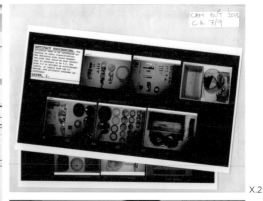

X.2

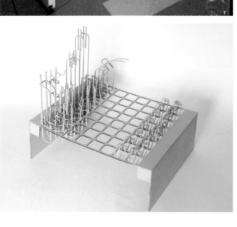

X.3

X.4

Fig. X.5 Amelie White, Artist's Palette (prototype model), alternative artist's palette designed through observation and discussion and made with a symbiotic combination of hand crafted and digital production techniques. **Fig. X.6** Seth Pimlott, So Exotic, So Homemade (appropriated Super 8 film, over-layed and scratched), see Fig. X.11 for more details. **Fig. X.7** Leonie Walker, Contemporary Archaeologies Conducted on Interior Domestic Spaces (archive folder), a method to observe, discover and at times imagine subtle stories and histories of a typical 1970's flat over a number of years, using the investigatory and archiving techniques of Archaeology adapted for the domestic environment.

X.5

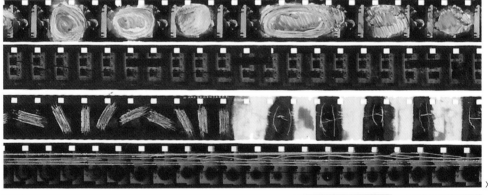

X.6

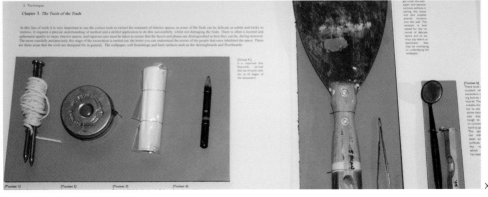

X.7

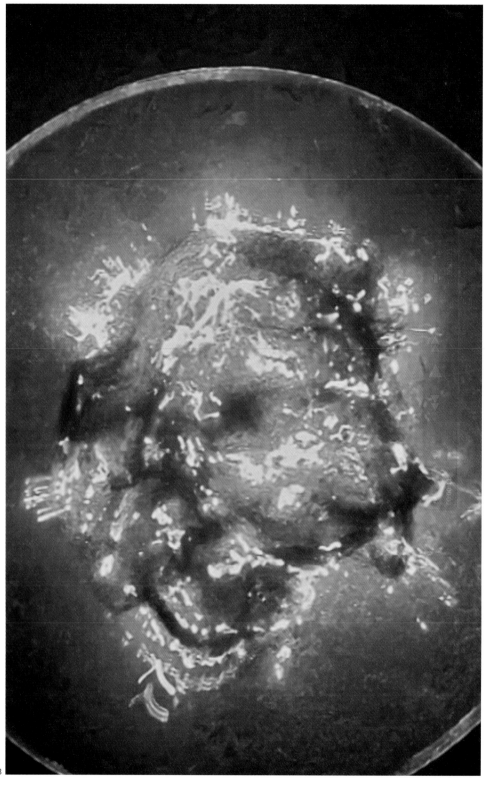

X.8

Fig. X.8 Amber Fahey, Interstellar Weather Moderated for Domesticity (film still, supernovae remnant, Somers Town Observatory), a project that works at a number of different scales and is tested through a surprising range of media to introduce and recreate rare astronomical events into the domestic environment through a carefully orchestrated combination of domestic alchemy, projection and sound. **Fig. X.9** Azuki Ichihashi, Zenbazuru (photograph, 1000 cranes), is a traditional Japanese event - the creation of 1000 paper Origami Cranes, that is orchestrated by a series of preparatory excursions and investigations. Unusually this project relies on a combination of social collaboration and the use of a range of social media and culminates in a public event that allows further meaning into the process of collaborative making to be discovered. **Fig. X.10** Kate Edwards, Caramel and Sugar at Play (photograph, teacup shipwreck), an investigation through a number of scales looking at our relationship and possible attitudes to childhood and play, working with sugar, caramel, installation and film. **Fig. X.11** Seth Pimlott, So Exotic, So Homemade (film still, construction site hoarding, EC2), Investigations using different film types and techniques and working with collage for both sound and image. The Barbican and Stratford are both the real and projected sites, observing a contemporary attitude to the future that can allow the spectator to see those places with a different and unexpected understanding.

X.9

X.10

X.11

MArch
Architecture

SF CITIES

CJ Lim, Bernd Felsinger

"…I chose to write science fiction in the beginning is that it offered me a way in which I could remake the landscapes of the England I knew in the 1960s and 1970s, in the way the surrealism worked, to make them resemble, unconsciously, the landscapes of wartime Shanghai… it's the psychological realm where science fiction is most valuable in its predictive function, and put the emotions into the future."

JG Ballard

Science fiction [SF] is prophetic - utopian visions in SF, have often predicted the future, as much as representing a past that was never possible. While SF has become mainstream, adopted by defence industries and food technology industries, it is treated with wariness in respect to architecture and urban design, leading to pejorative accusations of utopianism. Imaginative SF often predates modern technology and cities, and is much more than the narrow pop culture definition given to Star Trek and Dr Who. Ebenezer Howard's garden city, for example, was inspired by the utopian tract, 'Looking Backward: 2000-1887', by the American lawyer, Edward Bellamy. The third largest bestseller of its time when published in 1888, Bellamy's novel immediately spawned a political mass movement and several communities adopting its ideals. Letchworth Garden City and Welwyn Garden City in the UK, founded on Howard's concentric plan of open space, parkland and radial boulevards that carefully integrated housing, agriculture and industry, remain two of the few recognised realisations of utopia in existence.

Perhaps one of the most celebrated pieces of SF was Arthur C Clarke's prediction of a network of satellites in geostationary orbits. Jules Verne wrote about air, space and underwater travel before these forms of travel had been devised. The British philosopher and science fiction author, Olaf Stapledon anticipated the science of genetic engineering, predicted in 'Last and First Men: A Story of the Near and Far Future' (1930) that civilization might collapse as a result of resource depletion, a concept that was ridiculed as outlandish at the time. Science fiction always holds a mirror to the present, taking the notion 'If this goes on…' as its starting point. At its heart, science fiction questions how humanity adapts, and no process of change threatens us more radically than what we are doing now to a natural environment we entirely dependent upon. SF is often used to comment on the failings of the real world - in Jack Vance's 'Rumfuddle', a typical job is driving a bulldozer that shoves the detritus of industrial civilization through a portal into the oceans of a garbage world, restoring the earth to its pristineness. However, can the world ever be perfect? Frank Miller of 'Sin City' created Gotham City's noir perfection for 'Batman' by hybridizing Cincinnati, Pittsburgh, Chicago and fundamentally New York at night.

The SF genre might have been better described as 'speculative fiction', and need not have anything to do with science at all. A good SF story, HG Wells's 'Time Machine' for instance, must contain some element that is not present in 'the real world' - no human transporting time machines actually existed. Also, could history have turned out differently with a different decision on our lives and environment? In PROJECT 1, we speculated and invented alternative realities, creating utopian impossibilities. The basic argument is that depictions of the future that may include, but move beyond, dystopias offer us ways to reinvent ourselves and especially our perspectives on new environments. PROJECT 2, the city was informed by individual studies to establish core interests and formed the basis of a complex narrative and programme. For speculative fiction to become reality, its design development as an infrastructural strategy has become ever more urgent.

> "Logic will get you from A to B.
> Imagination will take you everywhere."
>
> Albert Einstein

Unit 10 would like to thank Simon Dickens for his teaching of the Design Realisation module.

Year 4: John (Yu Wei) Chang, Douglas Fenton, Thandiwe Loewenson, Steven McCloy, Sasha Smolin, Viktor Westerdahl

Year 5: Carmelo Arancon, Kwan Kit Franky Chan, Daniel Dale, James Kitson, Savan Patel, Ned Scott, Man Fai (Martin) Tang

10.1

10.2

10.3

10.4

Fig. 10.1 — 10.2 (Prevoius spread) Man Fai (Martin) Tang, Eternal Autumnal Micro-Climates of Kyoto. Maple trees and a thousand origami cranes across the skies form a dynamic environmental responsive urban infrastructure, painting the maple syrup filled city forever golden with the warm smell of autumn. Fig. 10.3 — 10.4 Kwan Kit (Franky) Chan, Pollution for Light. As Hoyle's Black Cloud engulfs London, the city engineers a symbiotic relationship, exchanging urban pollution for natural light in Hyde 'Beach' Park. Fig. 10.5 Carmelo Arancon, Domesti(city) — the Christmas City According to Kirstie Allsopp. Mayor Allsopp of London regenerates the city with domestic strategies adapted from the twelve days of Christmas. Fig. 10.6 Daniel Dale, From HE to SHE: The Northampton Recreational Gardens. The landscape explore the potential for radical re-generation of Northampton town by way of design for and through 'play'. Fig. 10.7 Savan Patel, The Urban Oasis for London 2100. Following its desertification, London is transformed into an oasis capturing water and solar energy for its depleted population.

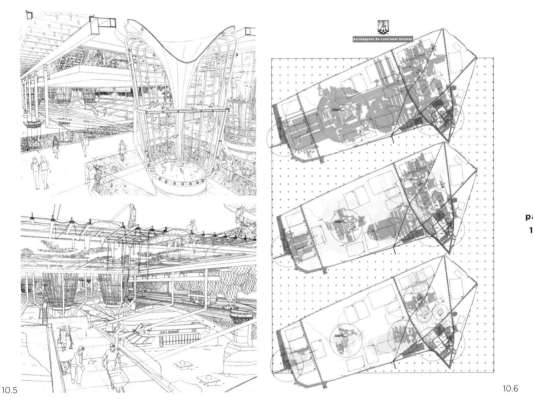

10.5

10.6

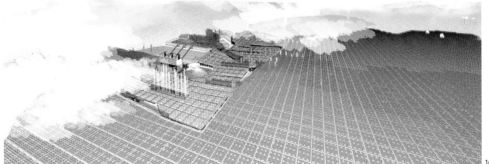

10.7

Fig. 10.8 — 10.10 Ned Scott, The War Rooms, St. James's Park London. An institutional framework to support the emergency decentralisation of the UK's infrastructural networks following an energy war in 2050 which operates on three simultaneous scales representative of the three protagonists from Clifford D. Simak's City: Man, Dog and Ant.

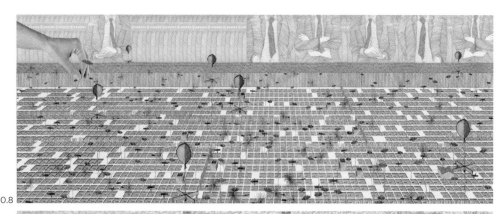

10.8

10.9

10.10>

Fig. 10.11 — 10.12 James Kitson, Duo Dimensiva. Located in the hills of Monuments Pass Utah the proposed city of Duo Dimensiva explores the concept of inhabiting a synthetic world of sensory manipulation; a development of a Foucauldian two-dimensional heterotopia explored through the narrative of Wim Wenders film Paris Texas.

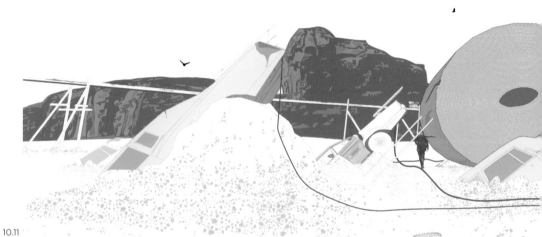

10.11

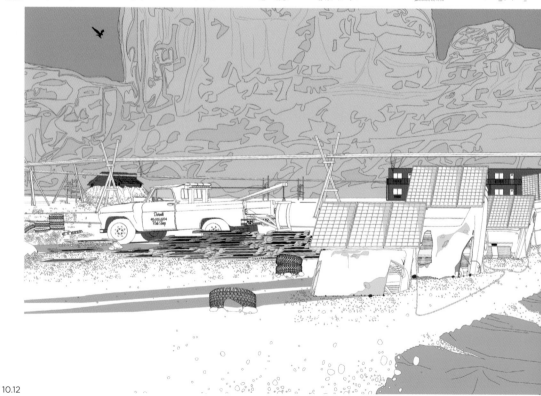

10.12

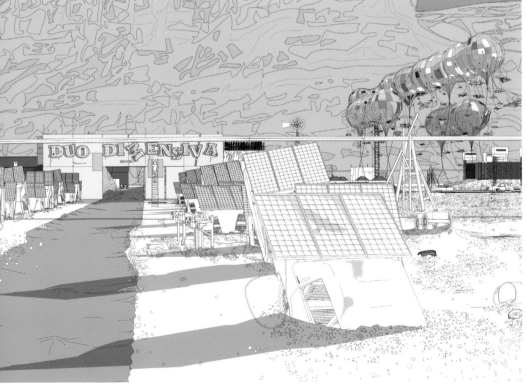

Unit 11

SUPER-URBAN-MEGA-LISTIC
Laura Allen, Mark Smout, Kyle Buchanan

"By its nature, the metropolis provides what otherwise could
be given only by travelling; namely, the strange."

Jane Jacobs, *The Death and Life of Great American Cities* (1961)

In recent years Unit 11 has looked at the responsiveness of architecture to natural landscape and how contrasting attitudes of nostalgia and tradition, policy and progress can be the stimulus for progressive architecture. This year we asked students to explore and exhibit the indivisibility of architecture and the infrastructural, social and natural landscapes of the urban world. We invited a miscellany of 'urban speciation' which synthesizes myth, mystery and the profound peculiarity of reality into intriguing and richly visualized Infrastructural Architectures and Mega-Urban Ecologies.

Forty years ago the Italian avant-garde architectural collective, Superstudio, created the Continuous Monument, a radical and dystopian proposition in which a global extrusion of the city, fashioned as a single piece of architecture, is laid over the metropolis and beyond. In the New York Extrusion project we see 'New New York' containing the built up form of Manhattan arranged into a 'great plain of ice, clouds or sky reflecting its surrounding and revealing little of itself' whilst forming 'a world rendered uniform by technology, culture and all the other inevitable forms of imperialism'. Many of the last century's speculative fantasies, visionary fictions and retroactive manifestos such as Buckminster Fuller's Manhattan Dome (1950), Ron Herron's Walking City (1964), the Lower Manhattan Express Way by Paul Rudolph (1967) and Rem Koolhaas' Delirious New York (1978) were sited in Manhattan. Then as now the city stood as a symbol of what is good and simultaneously what is bad about American urban culture, making the city apposite for utopian and dystopian megaschemes and super-structural projects as a response to the cultural pressures and architectural politics of the day.

The megascheme positions architecture at the convergence of urbanism, engineering and infrastructure. These conceptual speculations as well as New York's megastructural remnants such as the Washington Bridge Extension Complex and idealist visions such as the United Nations Headquarters and Rockefeller Centre, exploit the vertical and horizontal – three-dimensional – infrastructure of Manhattan's built and natural environments which overlap and entwine to form a nexus of the technological, cultural and natural world.

Manhattan's infrastructural systems of road, rail, power, water, communications, sanitation, commodity and waste are cited as the most complex and extensive of any developed city and exist in parallel with one another stretching across

Manhattan to the commercial, industrial and residential boroughs that surround it. They are fused into the everyday life of the city and its inhabitants to the extent that delivering fresh coffee, activating road crossings, monitoring drinking water and cleaning the streets form part of an invisible yet intrinsic system of provision, support and control.

The Past, Present and Future of Big Ideas

We began by looking at New York from afar. Following film screenings and readings, students examined the curious realities of the city's support structures, political manifestos, and avant-garde attitudes. They developed propositions that speculated about the actual and potential architectural impact of the systems that drive the everyday operation and formation of the urban reality. We sought to operate at the interface between architecture and the city's cultural, environmental and build infrastructures. The studio examined systems ranging from the New York steam network, brownouts, food distribution, water and waste management, to the potential for mineral extraction from the bedrock of Manhattan.

We then advanced initial investigations into definitive proposals: Year 5 developing thesis design projects; Year 4 design realization buildings on site in New York. Projects explored physical and systematic propositions at the scale of the city, whilst investigating the tectonic, lyrical, and architectural impact of these.

Following the success of last years 'Los Angeles Super-Workshop' we again collaborated with writer and blogger Geoff Manaugh (BLDGBLOG). Our New York trip was hosted by the GSAPP Columbia University's Manhattan based Studio-X venue, of which Manaugh is a Director. Guided by local experts we explored and visited ventilation systems, steam plants, and transport networks, many of which are rarely open or even known to the general public. The knowledge and experience of the characters who operate and manage these systems day to day was invaluable in animating the potential of infrastructure to impact on our experience of the city.

Thanks to our external consultants: Sarah Bell, Dan Cash, Stephen Foster, Murray Fraser, Daisy Froud, Ben Godber, Eva Macnamara, Barbara Penner, Jason Slocombe, and Oliver Wilton. Special thanks to John Lyall and Geoff Manaugh.

Year 4: Farah Badaruddin, Banksie Critchley, Alisan Dockerty, Rebecca Fode, Imogen Holden, Sonila Kadillari, Yee Yan (Adrienne) Lau, Tom Partridge, Biten Patel, Harriet Redman, Luke Royffe

Year 5: Janinder Bhatti, Emma Flynn, Theo Games Petrohilos, Victor Hadjikyriacou, Amy Hiley, Jonathan Kaminsky, Daniel Marmot, Marcus Todd

Fig. 11.1 Theo Games Petrohilos. The Air Futures Building, Wall Street, stands as the headquarters of the alchemic financial system that trades the air above Manhattan. Air bankers and their architecture of mania manipulate investments, investors and air flows to their own ends in this speculative future of the city's existing TDR (Transferable Development Rights) market. Regulation nodes and air column model. **Fig. 11.2** Yee Yan Adrienne Yau. The Inverted Street Market exploits Manhattan's strict street vendors regulations. **Fig. 11.3** Victor Hadjikyriacou. The Golden Core. A project investigating the expansion of the United Nations as a global economic organisation.

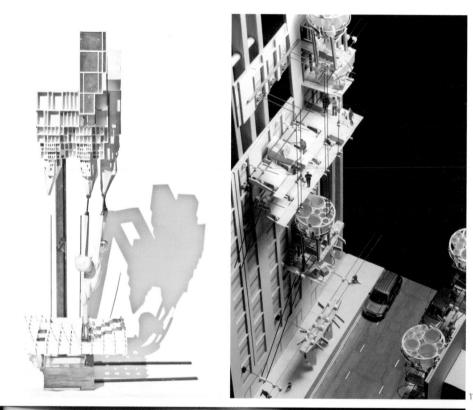

11.1

11.2

11.3

Fig. 11.4 Jon Kaminsky. Powered Parkland: The Museum of Steam. The parkland exposes the hidden infrastructure of NYC's district steam system providing an alternative to the city's extreme seasonality via tempered microclimates that smooth the winter climate at varying speeds. Warm areas are incorporated for the growth of tropical and unseasonal plants and crops, as well as warm lawns, heated bathing pools and walkways. **Fig. 11.5** Sonila Kadillari. Studies for a Blackout City. This model explores how darkness can be used to reveal and how light can hide. Studies for Madison Observatory celestial viewing corridors. **Fig. 11.6** Tom Partridge. The Manhattan Air Spa. Test model for an activated air-landscape, driven by the thermal vortices that form around tall buildings showing the flotation of elements. **Fig. 11.7** Harriet Redman. The Lock Inn, Amsterdam Avenue, Manhattan. Limited availability of fresh fruit and veg is a consistent issue in NYC, which has a inadequate network of supermarkets and food retailers. The project proposes a food distribution network that uses canals to reconnect Manhattan with its rural hinterland in New York State. Model showing a 'market-hub' where canal boats moor-up as market stalls.

11.4

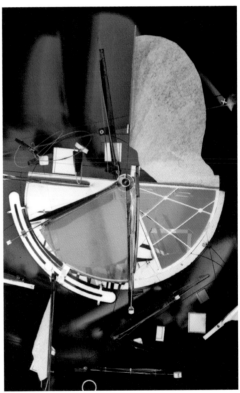

11.5

11.6

11.7

Fig. 11.8 Alisan Doherty. Watershed Public Toilet, J.P Morgan Chase Bank Plaza, Manhattan. This project develops a new take on the traditional NYC public plaza. Super-scale water harvesters collect and treat storm water and reuse it as a public spectacle and public toilet. **Fig. 11.9** Banksie Critchley. Landscape of Sleepless Light, Sara D Rooselvelt Park, Manhattan. Colour spectrum modelling exposing concealed routes over a subterranean landscape. **Fig. 11.10** Marcus Todd. Proximity without Presence. An exploration of New York as the original cinematic city, through readings of Alfred Hitchcock's New York-based films. Arced models investigate the conceptual and physical gap between interior and exterior in the construction of filmic space. **Fig. 11.11** Farah Badaruddin. Scriptorium Institute of Licensing, Farringdon, London. A building for the storage of copyrights, licenses, and secret recipes. Axonometric of the main core. **Fig. 11.12** Luke Royffe. Macy's Balloon Factory, Pier 75 NYC. A sectional model showing the assembly of 'Kermit' the largest inflatable character in the Macy's parade. The building is constructed from layered membranes hung on a lightweight frame, and can be expanded in response to the inflation (during the fabrication process) of the dirigibles within, transcribing the preparations for the parade into the consciousness of the city.

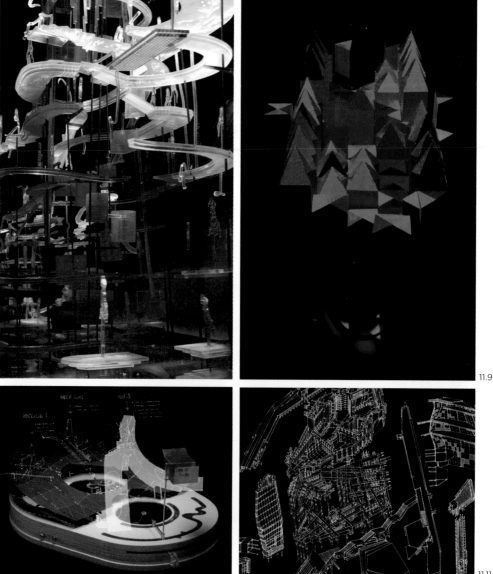

11.8

11.9

11.10

11.11

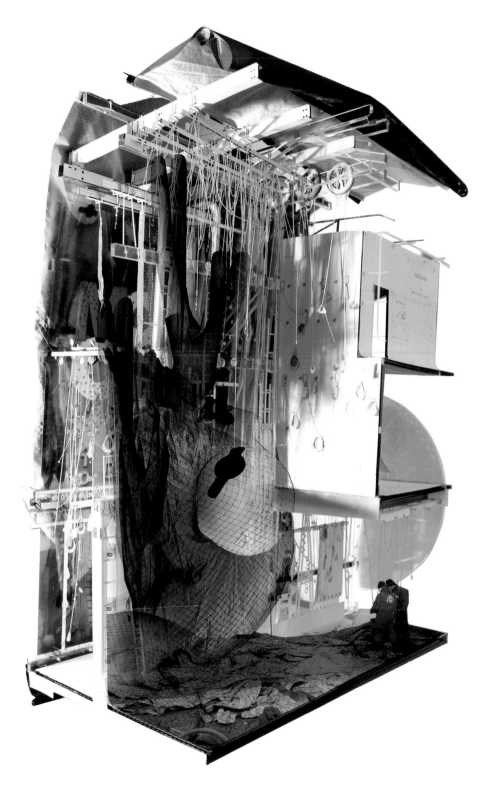

11.12

Fig. 11.13 — 11.14 Emma Flynn. Trash Can Utopias: Transforming the Waste Landscape of Long Island Suburbia, Hicksville, Long Island, NY. Since suburbia's proliferation in the U.S. more Americans now live in the suburbs than either the city or the country. Designed for a post war era and the collective American dream of the 1940s, the suburban typology is out of touch with the issues of today. Inherently wasteful and unsustainable, in terms of both space and resource consumption, the current suburban model needs to be readdressed in the face of increasing energy and environmental concerns. 'Trash Can Utopias' explores waste's historic role and future potential in the vision and creation of utopias, and how, in the specific case of Long Island suburbia, waste, and waste technologies, can transform the suburbs from a wasteful dystopia to its promised utopia. It explores the taboo and unpopular issue of garbage, challenging the invisibility and unsustainability of the current garbage infrastructure, it proposes that waste management should be brought closer to our everyday environments, increase energy efficiency and off-grid communities, whilst retaining the utopian image of suburbia to which many still aspire.

11.14

Fig. 11.15 Rebbeca Fode. L.E.S Quarry Tenement Museum. This project speculates that the Lower East Side's Inwood Marble geology is more valuable than real estate prices and proposes the excavation and subsequent redevelopment of cliff sites and memorialised spaces. **Fig. 11.16 — 11.17** Amy Hiley. Green Living City Wall, Hudson County, New Jersey. The 'City Wall' is an imagined super-dense vegetative structure; large greenhouses for food growth, interconnected with walkways and cycle paths, sky forest towers, recreational gardens, and farm market towers, fed through a circular metabolic method of managing and storing local water cycles. The wall wraps itself along the periphery of urban environments reflecting a sense of continuity, and synthesizing landscape, green infrastructure and architecture to create an ecological, recreational and social catalyst. **Fig. 11.18** Janinder Bhatti. Sacrificial Flooding: The Manhattan Island Bluebelt. Rock and Ramble detail. The scheme proposes the 'Sacrificial Flooding' of Central Park in order to deal with the problem of flooding in New York which results from the increasing climate extremes and the city's outdated water infrastructure. Central Park is redesigned as an inhabitable water infrastructure which collects, cleans and subsequently recycles and exploits storm water to produce microclimates, energy, food and drinking water for the inhabitants of the city.

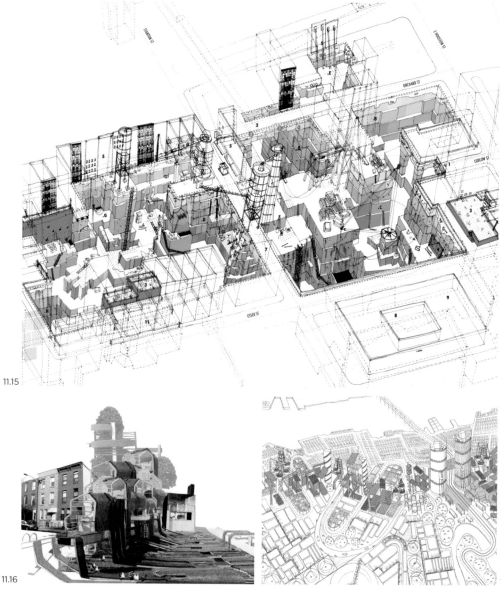

11.15

11.16

11.17

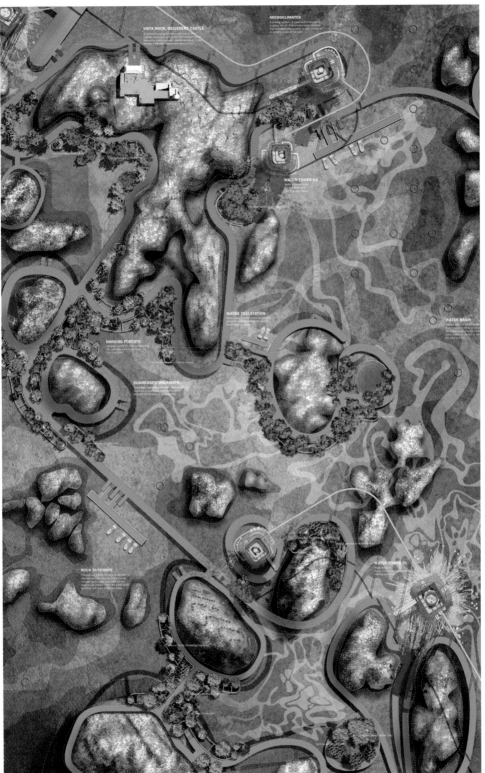

11.18

A NEW CREATIVE MYTH

Jonathan Hill, Matthew Butcher, Elizabeth Dow

Exceptional architects are exceptional storytellers, weaving a narrative that completely convinces the designer as well as the users. Denys Lasdun succinctly remarked that each architect must devise his or her 'own creative myth', a set of ideas, values and forms that are subjective but also have some objective basis that helps to make them believable. Lasdun concluded "My own myth … engages with history." Creative architects have always looked to the past to imagine the future, studying an earlier architecture not to replicate it but to understand and transform it, revealing its relevance to the present.

A city also needs a creative myth, which allows its inhabitants to understand it collectively and imagine its future. A new creative myth generates a new genius loci — genius of the place — an idea that originated in classical antiquity and has influenced architects for centuries. The genius of the place is made as much as it is found, formed from the fusion of new ideas, forms and spaces with those already in place. Edinburgh became the 'Athens of the North' and Rome is associated with La Dolce Vita, the good life. Sometimes a myth fades and a new myth must replace it for a city to prosper. To explore this idea each student developed their own 'creative myth' to allow them to design a building that could propose a new 'creative myth' and genius loci for the city it inhabits.

This year our site was Istanbul, a city whose character, name and architecture have changed many times. Once the capital of the Roman Empire and then the Ottoman Empire, it is now the principal city of the Turkish republic. As Byzantium, it was renamed Constantinople in honour of the Roman Emperor. Its modern title — Istanbul — derives from a Greek phrase that means both 'in the city' and 'to the city'. Istanbul's most famous building — Hagia Sophia — exemplifies the city's shifting image. First a church and then a mosque, it is now a museum and representative of Ataturk's secular republic. Located both in Europe and Asia, Turkey's future may lead towards the European Union or in a different direction.

Istanbul is a city of many dualities. From its location, the city straddles the Bosphorus Strait, the divide between East and West. To its religion, the secular state is overwhelmingly Muslim but has Christian and Jewish communities that connect to and provide an echo of Istanbul's many pasts. And finally to its economy, Istanbul is a city where great wealth is held by a few and poverty experienced by many.

Within this context, and key to our investigations, was an examination of distinct sites, spaces and economies within Istanbul that are under extreme pressures to re-invent or defend themselves for survival. As a starting point for these investigations we looked at, and researched, the waterfront area of Zeytinburnu and its attempts at economic regeneration after the disappearance of the area's tanneries. We examined underground economies within the city, including a previously state-supported black market. We looked at a city with its history of immigration and its many different communities, not all now welcome. We considered the place of religion and its architecture in a secular, but significantly Muslim, state. And lastly we sought to understand the slow extinction of the artisan industries in the area of Sishane, an old commercial centre in pre-Ottoman and Genoese times. Through this interrogation a deeper understanding of the city, its future as well as its past, has been established, acting as a catalyst to each student's individual approach to their architecture, their reading of site and understanding of history.

The following pages give a glimpse of the work of the unit produced within this last year. The work can also be seen as a continuation of themes that have developed within the unit over recent years, with each year having added something new to the unit's agenda, ambition and passions. Unit 12 has always encouraged the work of each student to be particular to his or her own interests, allowing them to develop a particular and distinct architectural voice that can be tested and developed through research, programme, drawing and making. This year, and in recent years, the work of the unit has also been able to continue a theme that we have become increasingly interested in: monumental buildings. In particular, those buildings designed and viewed under construction, in use and in ruin, with each phase to be seen as neither distinct, nor unique nor final. In Unit 12 we have continued to consider and develop a contemporary meaning of monumentality. Allowing a diverse range of influences, including social, political and meteorological, to play a part in the life and the material of the monument. Rather than static monuments as a unit we have proposed buildings that are in a state of flux, caught between the monument and the ruin, the material and the immaterial.

Unit 12 would like to thank Dominique Oliver, Carl Vann, Ben Godber; Rachel Cruise, Oliver Wilton, Shibboleth Shechter, Brendan Woods, Peg Rawes, Hilary Powell.

Year 4: Graham Burn, Charlotte Knight, Lulu Le Li, Anders Strand Lühr, Fiona Tan, Cassandra Tsolakis, Owain Williams, Kieran Wardle, Tim Zihong Yue

Year 5: Emily Farmer, Jerome Flinders, Patrick Hamdy, Benjamin Harriman, Ifigeneia Liangi, Yifei Song, Gabriel Warshafsky

12.1

Fig. 12.1 Gabriel Warshafsky, A Grotesque Public Body, Istanbul. Roof Plan, Detail. A new headquarters for Istanbul's public corporations, centring around the annual sponsorship and production of the world's largest feast. **Fig. 12.2** Patrick Hamdy, Saliferous Monastery, Istanbul. The Saliferous Monastery attempts to provide the city with a new urban pilgrimage site, incorporating an annual salt harvest, which will begin on an existing national holiday celebrated on 23rd April. The natural occurrence of decay conflicts with the man-made task of daily construction and maintenance of the monastery. **Fig. 12.3** Gabriel Warshafsky, A Grotesque Public Body, Istanbul. Long Section.

12.2

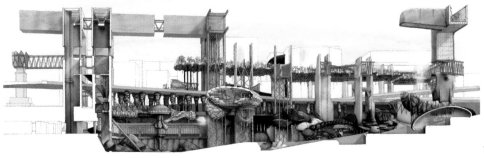

12.3

Fig. 12.4 Patrick Hamdy, Saliferous Monastery, Istanbul. Long Section. **Fig. 12.5** Charlotte Knight, The Nameless Monastery, Istanbul. Night Perspective. The Nameless Monastery conceals a theological school for the Eastern Orthodox Church of Constantinople, illegally continuing its teaching so that the ancient religion will not be lost. As the nuns retreat from the outer world, they see only the sky and are thrown back onto their solitary selves. **Fig. 12.6** Fiona Tan, The Lost and Found Power Station, Istanbul. Snapshots. A monument to the faceless migrant worker who built the city but remains excluded from it. It becomes an allegorical response to the fragile existence of the migrant class, and the government's refusal to grant them a settled identity by proposing a completely off- grid building which generates its independent source of power — a symbol for autonomy from the authority and power of the government.

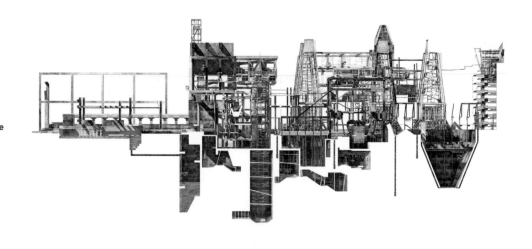

12.4

12.5

12.6

Fig. 12.7 Emily Farmer, The Writers' Harbour, Istanbul. The Authors' Lobby. The Writers' Harbour, which inhabits the interstitial site of Istanbul's main passenger port, is occupied as both a tourist thoroughfare and a safehouse for proscribed authors. The Harbour is the first purpose-built headquarters for an existing board, The European Writers' Parliament. **Fig. 12.8** Cassandra Tsolakis, Gateway into Phanar. Losing Your Marbles. Challenging the perceived value of location, the Gateway into Phanar encourages the returning Greek population to question the intrinsic connection between humans and their notions of 'home'. **Fig. 12.9** Tim Zihong Yue, The Institute of Leathercraft, Istanbul. From destruction of flesh and bones to the craft of skin, from nightmare to aspiration, the architecture is an allegory for the essential transition underlying the leathercraft industry.

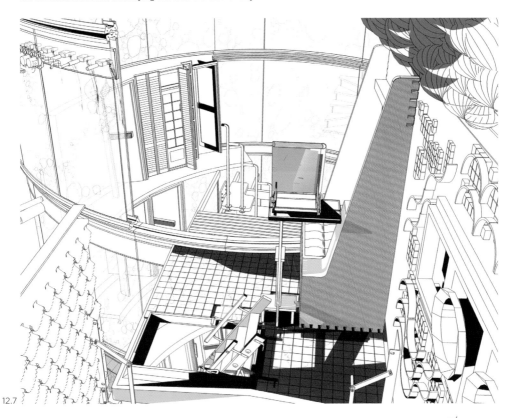

12.7

12.8

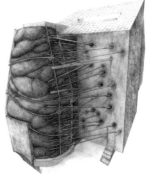

12.9

Fig. 12.10 Lulu Le Li, Water Theatre, Istanbul. Morning Perspective. A living body: breathing and sweating to modify its environment. The labyrinthine spaces within work with strategies of revealing and framing to blur the distinction between performer and spectator as they engage with filtered and artificial weather conditions. **Fig. 12.11** Graham Burn, ROCOR (MDF) Church of Aksaray, Istanbul. Large Etching. A Prototype Russian Orthodox Church is erected across a dormant construction site. Constructed entirely from MDF, the building weeps, warts and wilts in the Istanbul climate. Glossy paints and varnishes are applied religiously to preserve the church. **Fig. 12.12** Benjamin Harriman, A New British Consulate Typology, Istanbul. Wedding Chapel Model. Sited in Istanbul, it is a slow, unwieldy, but rapid to dismantle, networking and promotion facility. **Fig. 12.13** Owain Williams, Findikli Garden Foreign Office, Istanbul. Elevation Detail. Charged with cultivating planting for a picturesque garden, a centrepiece meeting room forms a loaded backdrop for Turkish foreign policy on the banks of the Bosphorus. **Fig. 12.14** Benjamin Harriman, A New British Consulate Typology, Istanbul. Courtroom Model. **Fig. 12.15** Benjamin Harriman, A New British Consulate Typology, Istanbul. Police Station Model.

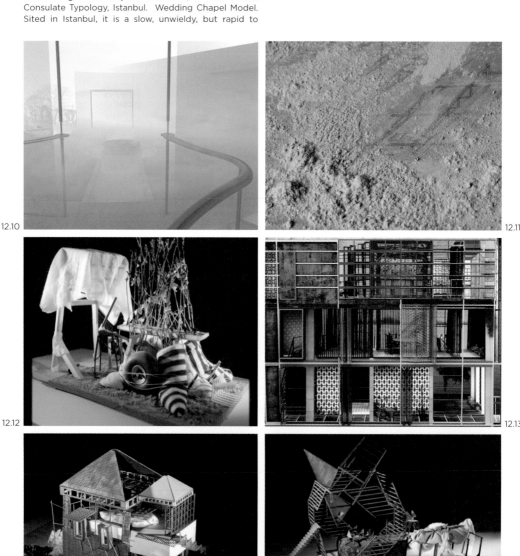

12.10

12.11

12.12

12.13

12.14

12.15

Fig. 12.16 Anders Strand Lühr, The Nation of Sivriada. Section: The Island is Carved out by the Quarry. Sited on an island of the coast of Istanbul in the Sea of Marmara, this project proposes an environment that is a symbiotic merging of nature and culture- whilst exploiting it for its resources through the reintroduction of quarrying. **Fig. 12.17** Kieran Wardle, Council for Territorial Exchange, Istanbul. Perspective. The Council investigates the attribution of authority, through architecture, to an invented political organization that attempts to govern questions of power and identity through discussion and compromise. **Fig. 12.18** Jerome Flinders, Hypoxic Complex, Istanbul. Perspective of Gateway to Complex. A Clumsy Climate Change Mitigation Strategy and Asthma Sanatorium in Istanbul.

12.16

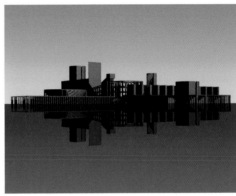

12.17

12.18

Fig. 12.19 Jerome Flinders, Hypoxic Complex, Istanbul. Roof Plan. **Fig. 12.20** Yifei Song, The Circus City, Istanbul. Plan. The project aims to re-introduce the circus programme to the City of Istanbul, searching for a new experience that reinterprets the traditional Turkish acts. The circus offers a fictional and nostalgic world which criticizes the contemporary nature of Istanbul's rapid urban transformation. **Fig. 12.21** Yifei Song, The Circus City, Istanbul. Spectator exploring the trapeze. **Fig. 12.22** Yifei Song, The Circus City, Istanbul. View of upper gallery. **Fig. 12.23** Ifigeneia Liangi, Nostalgia of the Future, 2013. The Lover's Tree House. The apartments of the area of Kipseli are particularly small and private space is limited. It is common for big families to use the living room as an extra bedroom, which causes difficulty in having sex. The lover's tree house is a response to limited private space. It is designed so that people would have to hold hands in order to climb on it.

12.19

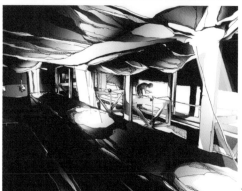

12.20

12.21

12.22

12.23

CHRONOTOPIA

James O'Leary, Paul Bavister

"We will give the name chronotope (literally, 'time-space') to the intrinsic connectedness of temporal and spatial relationships. In the artistic chronotope, spatial and temporal indicators are fused into one carefully thought-out, concrete whole. Time, as it were, thickens, takes on flesh, becomes artistically visible; likewise; space becomes charged and responsive to the movements of time, plot, and history."

Mikhail Bakhtin, *The Dialogical Imagination* (1975)

Unit 14 explores the creation of architectures of temporal awareness and sensitivity that are situated in an expanding field of architectural practice - one that touches the edges of related disciplines such as art installation, film, performance, interaction and experience design. We are interested in architecture that is developed through the realms of the phenomenal, the atmospheric and the ephemeral to engender spaces that are as focussed on the magic of the experiential, as much as the logic of the constructional.

In parallel with this immersive approach to architectural design, we are interested in the evident necessity to develop new tools and approaches to architectural representation required to project forward into this condition. Here, developments in performative scoring, storyboarding and time-based drawing take on more of an active role in the design process. Beyond the representational, the Unit is focused on the pursuit of the tangible in architectural design processes through rigorous testing of various material, tectonic and technological realities. Through building on the Units' culture of making, testing, fabrication and live projects, we aim to promote awareness of innovations in communications, sustainability and technology in architectural practice. We are interested in developing and promoting collaborative approaches to design that integrate teaching, learning and research practice; cultivating a rich context of architectural enquiry that is at ease with the critical thinking and reflection required to address a broad range of contemporary architectural issues.

We started the year with the development of the 'Chronotope', where we explored the idea of THICK TIME where 'Time, as it were, thickens, takes on flesh, becomes artistically visible'. Year 4 students collaborated with Year 5 students for an introductory project linking programme and process through a series of 600 mm cubic volumes. The aim of the project was to pass an electrical current from one corner of the complete volume to the other — answering the question "How many architects does it take to switch on a light bulb"? Between switch and bulb are student-devised circuits of handshaking machines, processors, hammers, connectors, weights, couplings and the like, all operating in manic collaboration toward the shared goal of mutual illumination.

For our Field Trip we journeyed to Scandinavia, travelling from Stockholm to Copenhagen; a 7-hour drive stretched in duration to 7 days. On our travels, we encountered projects with mesmerising connections between architecture and landscape, culture and nature. Amongst the most special were works by Gunnar Asplund, Sigurd Lewerentz, Tham & Videgård Hansson, Rafael Moneo, Jorn Utzon and Wohlert + Bo. We attended a conference on 'Architecture & Cybernetics' at CITA – Copenhagen, before returning to the UK, where all of our projects were sited. Year 4 students selected various sites around the environs of Snape Maltings in Suffolk, while Year 5 students had more varied site choices, depending on the conceptual, architectural or political intent of the project.

The next phase of work tackled the idea of CHARGED SPACE, where 'Space becomes charged and responsive to the movements of time, plot, and history.' Year 4 students progressed through their Design Realisation Project and Year 5 students evolved their Prototype Projects, before elaborating on these exercises for the final phase of the year, entitled THE DREAM OF THE UNIFIED FIELD. This expansive title, suggested by a book of poetry by Jorie Graham, became a touchstone for all final works this year.

What is evident from the work is that increasingly, the Unit is committed to exploring contemporary architecture as a space of flux and communication. Whether through narrative environments, reflexive spaces, cinematic architectures, perceptual fields, immaterial surfaces, augmented realities or dynamic structures, students this year have been fascinated by the endless possibilities of how spaces of meaning can be constructed through the strategic deployment of technology, media and material within an increasingly charged political and social realm.

The unit would like to thank: Dr. Ana Araujo, Phil Ayres, Julia Backhaus, Matthew Butcher, Jason Bruges, Dr. Marcos Cruz, Kate Davies, Prof. Stephen Gage, Ruairi Glynn, Simon Herron, Prof. Jonathan Hill, Bill Hodgson, Dr. Kristen Kreider, Dirk Krowlikowski, Chris Leung, Ollie Palmer, Dr. Vesna Petresin-Robert, Bob Sheil, Jason Slocombe, Emmanuel Vercruysse and Liam Young.

Design realization tutor: Dan Wright of Rogers Stirk Harbour + Partners. Structural Engineering support: Andy Toohey of Price & Myers.

Year 4: Ruben Alonso, Joohoon Kim, Chace Hong-Jin Leow, Andrew Walker, Suyang Xu

Year 5: Ariff Abd-Hamid, Jonathan Cohen, Matthew Donkersley, Sahar Fikouhi, Lewis James

Fig. 14.01 Jonathan Cohen, Intangible Fields. The project proposes a tangible yet immaterial sub-architecture that defines new dynamic spatial conditions within an existing environment. This sub-architecture consists of user-actuated phenomena perceived through aural and visual means. The proposal comprises of an arrayed field of 'enabling nodes' creating a distributed interface which is activated by an occupants' proximity. In operation, the Field establishes a set of continually changing boundary thresholds defined through the observer's interaction. Intangible Field deployed at night on Primrose Hill. **Fig. 14.02** Jonathan Cohen, Intangible Fields. The limits of deployability of the Field are tested in Bayhurst Wood in North London. **Fig. 14.03** Jonathan Cohen, Intangible Fields. Intangible Field tested at UCL's Research Department of Genetics, Evolution and Environment. **Fig. 14.04** Jonathan Cohen, Intangible Fields. Constructing the interactive nodes of the Field at the Bartlett Workshop.

14.02

14.03

14.04

Fig. 14.05 Joohoon Kim, Snape landscape observations. Joohoon's scheme analysed the idea of theatre as a site of multiple layered encounters between the scale of the personal and the scale of the landscape. **Fig. 14.06** Joohoon Kim, Shadow puppet Theatre. Initial studies of figure, lighting, staging apparatus and procenium. **Fig. 14.07** Ruben Alonso, Active facade study. Ruben's proposal for a forum for Snape Maltings sought to reconcile differing attitudes to urbanism in a historic setting. The facade becomes a wing sheltering various activities that are locked to the spine of the project. **Fig. 14.08** Chace Leow, Experience-Machine studies. Chace investigated the possibilities of steam acting as an architectural element, through rigourous qualitative tests of visual and environmental control in his Fenland steam bath project.

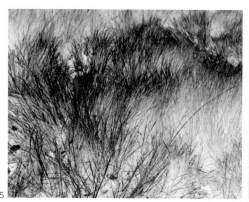

14.05

14.06

14.07

14.08

Fig. 14.09 Suyang Xu, Cinematic Space in The House of Moments. Suyang's project uses personal experience to develop a series of spatial environments that both archive and exhibit documentation of carefully calibrated moments on the site, from sunrise over the Alde to sunset at mid-winter. **Fig. 14.10** Suyang Xu, Entrance Foyer Study for The House of Moments **Fig. 14.11** Andrew Walker, Axonometric study of constructional elements of the Homeostatic Brewery. Andrew's project develops a systems-based architectural proposal that seeks to balance the relationship between the provider and inbiber of alcohol through the use of monitoring and projection technology. **Fig. 14.12** Andrew Walker, Plan study of servant and served spaces of the Homeostatic Brewery. **Fig. 14.13** Andrew Walker, Study of intelligent projector.

By manipulating the porosity, elasticity and kinetic energy of soft edge conditions using roaming robotic projectors one can create ephemeral, diffuse and adaptive in-between zones of occupation. **Fig. 14.14** Andrew Walker, Study of projection space. By setting these agents in an endoscopic landscape of brewing, they disseminate the hidden processes of alcohol production by projecting the footage back onto the system itself .

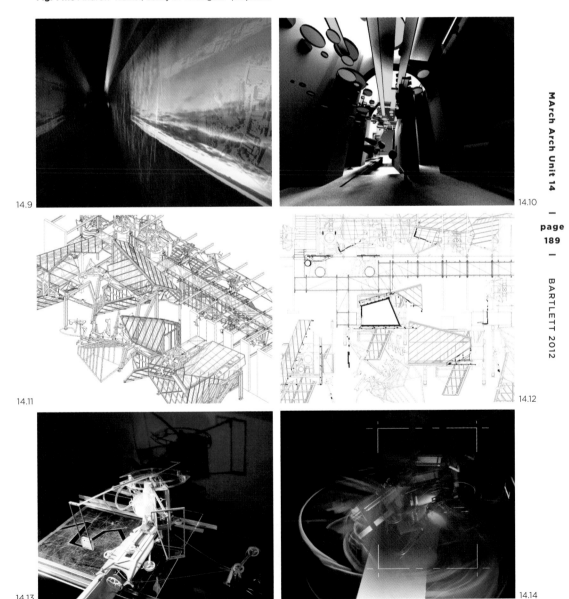

14.9

14.10

14.11

14.12

14.13

14.14

Fig. 14.15 Matt Donkersley, Haggerston Research Facility. The project seeks to fuse an existing industrial landscape with a creative and experimental local community by proposing a speculative platform for experimental building and materials research. Through the deployment of a flexible infrastructure, multiple test-sites play host to an ever-changing landscape upon which research, free experimentation and real world testing can be continually manifest. View of Gasworks materials bay showing rotating platforms. **Fig. 14.16** Matt Donkersley, Haggerston Research Facility. Material experiments are continually monitored by a system of communicating drones. **Fig. 14.17** Matt Donkersley, Haggerston Research Facility. A live landscape of continuously evolving architectural 'gardens' that are in constant flux, perpetually remaking themselves and acting as an interface to the future of material science and architectural construction. **Fig. 14.18** Matt Donkersley, Haggerston Research Facility. Exploded Axonometric of site components. **Fig. 14.19** Matt Donkersley, Haggerston Research Facility. View of ponding in the garden of redundant material tests. **Fig. 14.20** Matt Donkersley, Haggerston Research Facility. View of the Haggerston Research Facility from the Regents Canal.

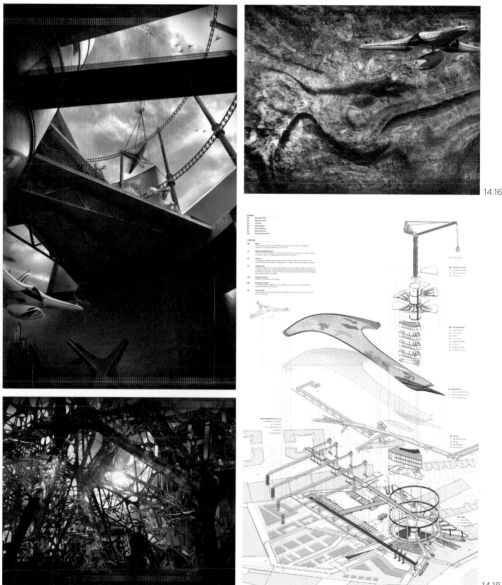

14.15

14.16

14.17

14.18

14.19

14.20

14.21

Fig. 14.21 Lewis James, A Catylytic Architecture Lewis proposes a temporary, flexible architecture developed to reanimate mothballed sites across London. The proposal utilizes automated systems to create an architecture with an indeterminate lifespan. These roaming devices spray clay slip on to fabric formwork, solidifying forms, which create new visual and acoustic enclosures that can be inhabited by the public, and assessed for practicality over time. Roaming devices generate new architectural forms. **Fig. 14.22** Lewis James, A Catylytic Architecture. Over time the clay shells crack and decay opening up new spatial possibilities for the system to begin again. The spectacle of decay is used as a catalyst to advertise the space and encourage use. **Fig. 14.23** Sahar Fikouhi, Detonator: Augmented Reality Playgrounds. Sahar's proposal creates gaming hot spots which utilize augmented reality to transform the city into a series of interactive playgrounds. The game design is based on key data relating to the use of landmines during war in many regions of the world, as well as the continued refusal of countries that have not joined an international convention to ban the use of landmines. Once the game is completed, the user is asked to sign a petition for the eradication of landmines throughout the world. Advertising the Detonator. Scan the QR code for a web download. **Fig. 14.24 — 14.26** Sahar Fikouhi, Detonator: Augmented Reality Playgrounds. Deploying detonator in politically charged areas of London.

14.23

14.24

14.25

14.26

ISLANDS
Josep Mias, Johan Berglund

"…in our ageographical existence, I am never entirely not in London,
entirely not in Tokyo. We all inhabit the meta city now, regardless
of our physical address."

William Gibson, *Life in the Meta City*, Scientific American (2011)

Islands are autonomous geographies, usually defined by their isolated location
in bodies of water. In the field of Island biogeography, this term is expanded
and can apply to any isolated or separate area of land or water, or any area of
suitable habitat surrounded by an expanse of unsuitable habitat. The isolated
nature of these islands has commonly encouraged the development of highly
specific ecologies.

Islands hold mythical powers as well. The phantom islands and lost islands of
old maps have for centuries spawned legends and myths, and generated stories of
hidden treasures and futuristic cities of old. We used this inherent mystique to
our advantage, and created our own imaginative islands of utopia. We speculated
on new architectural and urban ecologies that straddle the gap between our
physical world and the world of myth.

Second London
We began with a dissection of London, a city of autonomous towns operating as
political and social islands in the London 'archipelago'. We cut into the urban
fabric in order to generate an understanding of the underlying dynamic patterns
and layers of the city, the 'forces' that shape the physical city directly or
indirectly. It was also a study of the physical footprint of London. Through these
investigations, a new version of the city emerged, one that engaged with London
on many levels and beyond the purely physical. This was seen as a new layer of the
city, a 'Second London', existing within/above/below/around the existing city.

Terra Incognita
"In the Archipelago, the islands don't define the milieu but the
space in between: the routes, the streams, the currents and counter
currents, whirlpools and calms. This is the space of countless lines
of lights intersecting, converging, creating temporary assemblages.
This is the multitude.

…Sometimes people take refuge on islands. Or at least direct their
hopes towards them, the reason is simple: all systems (of belief)
require a fixed basis — islands represent that which is ideal and
permanent. Islands have edges. They are refuges for those who need

something to cling to. Most of the time, though, there are monsters
on the islands..."

Foucault's Sleep, Models for a Proposal, Iconoclast publications 8
(2005-06)

We examined the concept of the Self Sufficient City as a sustainable model
for future urban developments, as well as larger infrastructural cuts through
the city of Miami. We decided to look for the other Miami, far from the glitzy
beaches and hotel lobbies of Miami Beach. We examined Island conditions in
Little Havana, in the catastrophic urbanism of the Downtown, the homeless
veteran community of Overtown, and the disjointed relationship to the heavily
trafficked Port area. The self sufficient city was thought of as an island,
autonomous and isolated, an island inside Miami or London.

Proposals ranged from small acupunctural insertions into the existing urban
fabric, landscape proposals that slowly facilitated the re-introduction of
native species into the everglades, a new barrier Island to stem the effects of
longshore drift which is depleting the beach areas along Miami Beach, to the
re-planning of some of Miami's poorest and most crime-ridden areas. We looked
for proposals of the not yet known and the unexpected, unveiling possibilities
for the future of Architectural and Urban development.

We would like to thank Dean Pike for his invaluable teaching of the DR module,
and Andrew Best/Buro Happold for their generous technical support. Thank you
also to Dan Neal of DNEG, Factory Fifteen, and Jessam Al-Jahwad for showcasing
their work to the unit.

We would also like to extend our warmest gratitude to our visiting critics and
guests: Jack Newton, Bob Sheil, Graeme Williamson, James Harper, Melissa Dowler,
Jorge Lobos, Emmanuel Vercruysse, Sarah Custance, Ignacio Marti, Roberta Luna,
Patrick Fransen, Kate Davies, James O'Leary, Julia Backhaus and Markus Jatsch.

In 2012, Unit 16 will exhibit work in Miami, Stockholm, Barcelona and Mexico.

Year 4: Jonathan Blake, Ione Braddick, Isaac Eluwole,
Rachel Hearn, Etain Ho, Oliver Leech, Phil Poon, Samantha Rive

Year 5: Indre Baltusyte, Cristine Castilhos Balarine, Kyle Hyde,
Joyce (Cheuk Ling) Lau, Chris Thompson

Fig. 16.1 — 16.2 Samantha Rive, Veteran's Rehabilitation Centre, Miami. The project occupies a vacant lot in the heart of Miami's downtown area — a part of the city that houses an unusally large population of homeless veteran soldiers. Realising the difficulties the veterans are facing upon their return to America and a 'normal' life, Samantha proposes a Centre that would cater for treatment of both physical and psychological injury. Vibration therapy is the main treatment method, and the building is tailored to both harness the vibrations from the nearby Metromover train and the busy roads, as well as to produce its own vibrations in specially designed chambers for individual and group use. Perspective Section and Model photo.

16.1

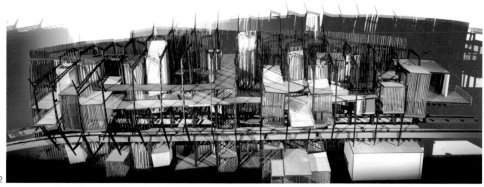

16.2

Fig. 16.3 — 16.4 Rachel Hearn, Water Taxi Terminal and Market, Port of Miami. An initial study of the particular techniques of Savile Row tailoring generated an interest in soft, folded, pleated, lined and stitched architectures. Rachel cleverly moves between the urban and the detail scale, and deploys her tailoring techniques to create a very comprehensive and bold proposal, aiming to create a stronger connection between the port area and the downtown district of Miami. Aerial overview drawing and model photo.

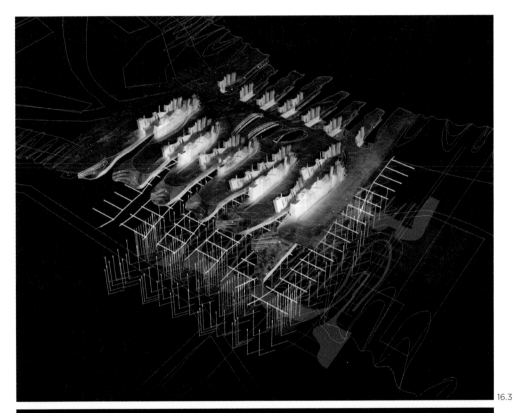

16.3

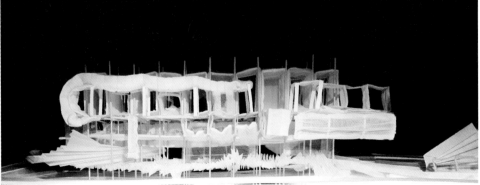

16.4

Fig. 16.5 Oliver Leech, Mental London, London. A study of the personal geographies of London. The model was seen as an active research tool, and was built and added to over time as Oliver set out to explore London during term 1. Additionally, it was beautifully animated to reinforce the way we perceive cities and places over time, and how our memory of a place is often different from the actual physical environment. Detail Model photo.

Fig. 16.6 Etain Ho, Youth Marine Centre, Miami. Set on the mainly ignored and forgotten Miami River, Etain's Marine Centre is proposed to regenerate the riverfront and at the same time provide activities for the inner city kids of Miami downtown and surrounding areas. Etain's preoccupation with the particular geology of the site generated an archeological approach where the ground was carefully excavated to allow water to penetrate and flood the site at high tide, while at the same time help to improve passive cooling in and around the building. Model photo.

Fig. 16.7 Ione Braddick, Entertainment Facility and Public Park, Miami. An obsession with the immense Miami Sky generated a project centred around the changing experience of the light and weather, set in Miami's new cultural district. Working through a series of prototypes, Ione developed an intricate roof within which a multitude of experimental structures were attached in order to harness, manipulate, and enhance the experience of the sky. Below, a 24 hour public park with cafés, bars and entertainment facilites blends in with, and reinforces the surrounding urban landscapes of nightclubs, museums and concert venues. Model photo.

16.5

16.6

16.7

Fig. 16.8 Jonathan Blake, A Research facility for the study of the Everglades Ecology, Miami. Jonathan's interest in the divide between the natural ecologies of the Everglades, and the urban expansion of Miami, led to a proposal for a research outpost that would monitor and regulate the city's effect on the natural ecosystems in the Everglades. Built as a lightweight and non-intrusive building, it proposes a respectful and light-footed relation to its surroundings, and suggest a possible way to build within a sensitive ecosystem. **Fig. 16.9** Kyle Hyde, A 50 year plan for the slow re-population of the Everglades. Kyle's in-depth research into the depletion and loss of native species within the Everglades led him to create a 50 year plan to help re-introduce sensitive species back into their natural habitat. As part of the study, Kyle developed a water farm, which would both help to regulate the water flow across a large area of landscape, and to allow for researchers to maintain and study the process. Masterplan drawing. **16.10** Kyle Hyde, A 50 year plan for the slow re-population of the Everglades. Study model of the Research Station.

16.8

16.9

16.10

Fig. 16.11 Indre Baltusyte, The City of M25, London. Indre spent the year researching and studying the M25 as an autonomous part of London, and its importance as both a thouroughfare and gateway in to, and out of, London. Projecting her project into a near future of hydrogen powered cars, and an increasing scarecity of water, her proposals transforms the M25 into a water harvesting plant, in which the cars become the main protagonists. Indre presented an uncannily real proposal, which was underpinned with her thesis, a highly detailed study into the feasibility of the proposal. Detail render, Road junction in construction. **Fig. 16.12** Indre Baltusyte, The Cadillac Palace, London. Inspired by the ascent and descent of the American Car industry, Indre created a beautiful and poignant commentary on our almost religious relationshop with the car, in the form of an animated short film. **Fig. 16.13** Cristine Castilhos, New Opa-Locka, Miami. In the 1920's, Opa-Locka was built to represent the American Dream. With a Hollywood-esque flair, it was supposed to promote a new kind of city, with a greater density and inspiration from middle eastern cities such as Bagdad. Only a few years later, a hurricane put an end to the dream as the area was badly damaged by the storm. Since then, the area has been in a state of disrepair, and is now home to some of the poorest people in Miami. Cristine's interest in the image of America, and her passion for social responsibility led her to re-plan parts of Opa-Locka, and to pave way for a densification of Miami. Aerial Overview showing housing clusters and public parks. **Fig. 16.14** Joyce Lau, Affordable housing and

16.11

16.12

Recycling Centre, Miami. After a study into the housing problem in Miami, Joyce proposed a new kind of urban typology, in which productive facilities and housing could co-exist in a symbiotic way. Using the existing Metro Mover train as a starting point, Joyce imagines a fantastical project in which houses are modular and easily extended, where urban gardening and recycling facilities are part of the everyday life, and life is lived above the old city, where the air is cleaner and cars are nowhere in sight. Detail of Long Section. **Fig. 16.15** (Overleaf, left) Samantha Rive, Veteran's Rehabilitation Centre, Miami. Model detail of the facade. **Fig. 16.16** (Overleaf, right) Chris Thompson, Financial Tribunal, City of London. A poetic and beautiful mediation on the value of Architecture and materials. Working with the Bank of England as a starting point,

Chris quickly developed an architectural language of chambers, convoluted corridors and monumental spaces, all intricately folded in on each other to create a complex sequence of spaces. The building was developed as a 'cloud' of elements rather than a defined external form, allowing the building to fluctuate with the marked as the more precious details of the buildings could be dismantled and used for investment and financial speculation. Overview of Model.

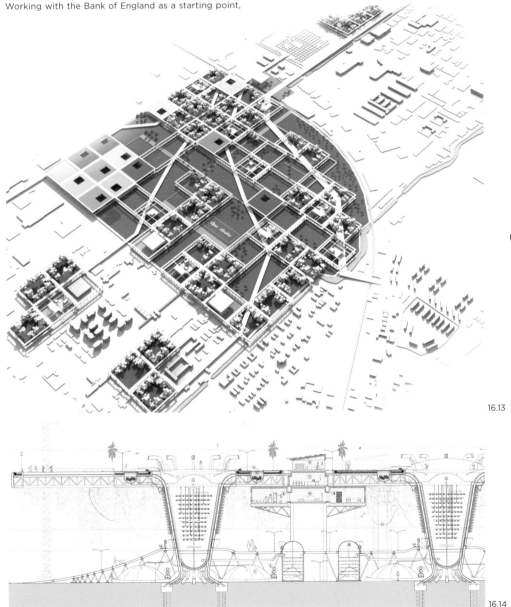

16.13

16.14

16.15

16.16

TAKE IT FROM THE TOP

Niall McLaughlin, Yeoryia Manolopoulou, Michiko Sumi

'Limit the sprawl of cities'. 'Use the existing building stock'. 'Replace, build on top and in-between, but do not expand'. These phrases are increasingly used to argue that the reuse of existing buildings and the restriction of urban sprawl is the new design 'solution' for architecture and the city. In a world that struggles to balance the forces of modernity with the current environmental challenges and with the histories and social desires of local places, what are the possibilities and limits of keeping buildings? To choose whether or not to build, what, how and for how long, requires a continuous and in-depth understanding of the physical, social and political realm. To preserve is first of all to find, learn how to actively observe, and collaborate.

The human need to keep and care for objects and places is as important as the urge to create new things. This tension is productive for architecture because it points to the limits of design. What exactly do we want to keep? Buildings? Landscapes? Experiences? Social organisations? In certain cases the continuation of meaning and experience may demand the demolition of buildings more than their conservation. In this context how, when and where can reuse be a radical design action? How can it operate within and against the authority of architecture? And is it ever necessary to make a totally clear start for buildings?

This year Unit 17 explored these questions in relation to Japan where the notion of 'keeping things' is cherished and handed over from generation to generation and where the Shinto Shrines are rebuilt every twenty years to symbolize both continuity and impermanence. A year ago the tsunami once again wiped out several coastal cities. How to begin again? 'Take it from the top' is what you say in music rehearsals when you restart after finishing or interrupting the previous attempt in order to create an improved or adjusted version. It can be used similarly in architecture to imply a symbiotic process of both keeping and changing.

The students started studying collaboratively different aspects of the Japanese contemporary society, its history and environment. In November we visited Tokyo, Sendai, Ise and Kyoto while many students also travelled to Osaka, Yokohama, Kamaishi, Ishinomaki and Tama New Town. They chose sites to carry out detailed research and develop individual design proposals. Year 4 were asked to experiment in order to open up possibilities for themes that they could bring forward to their final year whereas Year 5 brought their projects into a more complete state. Doubt and the process of constantly working between multiple and sometimes contradictory options were encouraged throughout.

Different interests were aroused during the course of the year but most fall under three main categories: projects based around observations of Japanese society looking at ageing, shrinking populations, primogeniture, weddings, divorce, pilgrimage, nursery care, homelessness and teenage isolation; projects looking at the impact of natural disasters on buildings, cities and landscapes; and, finally, projects looking at the material processes, innovations and traditions of the local building culture and technology. Students researched the current architectural discourse in Japan but there is not a great deal of formal borrowing in their projects. The writings of Atelier Bow Wow, however, offered them a way into the Japanese society that was not possible through the direct emulation of other resources.

We can now observe that many of the students' projects present Japan as a culture in crisis where economic, demographic, social and geotechnical factors combine to create a condition of almost intractable difficulty. In all of this they recognise the unique relationship between Britain and Japan in geographical, historic and financial terms. Perhaps that is why Japan is a potent place for us to visit. It is like our own place seen differently. This island off a major continental power with its history of imperialism and isolation is facing questions about twenty-first century predicaments that we are only beginning to consider.

Our very memorable visit in Japan would have not been possible without the generous hospitality of: Fumihiko Imamura, Abdul Muhari, from the Tohoku University, Tsunami Engineering Department; Kojiro Fukuda and Asako Matsushima from Sendai Tokio Marine Insurance; Inagaki Junya and Yumi Sato from Waseda University; Yoshimasa Yoshida and students from Kyoto University; Toyohiko Kobayashi and Julia Lee from Toyo Ito & Associates; Yoshiko Iwasaki from Atelier Bow-Wow; and Takayuki Kubo from the Mori Memorial Foundation.

Many thanks to our critics: Alessandro Ayuso, Julia Backhaus, Justine Bell, Johan Berglund, Pierre D'Avoine, James Daykin, Shin Egashira, Hiromi Fujii, Peter Grove, Yiorgos Hadjichristou, Maria Hadjisoteriou, Will Hunter, Murray Fraser, Chee-Kit Lai, Brian Macken, Matthew Mindrup, James O'Leary, Sophia Psarra, Joshua Scott, Elle Stevenson, Mike Tonkin, Nikolas Travasaros, Peg Rawes, Victoria Watson.

Design Realisation Tutors: Maria Fulford, David Hemingway and Joanna Karatzas.

Year 4 Consultants: Neil Daffin (Max Fordham Associates) and William Whitby (ARUP).

Year 4: Christine Bjerke, Alice Brownfield, Freya Cobbin, Tamsin Hanke, Ben Hayes, Francis Hunt, Shu Wai Charis Mok, Sash Reading.

Year 5: Pooja Agrawal, Alexandra Brooke, Canzy El-Gohary, Chiara Hall, Katherine Hegab, Louisa Danielle Hodgson, Mathew Leung, Paul Sidebottom, Richard Wood.

Fig. 17.1 — 17.2, Fig. 17.5 Katherine Hegab, Gaming Complex, Extension to Electric City, Shinobazu Pond, Ueno Park, Tokyo. The Gaming Complex reintroduces a proportion of Japan's Hikikomori to natural light in a video-gaming environment. The building seeks to engage light through the harness and distribution of natural and artificial sources from its surroundings as it responds to Japan's excessive light pollution. **Fig. 17.3** (From left to right) Year 4 projects by: Freya Cobbin, Tokyo Waterworks Bureau, Nihombashi, Tokyo; Tamsin Hanke, Minami-Ku Satellite Tax Office, Kyoto; Charis Mok, Bento Box Production Centre, Tokyo; Alice Brownfield, Civic Forum & Archive, Tama New Town, Tokyo. **Fig. 17.4** (From left to right) Sash Reading, Kamaishi Yakusho, Kamaishi, Iwate Prefecture; Francis Hunt, House of Binding, Futami; Ben Hayes, Kamagasaki Union, Nishinari District, Osaka; Christine Bjerke, A Shelter for Divorced Women, Asakusa, Tokyo.

17.1

17.2

17.3

17.4

17.5>

Fig. 17.4 — Fig. 17.5 Paul Sidebottom, An Agronomic Recovery: elementary school and call centre within a cotton growing memorial landscape, Miyagi Prefecture. Situated on the site of a farming town destroyed by the 3-11 tsunami the project proposes a strategic reconstruction model, confronting the socioeconomic paradox of agriculture in rural Japan. The project responds to the threatened cultural construct of part-time farming families whilst addressing the psychological issue of tsunami children and the importance of the family bond. **Fig. 17.6** Canzy El-gohary, A View to Mount Fuji, Nippori Fujimizaka ("slope for viewing Mount Fuji"), Tokyo. The last view of Fuji from ground level is threatened by encroaching developments and residents have consequently set up the 'Citizens Alliance to Preserve the View of Mount Fuji'. The building provides their offices and offers an elevated viewing landscape. **Fig. 17.7** Mat Leung, Inhabiting Chinatown, Yokohama, Japan. Chinese library, temporary housing and labour centre located at the border of Japan's largest Chinatown. **Fig. 17.8 — Fig. 17.9** Richard Wood, Reassembling The Past, New Kyoto Parliament Kiyomizu-dera Temple Complex. Situated within the complex of an amassing of ancient temples, the project considers a new technique towards contextual architecture. Reassembled from the component parts of other stultifying timber structure temples, the proposed city hall and chamber offer progression for the city while questioning established preservation principles.

17.4

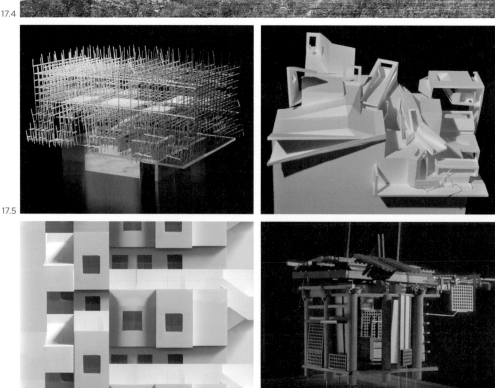

17.5

17.6

17.7

17.8

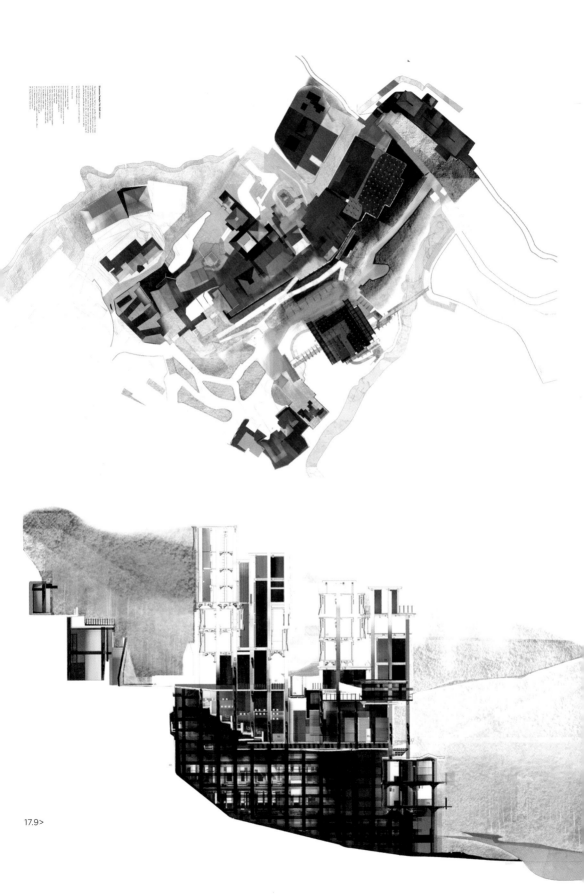

17.9>

Fig. 17.10 Chiara Hall: Revealing and Concealing the Ise Shrines through Storytelling, Ise. The project is inspired by Japanese narrative scroll paintings. Four stories describe the rituals of different social groups within the landscape: shrine priests, pilgrims/tourists, festival town people and shrine construction workers. The proposal for a public square interweaves these stories and a repair and storage workshop for deconstructed shrine material acts as a screen to the edge of the sacred forest, turning place into a spectacle within the twenty-year reconstruction timescale of the Shinto shrines. **Fig. 17.11, Fig. 17.12** Alex Brooke, Sugamo Fureai: Kindergarten and Assisted Living, Sugamo, Tokyo. The scheme seeks to positively address the problem of an ageing population and the breakdown of the traditional family care system in Japan. Conceived as a series of unfolding screens, interconnecting sight lines and shared spaces for young and old, the building provides a mutually inclusive framework for living. **Fig. 17.13 — 17.14** Pooja Agrawal, Song-Dance-Play-House, Tokyo. Within the ephemeral physical environment of Japan, ritual forms a means of continuity and permanence in Japanese culture. These rituals are performative in nature and preserve memories of society. Song-Dance-Play-House, a Kabuki playhouse in Tokyo, forms a seductive permeable framework for social play, celebrating cultural performance.

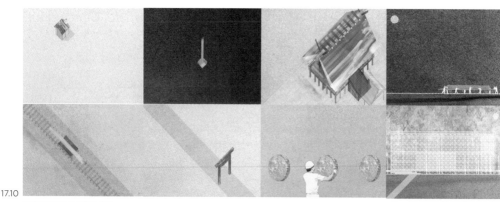

17.10

17.11

17.12

17.13

17.14

Fig. 17.15 — 17.19 Danielle Hodgson, Community Kura forms a critical response to the extinct Japanese clay-walled kura storehouse typology. In their performance and construction kura are unique to Japan and, as such, offer a particular insight into the relationship between safety and architecture in this country. Historically, the principle reason for the development of these buildings was the unsurpassed resilience to fire, typhoons, and earthquakes that their clay wall construction provided in the safe storage of valuable goods. In addition to this their influence can be recognized much further afield in the areas of city planning, social structure, and the transmission of culture. The proposed design is informed by an original body of research identifying the complex underlying structure of risk perception present in kura.

Through the material characteristics of plasticisation and ossification, inherent in the unfired clay used in their construction, the project reconsiders the material and cultural associations of this historic building type through the programmatic amalgamation of a self storage and emergency evacuation facility for Kitano Shrine Park, Kyoto. The design posits the contemporary use of unfired clay to provide an environmentally responsive and culturally relevant form of protection for the city.

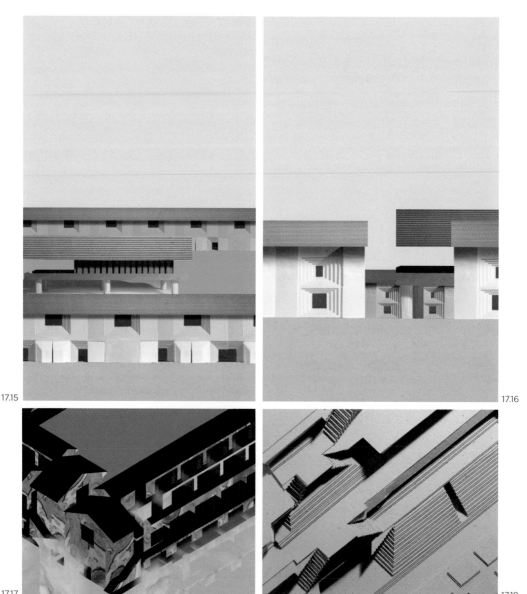

17.15

17.16

17.17

17.18

17

GENERATIONAL PHANTOMS
Nannette Jackowski, Ricardo de Ostos

Have you read the reviews yet? 'Brutally graphic' … 'wonderfully unpleasant' … 'underground classic' … 'notorious banned thriller' … 'hits the nerve!'… Name the in-between using your background imagination…

Unit 18 set up to study hellish zones of emerging social conditions and technological payload scenarios inherited in these zones. These are zones where urbanity has to be redefined simply because the dots in between are not differentiated enough from the headlines, social noise and techno craft archaeology for Wikipedia. Generational Phantoms, or Unit 18, studied the short and long-circuits that connect generations — generations lost or slowly fading into kingdom come for not being 'fit for purpose'. In our trip to South China these fading ghosts seemed abundant and manifested in different spatial forms and time events. From dying out fish farms near Shantou to the homogenisation of special cultures such as the ex-boat dwellers called Tanka to 'secret services' coercing us upon entrance to immediately leave again the e-waste town Guiyu to prevent any suggestive 'danger'.

We started the year by investigating three fiction and technology literature references in order to set up each individual's bandwidth of interest. Between territory recognition and tactics the first project included ventures into sentient environments, alternate presents and technological natures. Followed by a seven-day bus ride along many not-so-well-known spots in South China we experienced and started to articulate thought provoking pictures of China's social political horizon. In disease-beauty scenarios of e-waste dumps and quiet star-packed sky evenings amid hot noodle soups in ancestral courtyards students formed their own contextual maps, social constellations and technological tales. Understanding architecture not just as a building but as a built environment the final projects combine narratives of spatial commentary, digital speculation and social construct.

Interested in the phenomenon of mass art re-production, specifically in the area of Dafen Village in Shenzhen, where thousands of classic western paintings are reproduced daily, Aris Theodoropoulos created a digital myth of architecture as a multi-faceted process of sensorial experience. As a Dorian Gray of sorts the project reconnects visitors and painters in a process of infinite reproduction utilising a feedback loop of scanning and 3d projection mapping. The resulting architecture is in constant revolution due to the visitors and space relationship in a building of social ghosts and technological phantoms.

In a tale of an alternate present linked with crafts and social reality Michelle Lam speculated on the question of what if the Tanka people would not have been forced to leave their life on boats and become urban dwellers due to the events of the Mao's Land Reformation. Investigated through a series of innovative ceramic tests — including one of the first successful ceramic 3d prints — the project's materiality explores fragility, translucency and communicative patterns. Designed as a series of water dwellings that are specially arranged according to the moon light the ceramic roof interacts with the light and sea water revealing hidden messages about the dwellers' lost history and customs.

Encrusted in an ultra dense urban plot occupying the same land from the farm days of Guangzhou, now surrounded by rising towers of an emergent speculative market a small meandering building surveys and documents the demise of Shipai Urban Village. Designed by Adam Casey an extension to an existing ancestral hall acts as a digital reservoir of the urban village culture. Daily objects are 3d scanned and its data is used to carve into the buildings altar that is positioned at the highest point. Utilizing Microsoft Kinect, coding and traditional model making Adam tested and explored the design between digital crafts and environmental storytelling to create a project that discusses the inevitability of market forces against the resilience of popular culture.

Generational Phantoms is set up as a design think tank on how rapid social and technological developments can work not only predatorily under market forces but also collaboratively. Unit 18 discusses how long-circuits between generations can be ground for speculation but also long-term investment. Amid digital dreams and tense social zones students designed their own tales of hope and wonder. As active engagement to imagine not the future but short-circuits in the present its main goal was to 'hit the nerve'.

Thank you to our external consultants: Manuel Jimenez Garcia, Sara Klomps, Nicolas Sterling, Gary Grant, Guan Lee, Oliver Wilton, Vesna Petresin Robert. Thank you to our guest critics: Ben Masterton-Smith, Abel Maciel, Manuel Jimenez Garcia, Sara Klomps, Guvenc Topcuoglu, Barbara Campbell Lange, Lawrence Friesen, Goswin Schwendinger, Ana Araujo, Theo Sarantoglou Lalis, Marcos Cruz, Vesna Petresin Robert, Yael Reisner, Julia Backhaus, Paul Bavister, Nick Szczepaniak, Theo Spyropoulos, Claudia Pasquero, Kate Davies, Joao Wilbert

Year 4: Sonal Balasuriya, Adam Casey, Shao Jun Fan, Liang Shang, Anis Wan Kamaruddin, Rintaro Yoshida, Saman Ziaie

Year 5: Ming Fung Jeff Ng, Michelle Lam, Kaleigh Tirone Nunes, Aris Theodoropoulos

Fig. 18.1 Michelle Lam, 'The Tanka Archipelago', Pearl River Delta, China. Digitally printed ceramic prototype, first produced in UCL. **Fig. 18.2** Michelle Lam, The Tanka Archipelago, Pearl River Delta, China. Digitally printed ceramic prototype, first produced in UCL. **Fig. 18.3** Michelle Lam, The Tanka Archipelago, Pearl River Delta, China. Tessellated origami porcelain prototype. **Fig. 18.4** Michelle Lam, 'The Tanka Archipelago', Pearl River Delta, China. Translucency study of fired prototype. **Fig. 18.5** Michelle Lam, 'The Tanka Archipelago', Pearl River Delta, China. Lunar festival cluster. **Fig. 18.6** Michelle Lam, 'The Tanka Archipelago', Pearl River Delta, China. Tanka dwelling isometric. This project speculates an alternative timeline that hypothesises; what if the Tanka community had remained untouched during Mao's land reformation in the 1950s. The architectural proposition is manifested through the re-mastering of lost Ming dynasty eggshell porcelain. An alternative urban condition reincarnates mythical Lunar festival rituals in the Pearl River Delta, China.

18.1

18.2

18.3

18.4

18.5

THE TANKA ARCHIPELAGO
蛋家列島

18.6

Fig. 18.7 Saman Ziaie, 'Shipyard for Modular Offshore Habitation,' Pearl River Delta, China. The point of origin, as expressed through the model, for a self-replicating and evolving architecture that responds to proposals of a Megacity, combining major cities in the Pearl River Delta. Dwellers living in urban villages such as Shipai in Guangzhou expand out into the water, constructing more offshore homes from a shared platform via a collaborative process of living/working. **Fig. 18.8** Saman Ziaie, 'Shipyard for Modular Offshore Habitation,' Pearl River Delta, China. Over time, the nature of buildings and modules change, utilising newer technologies and customized elements, responding to the needs of the offshore settlers while urban density reaches the waters. **Fig. 18.9** ShaoJun Fan. Conceptual drawing of Chinese Tulou events happening in the building, generating new relationships between form and space and allowing the meaning of Tulou to be reinterpreted from its own culture. **Fig. 18.10** Anis Wan Kamaruddin, A view inside a phytomine in Guiyu, China – where gold particles from technological remnants are collected using plants, and the harvest processed in biochemical laboratories on site.

18.7

18.8

18.9

18.10

Fig. 18.11 Adam Casey, 'Ancestral Temple Extension', Guangzhou, China. Composition of the digitally manufactured Altar surface inspired by the transformation of Shipai urban village in Guangzhou, China. The surface becomes a diasporic depiction of a transcient landscape constructed from the artefacts collected from the rural and forgotten in the urban, creating an archive of future archaeology. **Fig. 18.12** Adam Casey, 'Ancestral Temple Extension', Guangzhou, China. Axonometric section depicting the ascension of the observer away from the street level to the Altar in transformation. Creating an architecture for capturing the temporality of the urban village as Traces of the migrating population are left in the architecture as those chosen progress beyond the boundary of the village, into the urban city; creating a surreal amalgamation of architectural references that reflect upon rural traditions. **Fig. 18.13** Adam Casey, Ancestral Temple Extension, Guangzhou, China. Digitally composed surface using processing and Kinect to extract fragments of the forgotten to be digitally recomposed into an adaptive architectural expression of the social changes of the urban village.

18.11

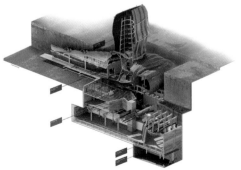

18.12

18.13

Fig. 18.14 Kaleigh Tirone Nunes, Illustrating the 'Tragedy of the Commons'. Cities are usually perceived as near utopias, by those who live outside them. However it seems, the more cities expand, the further the divide grows, between urban and rural realities. We rarely know where our food, clothes, water and energy come from, or what conditions prevail in the systems and chains that provide us with our daily needs. Furthermore, the 'Tragedy of the Commons', arising through the actions of multiple individuals independently and rationally consulting their own self-interest, inevitably leads to the destruction of shared limited resources, even when it is clear that it is not in anyone's long-term interest for this to happen. **Fig. 18.15** Kaleigh Tirone Nunes, Urban Ecosystem, the Habitation and Harvesting Units , The image speculates on a future, re-invented rural life in the city, motivated by the need to undo the harm caused by depleted ecosystems and resources, which affect both society and nature. **Fig. 18.16** Kaleigh Tirone Nunes, Urban Ecosystem, Project Overview, Roof Plan. Sited at a live Seafood Market in Guangzhou, China, the intervention forms a biophilic aquaponic urban farm inhabited/taken care of by agricultural experts — Rural Migrants. Water is purified from the neighbouring Pearl River in order to harvest seafood, vegetables and fruit for the local community. The project encourages the formation of a renewed socio-ecological relationship with nature in the city by allowing the existing natural resources to reappropriate and re-establish urban ground.

18.14

18.15

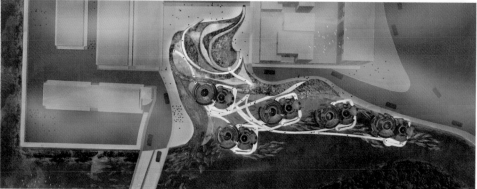

18.16

Fig. 18.17 Ming Fung Ng, Memory Archaeology, view towards the public recording hall for the public to record their narratives on clay tiles, as part of the institute to collect memories of the inhabitants in Guangxia village which suffers from a strong sense of collective amnesia about its past and uncertainty about its future. The space is appropriated by the urban villagers to create their own space to represent their humanity. **Fig. 18.18** Ming Fung Ng, The clay tablet prototype. to transcribe data on the wet clay to show how to engage villagers with the tactile experience of crafting with clay to record their narratives, which is then fired to become the building component to display and store data permanently, as opposed to the ephemeral contemporary culture in the fast-developing modern city bordering the village. **Fig. 18.19** Ming Fung Ng, The strata plaster cast. plaster is poured and cast in place layers by layers over time – to narrate how the narratives of the place are recorded and portrayed by the engravings on the clay tiles.

18.17

18.18

18.19

Fig. 18.20 Aris Theodoropoulos, 3D Prints. Dafen Artist Pixelation Portraits. Prosthetic Recall Memory Portraits. **Fig. 18.21** Aris Theodoropoulos, Dafen Artist Studio: 2D to 3D Spatial Experiment. Grasshopper Image sampler definition of image pixelation from a photograph of artist studio in Dafen. Image pixelation is generated from its RGB channel values. **Fig. 18.22** Aris Theodoropoulos, Tintoretto Nativity: 2D to 3D Spatial experiment. Grasshoper Image sampler definition of triangulation from the image luminance values. **Fig. 18.23** Aris Theodoropoulos, Prosthetic sensorial Dome. Anamorphosis of repetitive phenomena in a sensorial Image of recognition and prosthetic recall memories investigate the body memory and body self image.

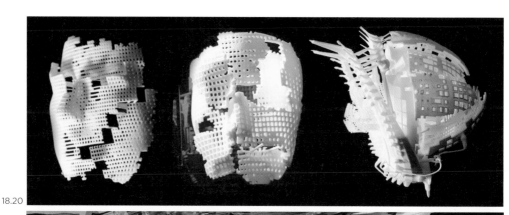

18.20

18.21

18.22

Dome's Engine

Projectors

3D Printer Engine

Synesthetic Dome

Gate

Prosthetic
Dome

18.23

SOFT, SENSUAL, SYNTHETIC:
GREEN PARADIGMS IN THE POST-DIGITAL ERA
Marcos Cruz, Hannes Mayer, Marjan Colletti

Unit 20 has formed a particular interest in crossing boundaries of the traditional architectural practice, envisioning innovative conditions in design. By looking into advances within a wide range from sciences to art — small-scale intelligence, bio-technology, new materiality and digital aesthetics — students are supported to develop an individual research field. The projects, on various scales, develop an architecture that is built up by many different strata of applied scientific knowledge, software based morphologies, urban contextualism, as well as local and global policies, traditions and cultures.

A critical positioning within today's architectural discourse

Most of the contemporary and fashionable "green" concepts are the collectively acceptable mainstream leftovers or technological implementations of avant-garde thoughts, which can be traced back to the oil crisis in the seventies and the subsequent emergence of a green movement. The radical and holistic thoughts of the beginning were most notably and globally voiced in 1992 as Agenda 21 at the United Nations Conference on Environment and Development held in Rio de Janeiro. However, the roots of such movement can be traced back to the 19th century with the formation of biology as a scientific subject coining the now commonly used words habitat, milieu and ecology.

Being in the teens of the 21st century challenges us to look for new alternatives and visionary thoughts that uncover and re-integrate a relationship which has been lost in translation: man-architecture-nature.

Modernity attempted to formulate a reality that was independent from nature, a replacement of 'sickly' nature with perfect technology; as a metaphor of this growing divide architecture was raised on pilotis and sought refuge in visual abstract art. In the recent past however, we have realised the limitations of such approach and nature has regained its place as a quintessential reference for technology, for scientific advances and thus, architecture. Natural complexity and exuberance succeeded classical simplicity and reduction. Instead of opposition, man-architecture-nature is now seen as a more intertwined formation of an overall environmental/cultural/architectural manifold.

More than anything, this reflects our post-digital condition in which architecture aims at a more human dimension in digital design. Following a notion that was first brought up by Nicholas Negroponte, "being digital" looses its appeal as a paradigm to "being human". This however, does not support the rejection of previous digital achievements as suggested by the crisis-benefiting advocates of analogue, orthogonal, handicraft architecture, rather, it calls for a shift from digital rationality to digital sensuality; a move towards a new fabricated materiality.

The question for architecture today is not so much about computational ability or whether designers are involved in scripting or other forms of mathematical processes that help manipulate complex geometries. Architecture goes beyond this. Future steps are about finding a new sense of materiality, one that allows us create new forms and spaces that ultimately engage us (the body) in a more intense way with our built environment. As a part of this exploration performative qualities of new materials are being tested: bio-concrete and high-performance concrete, bio-bricks, novel ceramics, a variety of silicon rubbers, fungal growth as binder of recycled materials.

Underlying is an understanding that programming has become an ubiquitous yet invisible element within our contemporary life whilst the interfaces become sensual, sensory, responsive, tangible — integrating digital, biological, cultural, spiritual and material systems. This is encouraging us to seek a hitherto unseen design approach, one that is soft, sensual and more synthetic.

This year our Unit trip went to Sao Paulo — Parati — Rio de Janeiro.

External Critics: Julia Backhaus, Nicolo Casas, Isaskun Chinchilla, Peter Cook, Oliver Domeisen, Colin Fournier, Linda Hagberg, Sean Hanna, Jonathan Hill, Branko Kolarevic, Justin Nicholls, Marco Poletto, Jose Sanchez, Sara Shafiei, Susana Soares.

Unit 20 would like to thank Justin Nicholls for his continuing unconditional support.

Archithese has also kindly supported the unit with additional Sponsorship.

Year 4: Steven Ascensao, Amittai Lee Antoine, Daphnie Costi, Neil Keogh, Joanna Pawlas, Era Savvides

Year 5: Chun Fatt Lee, Sheung Hok Lim, Rui Liu, Jiro Munechika, Barry Wark, Sam Welham, Maria Knutsson-Hall

Fig. 20.1 Steven Ascensao, Samba School, Morro da Providencia: Carnivalesque Flamboyance. **Fig. 20.2** Amittai Antonie, Ornamental Investigation: Divine, Sacred and Transcendent Order. **Fig. 20.3** Daphnie Costi, Carnival Museum, Morro De Providencia. **Fig. 20.4** Neil Keogh, Hackney Wick Suspended Gardens. **Fig. 20.5** Era Savvides, Museum of Primitive Art, Rio de Janeiro. **Fig. 20.6** Joanna Pawlas, Auditory transgression, Bio-Acoustics Research Centre, Rio de Janeiro. **Fig. 20.7** Sam Welham, Connect, Intersect, Redirect — Material mass versus digital linearity. Post-digital transitions at a textural scale. Mechanical marks and errors are scanned back into the digital interface, joints and components are modelled into tool paths; connecting stone to wires. The dual tooling tolerances exist within a single material articulation, obscuring and revealing details and geometry. **Fig. 20.8** Sam Welham, Masonic Lodge and Temple, Rio de Janeiro. Exposing a single elevation, the Masonic Temple occupies an interstice within the built mass. A focus on digital fabrication, as a craft, connects scales of milled-stone detail with a ritual passage of enlightenment; as degrees of initiation are reflected in strata of refined tooling.

20.1

20.2

20.3

20.4

20.5

20.6

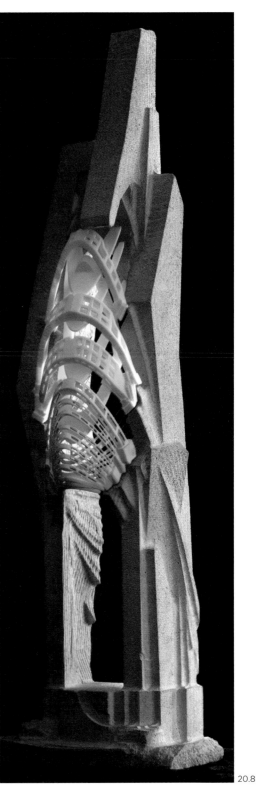

20.7

20.8

Fig. 20.9 Chun Fatt Lee, Rui Liu, Sam Welham, Terminate-Originate. The strategy projects a new layer of density around Central Station of Rio de Janeiro. A gradual pixelation articulates a scripted city grid, creating an urban language unique to Rio de Janeiro. This urban image identifies the cultural frontage and represents an international presentation of the city. **Fig. 20.10** Rui Liu, UN Water Conference Centre. The building is located on the Western end of the Avenida Presidente Vargas, which is a less developed spot of the avenue and an area prone to floods due to its very low topography. The building and surrounding landscape are planned for the 2012 Earth Summit in Rio De Janeiro, integrating a water purification plant and a flooding prevention system. **Fig. 20.11** Chun Fatt Lee, Grandstand for Samba. A new grandstand is proposed for the Sambadrome of Rio de Janeiro. The development aims to regenerate the surrounding area, whilst providing amenities and more comprehensive views of the parade. The curvilinear and sensual platforms rises from the ground, creating a museum for the Samba floats underneath. **Fig. 20.12** Jiro Munechika, Olympic Gateway Station Hackney Wick. **Fig. 20.13** Sheung Hok Lim, Guanabara Bay Transportation Hub — Lattice Landscapes. The project aims to create a new typology of transportations hubs where inhabitation of a complex lattice structure occurs on several scales. The subdivision of concourse and its multi-levelled continuity is designed to create a gradient of spaces from personal to anonymous are as well as the transgression of speed.

20.9

20.10

20.11

20.12

20.13

Fig. 20.14 Maria Knutsson-Hall, Olympic Forum for the Rio de Janeiro 2016 Olympics. The Forum is a public building for visitors to interact and communicate with the Olympic Committee both during and after the Olympics. The Forum will provide information about the Olympics and future Olympic venues with the aim to decentralise the decision making process of such complex structure to a more local level. The building works like a scaffold that integrates nature and growth throughout. During the Olympics the vegetated building will appear relatively controlled. Over time nature will slowly infiltrate the building structure and take over its full tectonics. **Fig. 20.15** Rui Liu, UN Water Conference Centre, Final Model.

20.14

20.15

Fig. 20.16 Maria Knutsson-Hall, Architecture and Nature — A symbiosis inspired by the sloth. Investigation into biophilic and biomorphic design has led to an evaluation of the experiential affect nature has on human beings. The sloth's aesthetic qualities and behavioural patterns within its environment have been analysed together with the spiritual mystification of nature. The project explores natural symbiotic systems and processes to construct an ecologically responsive architectural proposal. The idea of integrating nature in the architecture is seen as a reaction for the decrease of natural environment in the rapidly growing zones in the north part of Rio de Janeiro, Brazil. **Fig. 20.17** (Overleaf) Barry Wark, North Rio Pool Club, A Corpulent Architecture. The Pool Club provides public leisure space in the expansive North Zone of Rio that is devoid of such amenties and gives the area a sense of identity. The project explores the potential of digital design and fabrication to create a corpulent architecture. The materiality folds, sags and conforms to its inhabitants to create a soft space that has a sense of heightened engagement and tactility between man and architecture. This materiality is tested through utilising additive layered manufacturing technology to create complex moulds allowing for the creation of soft composite interfaces.

20.16

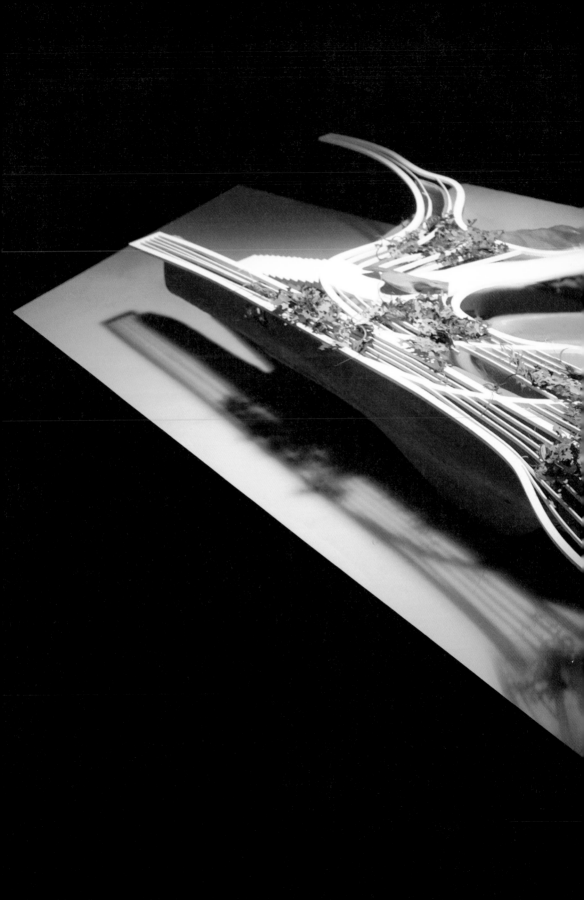

CONTINUOUS TRANSLATION

Abigail Ashton, Andrew Porter

"To translate is to convey. It is to move something without altering it. This is its original meaning and this is what happens in translatory motion. Such too, by analogy with translatory motion, the translation of languages. Yet the substratum across which the sense of words is translated from language to language does not appear to have the requisite evenness and continuity; things can get bent, broken or even lost on the way."

Robin Evans, *Translations from Drawings to Buildings and Other Essays* (1997)

It is inevitable that buildings will be constructed increasingly by factories, machine tools and other automata. However, as with traditional building methods, it is not inevitable that those buildings will also be architecture. The unit has sought to investigate and speculate on how such processes will ensure an outcome that is architecture.

The use of emerging digital technologies means there is an opportunity for the construction industry to move from its current, predominantly 19th century mode of operation, to one of super-industrialisation. In the last 50 years the role of the architect has been eroded and compartmentalised within the increasingly specialised fields of the construction industry. By understanding and developing the relationship between software (representation) and hardware (building), the architect is in a position to reclaim their role as both initiator and master builder. More importantly, as the architect will have a potentially more direct relationship between the drawing, production and the building there are new sets of creative opportunities and tactics to investigate and invent.

One of the key themes the unit focused on is the translation from software to hardware. In its simplest terms this might mean the translation from digital representation to physical object. However, the unit posited the idea that this may be an overly deterministic and simplified operation; we were therefore interested in the spillage in the system, in the same way that Evans refers to getting bent, broken or lost. It is possible that this mistranslation is a by-product of the processes you invent or it is a deliberate aim to re-contextualise or distort data. Equally, we welcomed the idea that these processes are not linear and self-contained. As always, we encouraged a layered approach which could just as easily incorporate analogue, visceral, political, environmental and cultural inputs; in any case we expected a hybridised approach which would allow for tactics of assemblage.

After the empowerment of Renaissance painting through perspective a new language of techniques was developed to nuance and manner the work. For example, sfumato was used to soften edges and to create the illusion of depth and chiaroscuro was the use of strong dark and light contrast to again further heighten the sense of perspective. There were also other techniques such as the cartoon (or large paper drawing) that allowed the transfer from sketch to canvas or plaster surface. This year the unit attempted to invent new terms and/or behaviours for the process of translation that has an equivalent contemporary status that sfumato or chiaroscuro has to perspective.

Further to which, as such historical techniques were deeply analogue they were both unrepeatable and one-way. The unit has considered how, using digital translation, the process could be reversible and interchangeable. In other words can we translate from digital to physical and back to digital to introduce a feedback into the process? In this way a building can be both dynamic (or animate) and responsive.

The unit continued to develop the idea from previous research that the city is treated as a landscape of data that can be harnessed and transformed onto a generator of architectural language. This year the city landscape under observation has been Berlin; a city of the 19th century, broken and reconnected in the 20th century and currently struggling to establish it's identity for the 21st century.

Unit 21 would like to thank our critics: Prof Christine Hawley, Prof Stephen Gage, Dr. Rachel Cruise, Tom Holberton, Godofedo Pereira, Narinder Sagoo, Tim Furzer, Luke Pearson, Peg Rawes.

Design Realisation Tutor: Julie Stewart. Unit Structural Engineer: Brian Eckersley

Year 4: Ka Lai Kylie Chan, Alexander Gazetas, Sara L'Espérance, Risa Nagasaki, Gordon O'Connor-Read, Shogo Sakimura

Year 5: Qing Gao, Mina Gospavic, Eleanor Hedley, Tia Randall, Yeung Piu So, Yi Su, Chun Ting Gabriel Lee, Anthony Smith, Sophie George, Ayaka Suzuki

21.1

Fig. 21.1 Sophie George, Opportunistic Geometries, The project tests whether bespoke digital methods can be used in a political and provocative way. It questions levels of chance and control within a design project and uses methods that embrace indeterminate outcomes. A new Federal Constitutional Court of Germany is proposed in Berlin on a site formerly occupied by the Berlin Wall. A single module of the Berlin Wall was modelled and scanned using a homemade 3d scanner. The homemade scanner contained nuances and inaccuracies, producing areas of slippage in the resulting 3d mesh. These areas of slippage, or 'opportunistic geometries' were used to design the key spaces of the new Court. The challenge of the project lay in combining these opportunistic geometries with the functional requirements of the Court.

Fig. 21.2 – 21.5 Mina Gospavic, Berlin Artspark, This project seeks to inquire what the civilian's image of the city is — using the film and photographic image as synonyms of subjective experience - to identify the qualities of repetitive and cyclical daily movement through Berlin, and subsequently how this can act as a strategy to design an alternative architectural proposal for the city. At the intersection of two subjective experiences, lies the architectural intervention of an Artspark which extracts the geometries from these views structurally and spatially into a landscape of performance areas, outdoor galleries and public spaces.

21.2

21.3

21.4

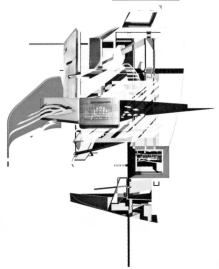

21.5

Fig. 21.6 — 21.9 Yeung Piu So, Karl Marx Allee Monument, "Perhaps spectators walking along the existing monument in Karl Marx Allee (KMA) is similar to the way Robert Smithson toured the monuments in New Jersey. However, not many of us can be as sensitive and imaginative as he did to read those monuments allegorically. Perhaps, we don't even want another Smithson to read the future KMA and say this is "a kind of self-destroying postcard world of failed immortality and oppressive grandeur." Accommodating more than 2,000 apartments, the present KMA deserves positive regeneration. Interacting with the existing Stalinist architecture built from 50s to60s, the proposal will be an anti-nostalgic scheme. Rather than being haunted by the unproductive nostalgia, it will mark the end of the GDR power, and transform it into a new park of possibilities by translating the existing motifs along the boulevard. To stop the unproductive and even dangerous nostalgia of the citizen, like the mother in the film Goodbye Lenin, the project made use of architecture as a tool to help people understand the condition of memory and their history. Meanwhile, it will regenerate the area as new urban recreational hub, putting emphasis on the present livelihood."

21.6

21.7

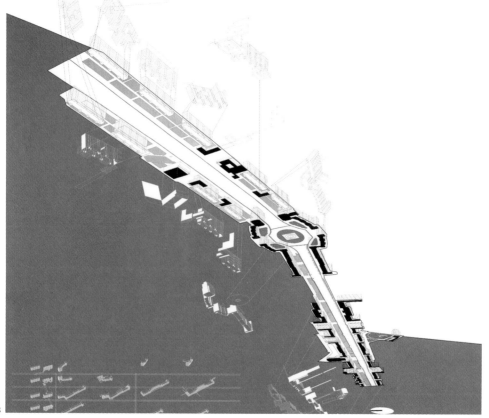

21.8

21.9 >

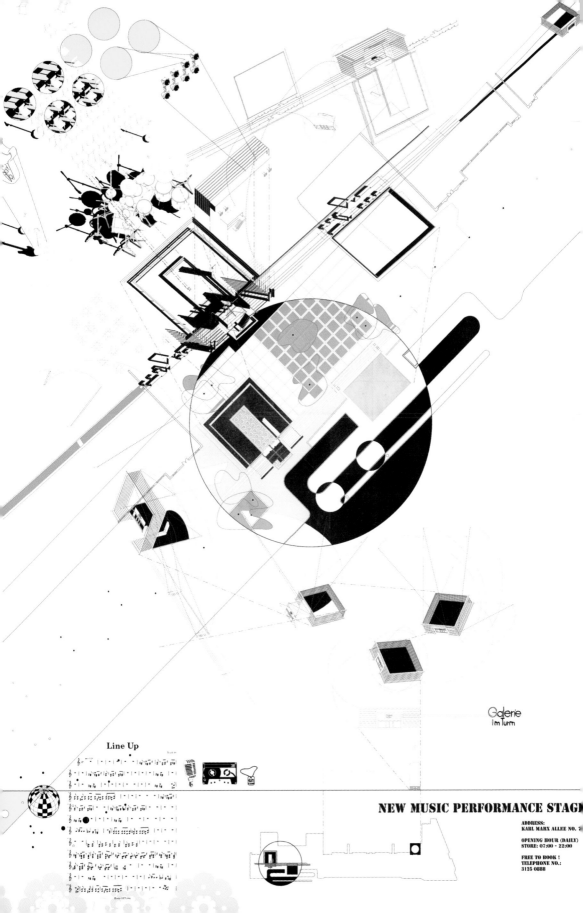

Line Up

Galerie
Im Turm

NEW MUSIC PERFORMANCE STAGE

ADDRESS:
KARL MARX ALLEE NO. 7

OPENING HOUR (DAILY)
STORE: 07:00 - 22:00

FREE TO BOOK !
TELEPHONE NO.:
3125 0888

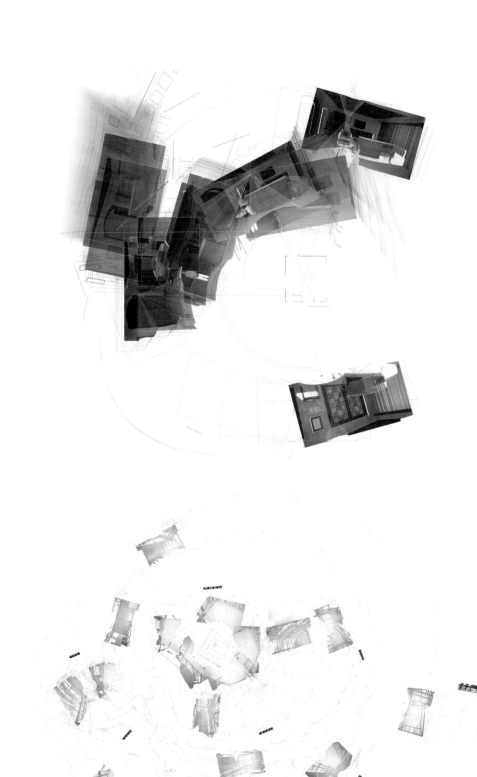

Fig. 21.10 Yi Su, Pina Bausch's Dance School, This dance school is equipped with special studios for practicing specific emotions in Pina Bausch's dance, and provides the audience with different viewing experiences for each studio according to the particular emotion in it. The dancers' and the audience's viewpoints are crucial in experiencing the building. A subjective strategy is applied in the design process, which relies on the designer's understanding from extracting emotions from Bausch's dance till transforming the emotions to dance studio design. **Fig. 21.11** Tia Randall, Die Engelbeckengärten, The Engelbeckengärten, a community agricultural gardens was designed to provide the infrastructure that enables a social framework to be developed by the local residents and users, over time. Within the landscape, we find objects of intrigue and invention, that allow for the manual manipulation of processes within the gardens. Users become physically entwined with the site, their constant presence and activities are required to animate and continue to develop the form of the proposal. At the same time, the individual objects of invention themselves create intimate event experiences with their users. Their language of inherent movement evokes curiosity in those who find them. Once the user has discovered their workings through child-like investigations, the enjoyment of the experience perpetuates their use.

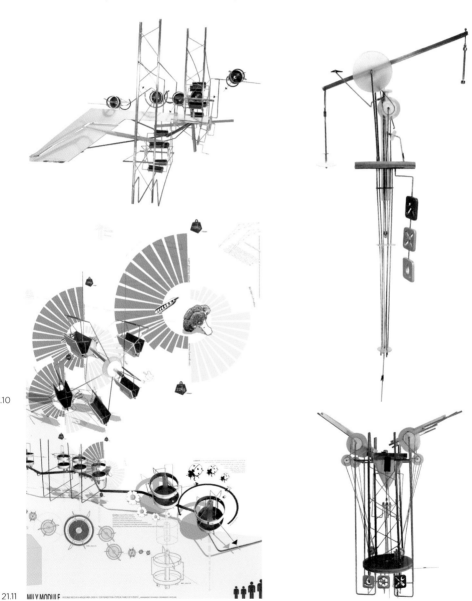

21.10

21.11 MILY MODULE

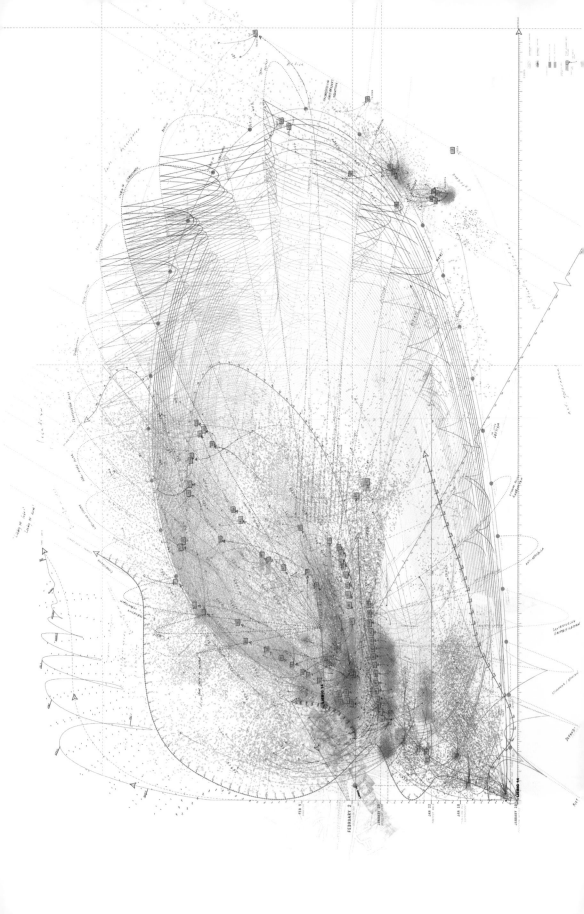

Fig. 21.12 Ayaka Suzuki, Place-Making, An investigation into the eviction of the collective housing residents in Berlin, the chain reaction of protests, with live uploads of videos and comments online is translated into the unfolded expression of the event. **Fig. 21.13** Sara L'Espérance, Urban Playground, The Urban Playground was designed to challenge the typical understanding of the playground's role in an urban context and redefine it as a space where 'play' can encompass all urban dwellers, not simply children. **Fig. 21.14** Qing Gao, The Museum of Domesticity, Metamorphosized from historical maps of Cockfosters in each decades, the evolution of suburban morphology is encrypted in the roofscape of the Museum of Domesticity. 3-d scanning of typical domestic items provided further materials with which to construct the galleries. **Fig. 21.15** Eleanor Hedley, The Theatrical Landscape, This project has sought to define an architecture of the view. This has been explored via the three characteristic viewing techniques displayed by the protagonists of Richard Wagner's opera 'Die Meistersinger von Nürnberg': empathetic, fragmented and unified viewing. **Fig. 21.16** Chun Ting Gabriel Lee, Place-Making, "We have attempted to present interior reality and exterior reality as two elements in process of unification, of finally becoming one" — André Breton. A series of analogue photographic experiments to explore the idea of superimposition of spaces, time and scale.

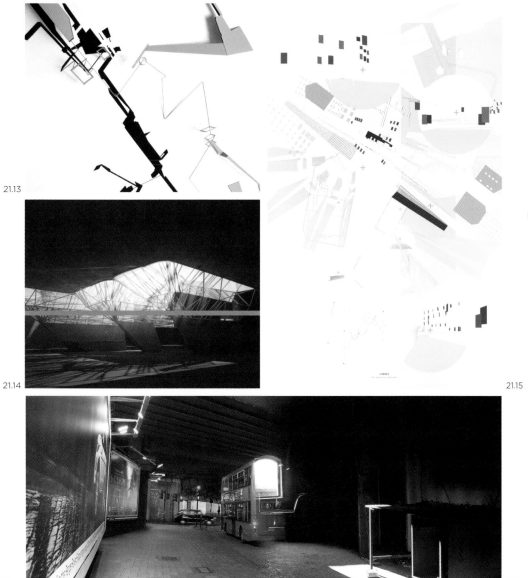

21.13

21.14

21.15

< 21.12

21.16

DARE TO CARE... THROUGH A YEAR

Izaskun Chinchilla, Carlos Jiménez with Helen&Hard

Technification pushed us to hold onto the illusion that humans are invulnerable. It has allowed economic privilege and the short-sightedness of the commercial sphere to overwhelm ecological and social circumstances. Modernity established an official language based on success, on the message that "everything is under control". Probably the main architectural expression of this tradition is the visual predominance: modern architecture is mostly the visual demonstration of what we can build as an act of dominance.

This year, Unit 22 has attempted to abandon the language of power and has embraced the language of care. To what extent we are enriching our context should be the main indicator of architectural quality. Through an architecture that Dares to Care, Unit 22 students have discovered the following:

Many of the public and economic systems associated with power and governmental control require amazing resources. Helping threatened minor communities inside these systems can provide flexibility. A good example is Kaowen's work, in which the private life of the British Monarchy helps the promotion of the UK car industry; or Julian's work, in which immigrant communities in London decrease public expenditure on health by providing domestic vernacular treatments.

Communal typologies will receive new benefits from preserving the particular intimacy and comfort of users renovating the archaic welfare state concept. Claire provided a double entrance and communication system to a dilapidated high rise enabling immigrant women to freely enjoy both public and intimate experiences together. By reassembling halls, stairs, courtyards and gardens in an office buildings, William went beyond the pure commercial image of the British office, instead providing a 'landscape office'; thus ensuring a healthy and larger rentable working space.

Building materials have been traditionally chosen for their mechanics. A more integral approach to materials, that takes time into account, adds new capacities relating material and shape with further processes. Clarissa worked with existing site materials to improve their performance by changing their state. She is using only soft techniques, such as transforming mud into footings with 'jet grouting'. Negin created a modular system suitable for organic urban evolution. Self-supported frames are designed only for their own weight while lightweight screens absorb efforts due to their position in a bigger scheme. Users have the opportunity to overlap screens providing all for family changes through their lifetime.

Cross design effects on different scales prevents sources of vulnerability. Urban architecture relies on the surrounding territory. Context not only provides ingredients for city construction, but it is also the source of energy, logistics and materials for maintenance. Paul's Food Banks react to scarcity in the agricultural belt around cities, learning how it can affect supplies. Insects and Kombucha tea provides a successful urban daily diet while providing independency from the surrounding territory. Liwei developed a housing project in which the necessary footprint for recycling waste is absorbed on-site.

Understanding bodies can detail biological dimensions, which in turn gives enormous clues to reinforcing the ecosystem's fragile balance. Preserving biological bodies help us to empower ecosystems when environmental complexity overwhelms our analytical capacity. Akmal prevents insomnia by living on the wild British coastline subjugating human behavior to natural rhythms. Rachel developed a way to promote laws for preserving American Landscapes by recording and playing back images and perceptions humans used to have.

Our goals should be small but related to different issues, incorporating varied range of materiality, they should be based on existing structures and create new patterns that are partly made out of analogies from visible and non visible parts of reality. Megan S. transformed Essex Road into a homestead facility to provide ingredients to Upper Street restaurants. Michelle combined two programs that together raise awareness on the relationship between the preservation of intangible heritages and climate change. An urban quarry is used to refurbish Paris monuments and provides a new type of performance space. Megan T. created an urban market that offers new ways of neighbours' development through participation in the production of the distributed goods and the use of the market over night.

Preserving vulnerability requires other methods than just drawing plans and sections. ZOETROPES are a good alternative example. These devices produce the illusion of motion from a rapid evolution of static figures. Each zoetrope accompanies users in a time-based activity focusing on parts of architecture that interacts with human actions in a continuous space, the space of life. Zoetropes force a dynamic vision on a scale that connects industrial design with landscape. Let's dare to try.

ROCA, VIDAL Y ASOCIADOS ARQUITECTOS and ARTEMIDE generously supported Unit 22. Richard Hyams has been practice tutor and Roberto Marin Sampalo has been structural consultant.

Year 4: Megan Smedy, Akmal Afandi Azhar, Clarissa Yee, Michelle Young, Megan Townsend, Claire Taggart, Kaowen Ho, Paul Leader-Williams

Year 5: Sung-Hwa Rachel Cha, Liwei Deng, William Fisher, Negin Ghorbani-Moghaddam, Julian Zi Liang Huang, Paul McManamon, Sinan Pirie

Fig. 22.1 UNIT22, Zoetrope device. **Fig. 22.2** Akmal-Afandi Azhar, Cuptopus. Cupping bath tub based on the traditional cupping method to remove the contaminant in the vulnerable heart. **Fig. 22.3** Michelle Young, UNESCO Centre of Intangible Cultural Heritage, Paris. Weather defined as the state of the atmosphere. In the new museum the building will aim to recreate the contexts, or most specifically the atmospheres, of the heritages that are being showcased. **Fig. 22.4** Michelle Young, UNESCO Centre of Intangible Cultural Heritage, Paris. Arrangement of Exhibition Spaces, within the building, the exhibition spaces have been organized so that opportunities arise where visitors can view other visitors engaging in a performance of cultural heritage. **Fig. 22.5** Megan Smedy, The High Street Homestead, London. Collection of traditional atmospheres and popular knowledge to organize Housing Units, Farms, Edible Gardens & Test Labs, Existing Architectures and Public Kitchen. **Fig. 22.6** Megan Smedy, The High Street Homestead, London. Façade study, composition of casted windows from Essex Road traditional shops facades.

22.1

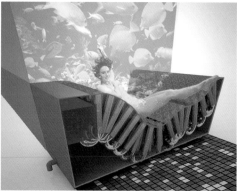

22.2

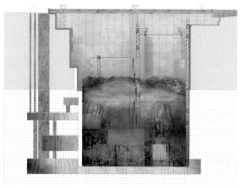

22.3

22.4

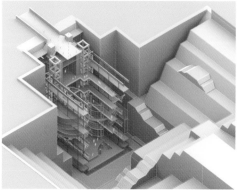

22.5

22.6

Fig. 22.7 Megan Smedy, The High Street Homestead, London. House Units plan. Vernacular and traditional techniques are combined with contemporary ones. **Fig. 22.8** Megan Smedy, The High Street Homestead, London. The goat turrets are constructed of pre fabricated water tower components, however the wall system is bespoke. It is simply a double cable system that supports and constrains hay bales that sit between the two. **Fig. 22.9** Megan Townsend. A Manifesto for a Local Consumerism Movement, Tower Hamlets Permanent Market and New Town Square, London. Long section (and small roof plan) of my building cutting through one of the germination towers and the main market and trading building, highlighting the community interaction with each of the buildings, as well as how the building interacts with existing infrastructure, and the new landscaped area around the site. **Fig. 22.10 — 22. 11** Clarissa Yee, Slow Housing Typology, Lancashire, UK. Familiar Kitchen and Comunal Kitchen desined to optimize the cooking procedures, maintining the highest level of vitamines.

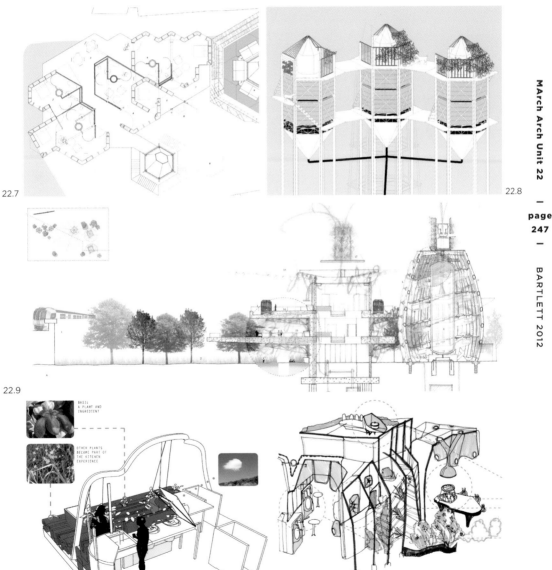

22.7

22.8

22.9

22.10

22.11

Fig. 22.12 Clarissa Yee, Slow Housing Typology, Lancashire, UK. Communal kitchen modelled for video to explore user experience within internal spaces. **Fig. 22.13** Claire Taggart, Social Housing, Creating social and extended community living spaces for a more sociable housing strategy in Ampthill Square Estate, Somers Town. London. **Fig. 22.14** Claire Taggart, Social Housing- retrofit extensions to existing residential tower blocks in Ampthill Square housing estate, Somers Town stretch private social spaces into new connecting back garden balconies. **Fig. 22.15** Claire Taggart, Social Housing — sequence model showing a typical day's route through extended living spaces, play tower and library in Ampthill Square housing estate, Somers Town. **Fig. 22.16** Claire Taggart, Social Housing- secondary façades extend existing living spaces in Ampthill Square housing estate, Somers Town whilst new towers and decks provide library, exercise, childcare, garden and community hall spaces.

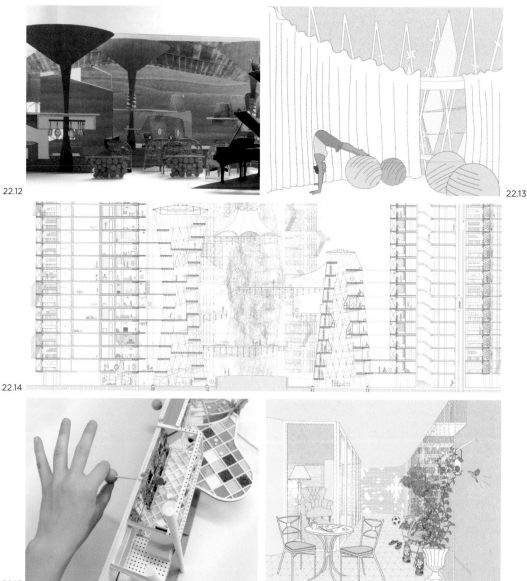

22.12

22.13

22.14

22.15

22.16

Fig. 22.17 Kaowen Ho, The Vulnerable Queen, London. An Investigation into the symbiotic relationship of HRM The Queen and her people. **Fig. 22.18** Kaowen Ho, The Vulnerable Queen, London. Inside the media machine. **Fig. 22.19** Kaowen Ho, The Vulnerable Queen, London. The Queen and the media; perspective long section. **Fig. 22.20** Kaowen Ho, The Vulnerable Queen, London. HRM vehicle display and maintenance. **Fig. 22.21** Kaowen Ho, The Vulnerable Queen, London. speculative views of Buckingham Palace interiors.

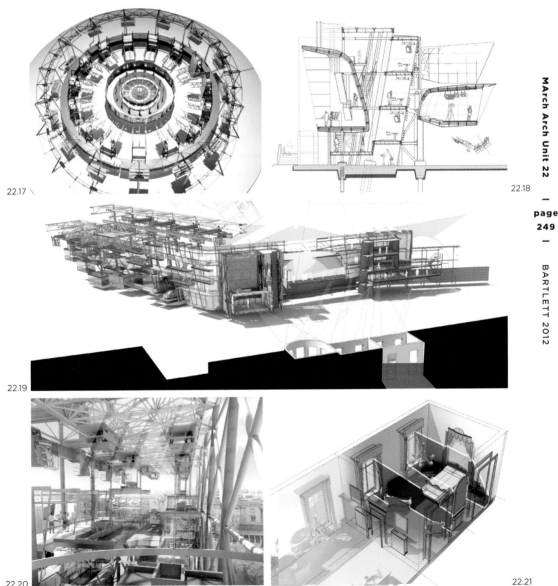

22.17

22.18

22.19

22.20

22.21

Fig. 22.22 Negin Ghorbani-Moghaddam, Modular Social Housing in Southall, London. Descriptions of a series of modifications of a privet modular dwelling following the needs of a family all through their life. **Fig. 22.23** William Fisher. Cooperative office space in Euston, London.The project investigates how spaces in which people carry out office work can enable them to be more productive, more in control and happy with their work, and better placed to integrate work into a balanced life. Fig. **Fig. 22.24** Sung Hwa Cha. Image Productions using Materials and Spaces. Pinhole camera photography Installation displayed in the lost landscape. The new artificial landscape integrated in the urban space allows Landscape Photographers to recreate impossible nature without digital technology. **Fig. 22.25** Liwei Deng. Waste Issues And Vulnerable Community. Newham, London. House typology designed thaking into consideration the collection and management of the domestic waste production in the UK. Recycling activities start just after consumption. The modifications, enlargements and dwelling improvements are encouraged by the regulations.

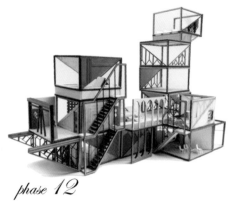

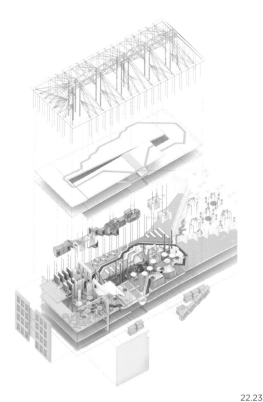

22.22

22.23

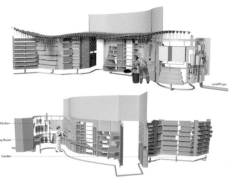

22.24

22.25

Fig. 22.26 Paul McManamon, FOOD BANK #4 Project, London. The project is a model for the extension of London's ailing infrastructure which supports the urban dweller, and thus is a response to the classification of London as a city of serious food and energy shortages. The proposal looks towards the future when London's consumption is expected to be unable to meet demand and when the global population reaches 8.3 billion. This project introduces a half organic, half industrial architecture supplying the City of London with a new series of production and distribution network hubs that adapt their sizes to the amount of resources contained inside of them, feeding the city, providing jobs and re-using the existing architectural infrastructure. **Fig. 22.27** Paul McManamon, FOOD BANK #4 Project, London.

The project creates an alternative sharing scheme which provides a rapid and dedicated distribution route network across London via the reinvention of the London post office railway as the 'Resource-Rail'. Kombucha Towers producing organic cellulose and gas. **Fig. 22.28** Paul McManamon, FOOD BANK #4 Project, London. The project envisages a municipal food production and energy system located in the abandoned royal mail centres across London, giving a purposeful and sustainable legacy to the mail infrastructure in the City.

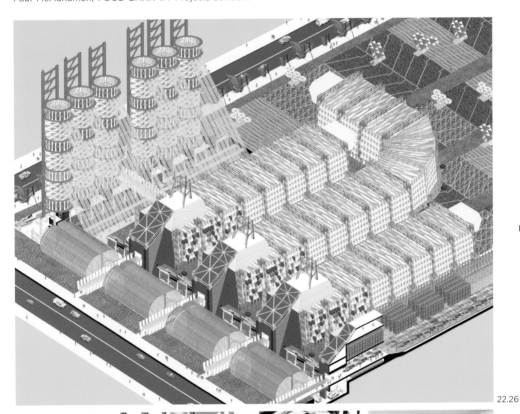

22.26

22.27

22.28

Fig. 22.29 Julian Huang. Instant Alternative Healthcare Service in Peckham, London. The proposal is set 50 years ahead in the future in 2060, when the NHS is predicted to have been fully privatised from the government. Instead it would be operated and ran by pharmaceutical corporations, who controls and manipulates who, why and how we access its health service. Collection of movable, semi-permanent and permanent Clinics. Each Clinic unit uses an specific medical procedure of the Peckham population. **Fig. 22.30** Julian Huang. Instant Alternative Healthcare Service in Peckham, London. Instant access to healthcare procedures. Diagrams illustrating how local residents would be able to obtain healthcare as part of their everyday process; such as visiting the 'Shiro Dhara' clinic above the clothing store, the 'Swedana' clinic behind the hair salon, the 'Pizhichil'

clinic directly from the patient's own home and the 'fire-cupping' clinic above the supermarket. A critical goal of the AHS is to provide treatment methods that are based on the local demographics, as future health care should consider not just who, but what type of health service could be administered. As our society is becoming ever more multi-cultural, our health service need evolve and reflect this change, and adapt fully to the different needs of its patients.

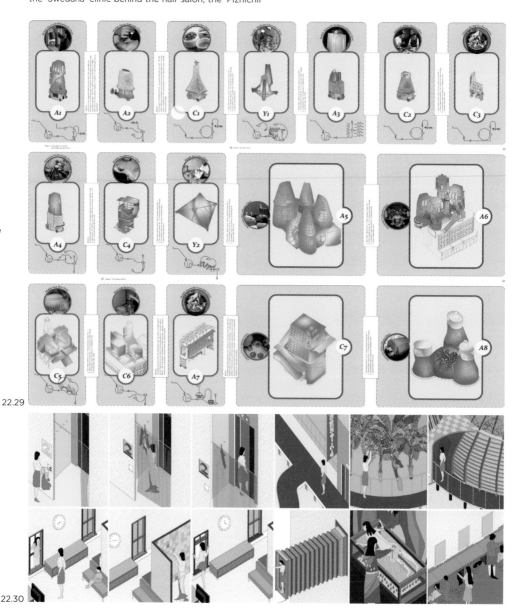

22.29

22.30

Fig. 22.31 Julian Huang. Instant Alternative Healthcare Service in Peckham, London. Axonometric of Peckham showing the relationship between the various health clinics and the local urban fabric, and how the implementation of an alternative health service would alter the urban landscape of the area. A network of over 25 mobile, temporary and semi-permanent alternative health clinics would offer instant access of health service to its local population, as opposed to the often arduous and long waiting time offered by the NHS. These health clinics would be diffused and saturated into the everyday places of the urban fabric. These include a variety of shops, bars, gyms, restaurants and entertainments complexes, the aim of this is to create a much more dynamic health care system, where places of medical practice is not an end destination where one goes to fix one's health, but an on-going, continuous process that can interact/intervene with our daily lives.

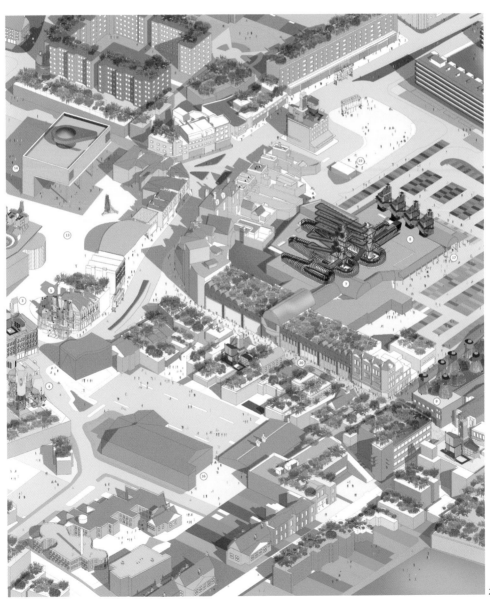

22.31

Unit 23

FABRICATING THE REAL

Bob Sheil, Emmanuel Vercruysse, Kate Davies

MArch Arch Unit 23

—

page
254

—

BARTLETT 2012

In the film studios of Pinewood, Shepperton and Ealing, and in the television studios of White City, Portland Place and Horseferry Road, reality is constructed and reconstructed – rewritten, recomposed, revealed and obscured, cut and remixed – fabricated. Recordings that lie fragmented across the city in banks of wax, celluloid, nitrate, tape and data, are embroidered for artistic, political or commercial ends. This year the unit explored the slippery, devious and creative world that exists between the real and the unreal by investigating architectural subjects associated with the processing and production of public media. Elusive and pervasive, brand new and rich with tradition, the media industry is both crumbling and blossoming. It embodies technique and technology, artistry and piracy, flamboyant show and global business. Viewing this industry through the unit's lens, we developed speculative propositions in three acts: 'Splice', 'The MacGuffin* Projects' and 'The Broadcasting House', constructing along our way a series of digital-analog chimeras that venture into pockets of unreal, imaginary and fabricated realities.

Framed as a speculative and polemic enquiry on spaces for the production of broadcast media, The Broadcasting House acts as a scaffold for the unit to question the act of viewing, the role of the viewer and the validity of that which is being viewed. Channel-hopping through the fragmented city, we set out to interrogate the mechanisms behind a set of fabricated realities, exploring slippages and transgressions between the actual and the imagined, the here and there, and the now and then, as the capital becomes backdrop, prop and plot device to a series of tall tales. Acting playfully into the physical and operating dextrously in the digital, the unit's work acts within the space of the imagination, of control, of voyeurism, consumerism and power, of dreaming and trickery.

Unit 23 operates as a critical practice to establish and evolve the agendas, methods, attitudes and directions its graduates will take beyond the institution. We approach the subject and discipline of architectural production as a broad and curious field that oscillates between meaning and means, representation and realisation, experience and expertise. We investigate and experiment within the operations, protocols, roles, deceptions and tales of making experimental architecture. Students are expected to take possession of their work as critical research in developing their knowledge, skill and ideas.

Fabrication is a deliberately ambiguous term that provides a backdrop to the year's questions. The Unit is a forum for in-depth design investigation. Closely aligned with the Bartlett's advanced fabrication labs, it spans the gulf between the speculative and the tangible and places a strong emphasis on the exploration of ideas through elaborations of craft, rigorous physical testing and experimental production in order to test and explore directly the material consequences of our speculations. The unit's work is diverse and personal and is driven by individuality and flair. It exists in twin digital and physical states. It is hand crafted, emerges from code and dissolves into point cloud. It lurks at the edges of perception and interferes within distortions of the senses. It sets its own terms of engagement, deploying active transgressions across the fertile territory between the actual and its many manifestations.

*A MacGuffin is a plot element that catches the viewer's attention or drives the plot of a work of fiction. Its specific nature may be ambiguous, undefined, generic, left open to interpretation or otherwise completely unimportant to the plot.

Special thanks to our critics and guests: Paul Bavister, Richard Beckett, Johan Berglund, Mark Burry, Matthew Butcher, Nat Chard, Ming Chung, Xavier De Kestelier, Mike Dean, William Firebrace, Stephen Gage, Ilona Gaynor, Oliviu Lugojan-Ghenciu, Bastian Glassner, Ruairi Glynn, Andy Hudson-Smith, Simon Kennedy, Asif Khan, Guan Lee, Luke Lowings, Yeoryia Manolopoulou, Matteo Melioli, Josep Mias, Ed Moseley, James O'Leary, Pernilla Ohrstedt, Alan Penn, Chris Pierce, Ru Scott, Matt Shaw, Gabby Shawcross, Marilena Skavara, Misha Smith, Matthias Suchert, Will Trossell, Nic Tyson, Peter Vaughan, Graeme Williamson.

Year 4: Mihir Benodekar, Behnaz Berengi, Kevin Chen, Stuart Colaco, Jacob Down, Meng Lui, Nurlina Marof, Richard Northcroft, Megan Passey, Tom Svilans

Year 5: Peaker (Chi Wai) Chu, Thais Kvejborg Espersen, Tom Harvey, Birgir Örn Jónsson, Madhav Kidao, Joseph Ransom Shaw, Thomas Smith

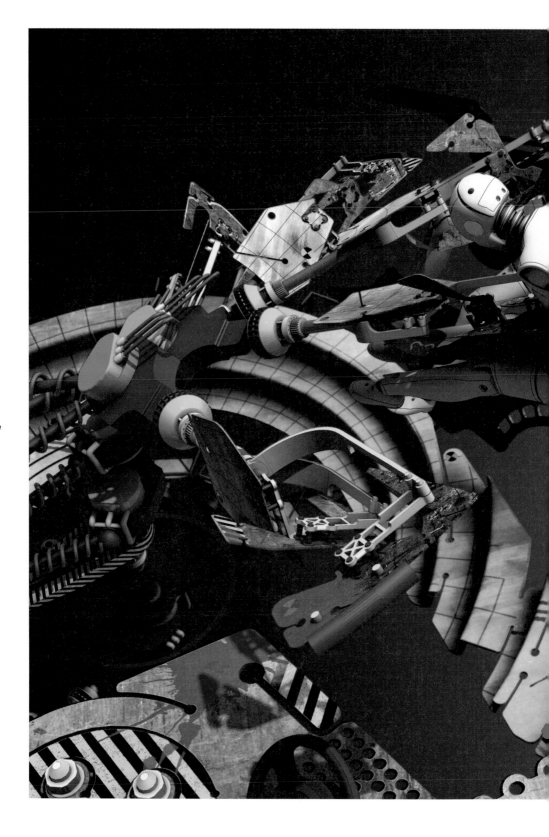

23.1

Fig. 23.1 (Previous spread) Tom Smith, Simulating a Crashed Architecture. An animated world of twisted spaces is constructed from four crash simulations, forming a technological ballet designed to choreograph its own violent destruction. The project is a richly saturated orgy of fetishism and precision inspired by both the meticulous reconstructions of crash-test simulation rigs and the mouth-watering collisions that unfold in slow motion across the cinema screen. **Fig. 23.2** Richard Northcroft and Megan Passey, The Factory of Unmade Films. Architectural 'scripts' describe tactical propositions for a playful rehousing of Stanley Kubrick's archive as a sequence of cinematic spaces inspired by iconic Kubrick film sets and viewed as a vast tracking shot from the Westway **Fig. 23.3** Jacob Down, Non-locomotive motion trace: A specifically constructed body prosthetic and a 30-second long exposure photograph reconstruct the motion and boundaries of the human form through time, drawing out spaces of action but erasing the actor. **Fig. 23.4** Jacob Down, Westway Dynamics: A 45-second long exposure photograph explores the prescribed vehicular motions and speeds of an underpass below the Westway. **Fig. 23.5** Tom Svilans, Prototyping a Myth: The objects, fragments from the Guild of Redundant Technology, are made to be viewed in subdued light and are explorations of shadow on material surface. The Guild reclaims precious metals from prosaic objects, and recasts them in spectacular illusory interiors for the grand hall. The mark of the digitally guided tool is both a sign of precision and a device for optical effect. **Fig. 23.6** Tom Svilans, Study model for the Guild of Redundant Technology.

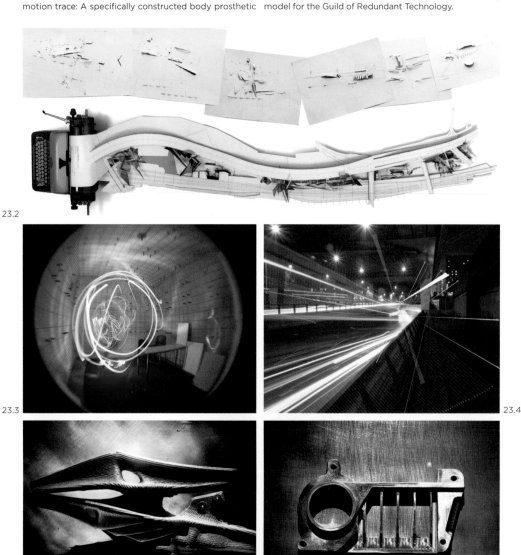

23.2

23.3

23.4

23.5

23.6

Fig. 23.7 Tom Harvey, Vertigo: Instrumentalising Perception Through Durations Of Spatial Temporal Realignment. The year's work explored architectural design as a means to distort and disrupt experiences and memories, overlapping real and subjective spatial scenarios which overwhelm frequently and unexpectedly. Playing with the shifting paradigms of consciousness, vertigo was seen as an emblem for the manipulation of space-time. In this context, the design process was an opportunity to test the limits of reality, to test the dissonance between subjective experience and cultural assumptions, to short-circuit the dependable physiological tendency to conform consciousness to outer reality and to instigate a sense of freedom. These overlapping spatial conditions were seen as the remit of the architect and the intention of the project was to propose the overlapping milieu as spaces for experimentation that question the traditional contradiction of architecture as a profession guised as an art form and propose the design process as a means of research conducted within the frame of a playful artistic pursuit. In this vein, models explored notions of the multisensory and multiperspective, primarily through both spatial distortions instigated through mismatch in the senses and disequilibrium between the expected and actually perceived. This allowed for ambiguous impressions of motion in both the external and internal process, leaving the world and body to slip out of harmony and in doing so creating a gap in which one could fall infinitely.

23.7

Fig. 23.8 — 23.9 Madhav Kidao, The Theatre of Synthetic Realities. A series of real and fictitious locations and events, actors and devices, that attempts to question our production, embodiment and perception of social space as mediated through technology. Through the use of ubiquitous personal and mobile computing we have become both constant consumers and producers of information, both live receiver and transmitter. We, and our environments, exist simultaneously as physical and real-time digital manifestations, as such augmenting our relationship to space, time and experience.

23.8

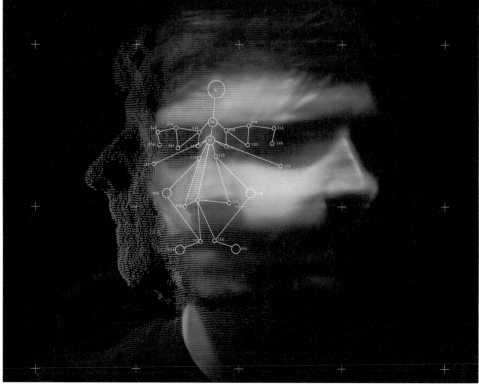

23.9

Fig. 23.10 — 23.11 Birgir Örn Jónsson, Islands of Vision. Research suggests that life in technologically-intensive cultures is becoming increasingly guided by a foveal character of vision. The fovea is primarily involved with the processing of objects and detail, while peripheral vision deals with the gathering of environmental context, and is inherently spatial. The project questions this centre-biased consumption of space by seeking to occupy the more mysterious periphery. A field laboratory for spatial perception, it was tested through the making of tools that address peripheral vision and the dynamics of the visual field. It suggests architecture that encourages a more curious, playful gaze and seeks to reconnect with the observer by providing for a heightened sense of peripheral awareness. The scheme reveals itself to the observer in layers interacting within specific zones in the field of vision. It skirts the edges and hides in blind spots, acting out a sequence of carefully constructed and cunning diversions in order to exist there at all.

23.10

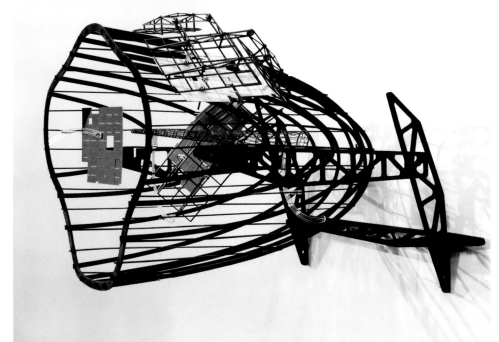

23.11

Fig. 23.12 — 23.13 Joseph Ransom Shaw, The Unnatural History Unit. A polemical enquiry into notions of authenticity, the project unpacks iconic BBC nature documentaries, revealing an elaborate artifice. A sequence of spectacular studio sets is carefully tailored for the precise construction of these seemingly seamless natural wonders. It is architecture as 'the making of' documentary, offering us a glimpse behind the scenes of the factories supplying the natural world to our living rooms. **Fig. 23.14** Thais Kvejborg Espersen, Twilight Theatre. The project is a series of performance spaces re-articulated by a sequence of architectural choreographies across time. The architecture is born from notation systems delineating the 3 phases of twilight. Two stages slowly track twilight, one at dawn, one at dusk, while a third is positioned to celebrate midsummers day. The made pieces and mechanisms act as both kinetic models and dynamic spatial notation. **Fig. 23.15** Peaker Chu, Cinematic Dreamscape. Inspired by abstract cinema, the project harvests and harnesses artificial light from the Westway to create a cinematic experience. A series of filmic architectural fragments are strategically located in relation to the sweeping arcs of passing traffic and feed off the shifting palette of colours and light qualities to create a distorted fluorescent and incandescent world; an abstract cinema driven by the buzz and flicker of the nocturnal city.

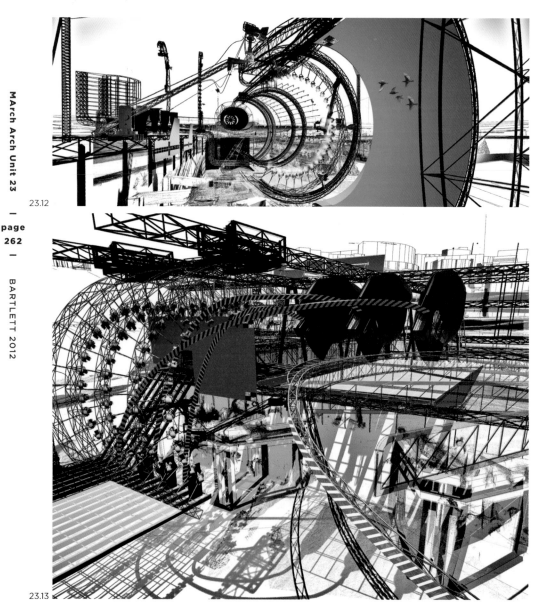

23.12

23.13

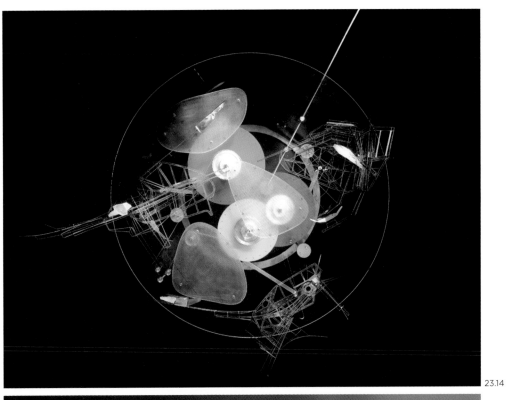

YEAR 5 MArch THESIS

Peg Rawes, Mark Smout

The thesis is the place where Year 5 students have the opportunity to develop a series of focused research questions that underpin their design work. These questions may be informed by disciplines such as architectural history, physical and biological sciences, cultural theory, technology, literary theory or philosophy. As a result, a reflexive relationship is created between the portfolio and thesis, each informing the other.

JEROME FLINDERS

Hypoxic Landscape: A Clumsy Solution for Climate Change Mitigation in Istanbul

The central theme of this thesis is to discuss the question: how can architecture adequately respond to the complexity of climate change science, and provide a clear built environment solution?

By examining the work of climate scientist, Mike Hulme, I show how climate change is as much a problem of our conception of 'truth', as it is a problem of science. I then consider Hulme in tandem with Quentin Meillassoux's 'object-oriented' philosophy, to show that rather than climate change being understood as an 'objective' scientific idea in the conventional sense, our understanding inherently relies upon subjective notions of space and place.

These ideas are then used to explore how architecture mitigates climate change in the conventional sense, as well as helping to frame its complexity by embodying broader questions of 'truth' and 'object'. The proposal is located in Turkey, west of Istanbul. It consists of an artificial oxygen-deficient wetland on an otherwise fertile piece of flat land. By diverting rainwater onto a site, and strategically injecting it into the landscape,

the site becomes artificially saturated, ombrotrophic (fed exclusively by rainwater) and slightly acidic. These conditions generate an oxygen-deficient soil that inhibits the decomposition of carbon-based matter embedded within it; it stops the soil's carbon content from being released into the atmosphere as CO_2 which means that the saturated land becomes a highly efficient carbon-reservoir. Carbon trapped in wetlands in this fashion, is a more significant source of trapped carbon globally than woodland and wetland alteration and drainage is one of the biggest causes of anthropomorphic carbon dioxide emission worldwide.

Finally, I consider the impact of architecture on our notion of climate change. Climate change represents a fascinating and unique condition where ideology and truth are forced to have an impact on our conception of space (and architecture). Whether it is double-glazing or the creation of estuaries or bogs as 'hypoxic' landscapes, changes in the way we deploy and read space may not be a consequence of climate change but what, in fact, determines our notion of climate change itself.

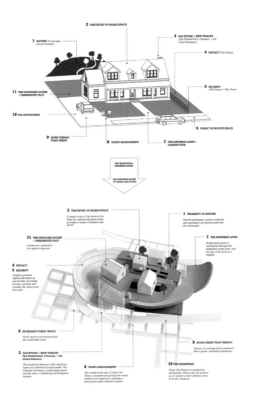

EMMA FLYNN

Trash Can Utopias: Transforming the Waste Landscape of Long Island Suburbia (Hicksville, Long Island, NY)

This thesis explores the potential role of waste and its accompanying technologies in the vision and creation of utopian and sustainable communities. With a focus on residential waste and suburban housing, the ideas and research explored here are ultimately demonstrated through the design concepts and waste technologies present in the accompanying design proposal, Trash Can Utopia.

Since suburbia's proliferation in the U.S. more Americans now live in the suburbs than either the city or the country, with the process of suburbanisation continuing to evolve. However building suburbia the old way is no longer working on Long Island. Designed for a post-war era and the collective American dream of the 1940s, the suburban typology is out of touch with the issues of today. With energy prices due to skyrocket, the car-dependant, energy-intensive suburbs may not be able to survive in the absence of low-cost petroleum. Inherently wasteful and unsustainable, in terms of both space and resource consumption, the current suburban model needs to be readdressed in the face of increasing energy and environmental concerns.

In response to this problem Trash Can Utopias explores waste's historic role and future potential in the vision and creation of utopias, and how, in the specific case of Long Island suburbia, waste, and waste technologies, can transform the suburbs from a wasteful dystopia to its promised utopia. It explores how the taboo and unpopular issue of garbage can be worked with in a positive way, with the aim of tackling the specific garbage problem in Long Island and the inherent wastefulness of the suburban model. Challenging the invisibility and unsustainability of the current garbage infrastructure, it proposes that waste management should be brought closer to our everyday environments, incorporated and become productive.

With the future of Long Island suburbia looking increasingly uncertain, this project explores how waste and its technologies can revitalise an area, increase energy efficiency and off-grid communities, whilst retaining the utopian image of suburbia to which many still aspire. Ultimately, the project proposes a new way of living and working with garbage, and through this admittedly polemical investigation, hopes to challenge our relationship with waste and wasting.

MATHEW LEUNG

Oriental Orientalism in Japan — The Case of Yokohama Chinatown

The concept of an innate 'Japanese spirit', distinct from those of all other countries and ethnicities, is an idea that appears to fascinate many; both in the West and within Japan itself. While such views may be overstated, there is a real sense of ethnic homogeneity within Japan. However, noted for their ability to create communities around the world that appear disconnected and detached from their 'host' societies, the Chinese have become the largest ethnic minority in Japan.

Within this context, the presence of Chinatown in Yokohama, the port city which merges with Tokyo, can be seen an island of 'Chinese-ness' in a sea of 'Japan-ness', especially given the strength of the identities involved. Yet, the coexistence of these two oriental neighbours is much more complex, including: centuries of cooperation and interchange; sustained, full-scale warfare; colonisation and tumultuous upheavals in the political and economic fortunes of both parties.

The thesis therefore examines the history of Yokohama, showing how it came to be a key point of cultural confluence, and documenting the historical development of its Chinatown. Introduced through concepts of 'orientalism' and 'hybridity' in relation to the context of other Chinatowns around the world, I argue that the term 'Chinatown' describes a social construct as much as physical space, and that the role of each 'host' society is intrinsic to this cultural construction. Yokohama Chinatown exists in relation to Japanese national identity, which has been moulded deliberately as a result of Japan's first encounters with western countries after its self-imposed isolation was brought to an end in the mid-nineteenth century. In turn, the Japanese perspective on the rest of Asia, specifically China, needs to be seen as a form of 'Oriental Orientalism' in which a single, exotic image of a culture is created, to serve the purposes of Japan. These themes are manifested in the physical fabric of contemporary Yokohama Chinatown in drawings, maps, photographs and textual analysis. Yokohama Chinatown is also the complex result of the constant processes of negotiation involved in the formation of cultural identity. Intrinsic to my analysis is the idea that architecture is intimately connected with its wider context, both in a physical and socio-political sense. This conclusion acknowledges the range of issues involved in this particular case study of urban hybridity in Yokohama, and outlines the repercussions of this research topic.

TIA RANDALL
THE RITUAL: The May Day Riots — Kreuzberg's role in Berlin's Identity

On International Labour Day, 1st May 1987, after apparently unprovoked police attacks on protest groups in Berlin during annual demonstrations, the radical left sought cover at the Kreuzberg peoples-fest. The situation escalated into the first of the famous 'Mai Krawalle' after almost a thousand people returned the attack. In the following days, the district of Kreuzberg made national and international news, reinforcing a now familiar portrayal of it as the volatile cradle of West Germany's radical left community. Today the riots have become a tradition in Kreuzberg, recurring every May Day since, but never with the fatalities of the first two years. This annual repetition has contributed to the transformation of the riots into something of legend, one that is irrefutably connected to the district and its political and cultural development, not only of its residents but also the built form of the urban environment.

This thesis traces the process of new German identity formation through its direct effects on the urban fabric of the district of Kreuzberg in West and reunified Berlin. Despite their differences, both East and West Berlin shared the problem of how to differentiate themselves with Germany of the Third Reich. The Cold War was yet another epoch that focused German concerns about identity, with solutions offered by the famous modernist urban planners and architects of the age. These were later contested by the alternative presented in Kreuzberg.

Today, those young enough for the memories of the Second World War not to haunt them directly, no longer wish to be constantly apologizing for the atrocities of the previous generation. They are looking for a way that they can be proud of the city they belong to. This problem of 'being German' may ultimately be tested, contested and resolved in Berlin. The German people will inevitably look to their capital for direction: 'Berlin is where we will see whether the Germans succeed in finding the way from the tragedy of division to a new identity' (Stimmann, 1991). The city today has become a lens through which it is possible to explore issues such as architecture and urbanism, identity and belonging, cultural historical memory and forgetting.

MArch DESIGN REALISATION
James O'Leary, Dirk Krolikowski

The Design Realisation course provides the opportunity for all Year 4 students to consider how buildings are designed, constructed and delivered. Students are asked to reflect upon their relationship with technology, the environment and the profession. This is explored through an iterative critical examination of the major building design project taught within the context of individual design units in 4th year. The course runs concurrently with The Building Project and is supported by an extensive lecture series, seminars, cross unit crits, with each design unit being supported by a dedicated practice based tutor.

The course aims to introduce students to core knowledge that is required in the realisation of buildings in professional architectural design practice. Students are asked to consider the influence of and develop an attitude towards construction, technology and the profession, which are all seen as having an integral role within the creative design process.

We would like to thank our lecturers and practice tutors. DR Lecturers: Rhys Cannon & Ben Addy (Moxon Architects), Andy Hudson-Smith (Centre for Advanced Spatial Analysis, UCL), Matt Shaw & Will Trossell (Scanlab), Jake Hacker (Arup), Salmaan Craig (Foster + Partners), Mark Whitby (Ramboll Whitbybird), Ed Clark (Arups), Tim Lucas & Andy Toohey (Price & Myers), Soo Ware (UCL), Simon Allford (AHMM), Cristiano Ceccato (Zaha Hadid Architects), Asa Bruno (Ron Arad Associates), John Lyall (John Lyall Architects), Phil Ayres (CITA Copenhagen), Robert Lowe (UCL), Hareth Pochee (Max Fordham), Sara Klomps (Zaha Hadid Architects), Andrew Nicholson (WSP), Felix Weber (ARUP), Dr. Mark Miodownik (The Institute of Making, UCL), Ozan Yalniz (ARUP), Prof. Alan Penn (UCL), Nathalie Rozencwajg (R-are), Takeshi Hayatsu (6A architects), Katerina Dionysopoulou (THS), Dirk Krolikowski (Rogers Stirk Harbour + Partners), James O'Leary (UCL), Nick Callicott (Stahlbogen), Bob Sheil (UCL), Peter Scully (AB3), Graeme Williamson (NORD), Dheeraj Bhardwa (Laing O'Rourke), Pernilla Ohrstedt & Asif Khan (Pernilla + Asif).

DR Practice Tutors: Simon Dickens (Youmeheshe Architects), John Lyall (John Lyall Architects), Carl Vann, Domi Oliver (Pollard Thomas Edwards Architects), Daniel Wright (Rogers Stirk Harbour + Partners), Peter Vaughan (Pernilla + Asif). Dean Pike (David Chipperfield Architects), Maria Fulford, David Hemingway, Joanna Karatzas (Niall McLaughlin Architects), Sara Klomps (Zaha Hadid Architects), Justin Nichols (Make), Julie Stewart (Eric Parry Architects), Richard Hyams (Astudio).

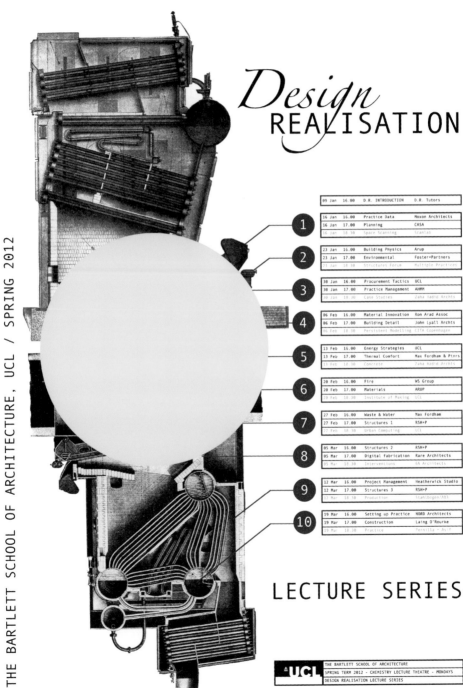

Design REALISATION

THE BARTLETT SCHOOL OF ARCHITECTURE, UCL / SPRING 2012

09 Jan	16.00	D.R. INTRODUCTION	D.R. Tutors

1

16 Jan	16.00	Practice Data	Moxon Architects
16 Jan	17.00	Planning	CASA
16 Jan	18.30	Space Scanning	Scanlab

2

23 Jan	16.00	Building Physics	Arup
23 Jan	17.00	Environmental	Foster+Partners
23 Jan	18.30	Structures Forum	Multiple Practices

3

30 Jan	16.00	Procurement Tactics	UCL
30 Jan	17.00	Practice Management	AHMM
30 Jan	18.30	Case Studies	Zaha Hadid Archts

4

06 Feb	16.00	Material Innovation	Ron Arad Assoc
06 Feb	17.00	Building Detail	John Lyall Archts
06 Feb	18.30	Persistent Modelling	CITA Copenhagen

5

13 Feb	16.00	Energy Strategies	UCL
13 Feb	17.00	Thermal Comfort	Max Fordham & Ptnrs
13 Feb	18.30	Concrete	Zaha Hadid Archts

6

20 Feb	16.00	Fire	WS Group
20 Feb	17.00	Materials	ARUP
20 Feb	18.30	Institute of Making	UCL

7

27 Feb	16.00	Waste & Water	Max Fordham
27 Feb	17.00	Structures 1	RSH+P
27 Feb	18.30	Urban Computing	UCL

8

05 Mar	16.00	Structures 2	RSH+P
05 Mar	17.00	Digital Fabrication	Rare Architects
05 Mar	18.30	Interventions	6A Architects

9

12 Mar	16.00	Project Management	Heatherwick Studio
12 Mar	17.00	Structures 3	RSH+P
12 Mar	18.30	Production	Stahlbogen/AB3

10

19 Mar	16.00	Setting up Practice	NORD Architects
19 Mar	17.00	Construction	Laing O'Rourke
19 Mar	18.30	Practice	Pernilla - Asif

LECTURE SERIES

UCL
THE BARTLETT SCHOOL OF ARCHITECTURE
SPRING TERM 2012 - CHEMISTRY LECTURE THEATRE - MONDAYS
DESIGN REALISATION LECTURE SERIES

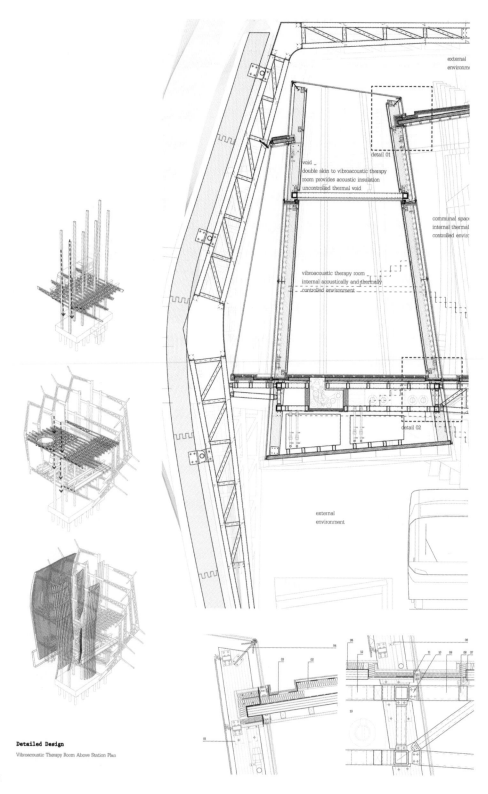

external
environme

void _
double skin to vibroacoustic therapy
room provides acoustic insulation
uncontrolled thermal void

detail 01

communal space
internal thermal
controlled enviro

vibroacoustic therapy room
internal acoustically and thermally
controlled environment

detail 02

external
environment

Detailed Design

Vibroacoustic Therapy Room Above Station Plan

Fig. DR.01 Samantha Rive, Miami Veteran Rehabilitation Centre. Left: Primary, secondary and tertiary structural components, layering and assembly strategy. Right: Detailed Sections through therapy rooms. **Fig. DR.02** Tamsin Hanke, Kyoto Tax Office. Translucent Porcelain prototypes and test pieces to assess potential structural strength. **Fig. DR.03** Tom Svilans, Guild of Redundant Technology. Cast aluminium junction details and truss components of roof assembly. **Fig. DR.04** Tamsin Hanke, Kyoto Tax Office. 3D Card Model for slip-cast porcelain shoji screen component. **Fig. DR.05** Tom Svilans, Guild of Redundant Technology. 3D sketch of cast truss components and roof truss assembly detail. **Fig. DR.06** Stephen Mc Cloy, Tea for Two (hundred). Environmental Strategy Overview showing water and heating systems.

Fig. DR.07 Graham Burn, Church of Aksaray. Left: 1:5 MDF roof truss assembly details. Right: Controlled deformation and surface blistering test panels to assess impact of weathering on the all MDF church construction. Panels are of untreated, varnished, painted and sealed MDF.

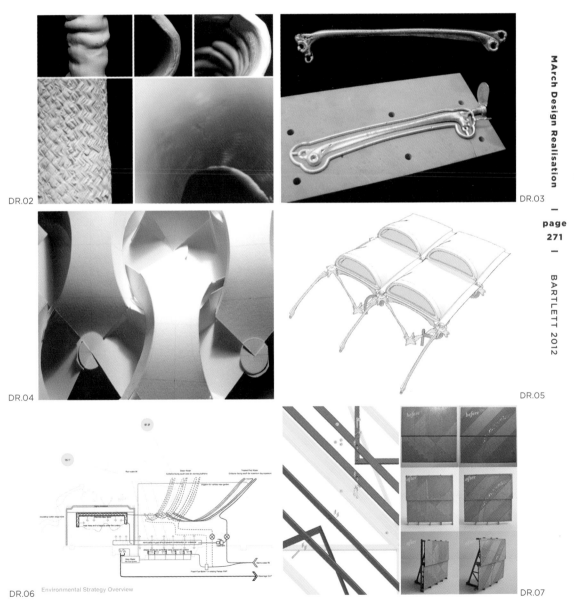

DR.02

DR.03

DR.04

DR.05

DR.06 Environmental Strategy Overview

DR.07

PART 3

Programmes leading to
professional registration
at the Bartlett School
of Architecture

POSTGRADUATE DIPLOMA IN PROFESSIONAL PRACTICE & MANAGEMENT IN ARCHITECTURE (ARB/RIBA PART 3)

Susan Ware

In January 2012, the Bartlett School of Architecture introduced a new Part 3 programme to meet the requirements of the new ARB/RIBA Criteria for Part 3 and the new practical experience requirements.

This six-module part-time programme can be taken over 12, 18 or 24 months to suit students' employment and work/life commitments. The programme is made up of five modules, each delivered over a 6-week period, and which can be taken in any order; each module is assessed in a different format. The sixth module is composed of a case study, career appraisal and evidence of work experience. Each student's experience of learning and development in professional practice will differ, depending upon the type of project, type and location of practice and management processes undertaken, and the preparation for the examination must therefore be approached in a structured way, whilst recognising the diversity of the profession and the construction industry. Module 6 is delivered through one-to-one tutorials where students have the opportunity to explore, analyse and reflect upon their professional education and experience with their tutor.

We aim to educate a generation of architects who are equipped to practice in an increasingly challenging environment. We do this by providing teaching and learning which encourages students to develop the skills beyond those required at threshold level by the professional criteria through reflection, appraisal, critical inquiry and research. We ask students to examine the role of the architect in the changing global construction industry and to examine the effect of politics and economics on the design and procurement of the built environment in future practice.

The programme is delivered through a comprehensive series of 50 lectures given

The programme is delivered through a comprehensive series of 50 lectures given by experts from practice and from within the Faculty. In addition, the teaching in each module is led by a director who is either a member of the Professional Studies team or an expert from practice. The school draws extensively from long standing connections with practice and the construction industry.

The programme aims to provide students with the skills to be competent to practice and demonstrate the knowledge, ability, judgment and integrity needed to fit an architect for his or her professional duties and to understand how an office organisation is managed for this purpose. Professional criteria are used to establish evidence of candidates' fitness to practice, demonstrated through their professional, procedural and technical awareness, understanding, knowledge and ability and have achieved a threshold of competence (in terms of knowledge and ability) and professionalism (in terms of conduct and responsibility) that is consistent and relevant, and will safeguard clients, building users and society at large.

BARTLETT INTERNATIONAL LECTURE SERIES

Supported by the Fletcher Priest Trust.

The Bartlett International Lecture Series features speakers from across the world. Lectures in the series are open to the public and free to attend. Forthcoming lectures are publicised on the Bartlett Architecture Listing.

LECTURES THIS YEAR:

CJ LIM
ADRIAN LAHOUD
ALISA ANDRASEK
TOM WISCOMBE
MICHAEL HANSMEYER
CAMPO MANNINGER
RUY KLEIN
AKIHISA HIRATA
PHILIPPE MOREL
DANIEL WIDRIG
JOSEP MIAS
EZIO BLASETTI
MIKE WEBB
SKYLAR TIBBITS

PERRY HALL
DANIEL WIDRIG
SOU FUJIMOTO
CHRISTIAN KEREZ
ATELIER BOWWOW
FRANCK VARENNE
JAKOB MACFARLANE
PHILIP BEESLEY
PRESTON SCOTT COHEN
ROSI BRAIDOTTI
HITOSHI ABE
ED KELLER
BRANKO KOLAREVIC
PETER COOK

For more info see: Email: archlist@ucl.ac.uk
URL: http://www.bartlett.ucl.ac.uk/architecture/latest/events/lectures

PGCAAR
MArch GAD
MArch UD
MA ARCH HISTORY
MPhil/PhD AD
MPhil/PhD H&T
SUMMER SCHOOL
SUMMER FOUNDATION

POSTGRADUATE CERTIFICATE IN ADVANCED ARCHITECTURAL RESEARCH

Stephen Gage

Architecture and engineering have a history where research and practice go hand in hand, where many great practices have grown as a result of fundamental research and where many research projects arise from groundbreaking design. This is especially true during periods of economic inactivity when recent modes of working are called into question and new modes (sometimes based on rediscovered historical precedent) are established. This can lead to the formation of innovative practices and to the start of academic careers in research and teaching.

The Postgraduate Certificate in Advanced Architectural Research gives students with appropriate graduate degrees the opportunity to take their work to a further stage development. Part of its production are group exhibitions, such as Constructing Realities, which was organised at the Arup's Phase 2 Gallery in central London in 2011 (curated by Stephen Gage and Ruairi Glynn; designed by Nick Westby). It showed how some of the best Masters portfolios and thesis contain the seeds of serious design research proposals, and how these might be taken forward to create new types of place, novel interactive building elements and new façade and structural systems.

Students: Richard Beckett, Chris Hildrey, Thomas Dunn, David Scott, WIlliam Trossell, Nicholas Wood, Nicholas Westby

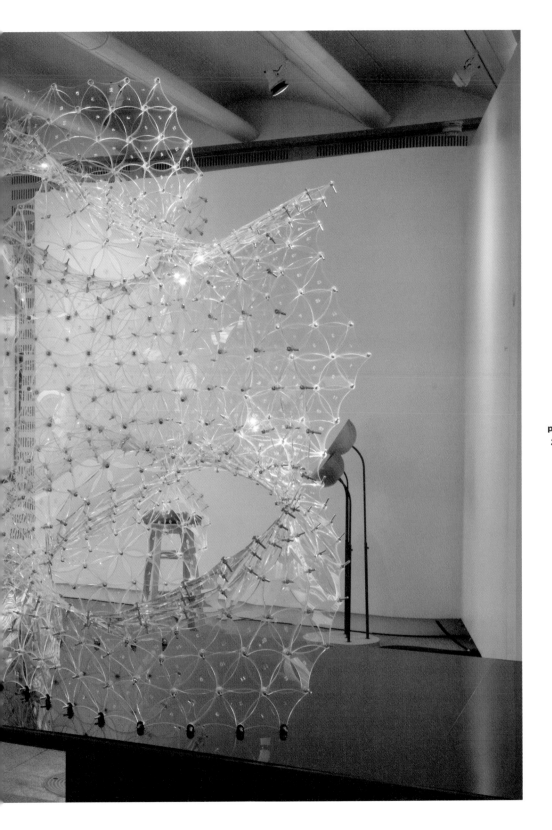

MArch GRADUATE ARCHITECTURAL DESIGN

Frédéric Migayrou

Deputy Director: **Andrew Porter**. Report Co-ordinator: **Professor Stephen Gage**.
Research Cluster Staff: **RC1: Alisa Andrasek and Jose Sanchez RC2: Marjan Coletti, Tea Lim and Guan Lee RC3: Professor Stephen Gage and Ruairi Glynn. RC4: Xavier de Kestelier and Jethro Hon. RC5: Andrew Porter and Luke Pearson. RC6: Daniel Widrig and Fulvio Wirz.**

The Masters studio in Graduate Architectural Design is a 12-month full-time programme concentrating on advanced architectural design. This program offers the opportunity to be involved in the world of advanced speculative research and to develop the possibility of a personal involvement and implication in the challenging aspects of prospective architecture.

For this academic year Professor Migayrou decided to open out the programme to offer a larger diversity of courses, in the form of Research Clusters, and focused on a better comprehension of heterogeneous language and the tools of production and fabrication which will radically change the shape of architecture, its social and economical role in the industrial world and its effectiveness as an active agent in the city. Through new developments such as the role of artificiality and simulation, the borders of many disciplines are more and more porous with emerging languages (computational and technological), which redefine the status and the territory of architecture, the understanding of the traditional architectural typologies and the mutations of urban morphologies. The six Research Clusters of the MArch GAD programme offer a large range of approaches to interrelated domains created by the dialogue between architecture and other disciplines (Biology, Physical science...) as well as structural mutations in industrialisation (Robotics, new materials, prototyping…). The notion of design is extended into the domain of these and other associated fields which are working with the same tools of production and conception. The programme opens a dialogue with a broad range of disciplines that will themselves become increasingly defined by such advanced design methods.

The programme is structured so that the first three months introduce students to the theoretical concepts through lectures and initial design projects. During this period students confirm the subject of their thesis project and report and then work in specialist teaching groups. There is continuous discussion of work via tutorials and reviews. In a second period they develop their own projects individually or in small groups depending on the structure of each cluster. This allows the individual to discover his or her individual expression; it takes many forms from speculative projects through drawings, models, printed objects, to the construction of working prototypes.

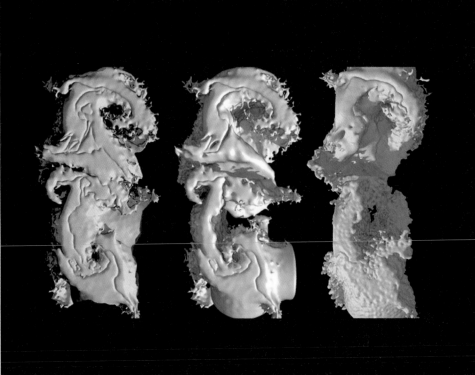

GAD.3

Fig. GAD.1 (Previous page) Chimera, RC2 group project. Shown as part of "By all means — analogue/digital experimental settings' an exhibition at the Haus der Architektur in Graz, together with the Academy of Arts Vienna and the TU Graz. **Fig. GAD.2** The Shrinking Tower, Ivan Linares & Long Cheng from RC4. A flexible structure for a floating society with two stable states. It is based on the works of the American inventor Chuck Hoberman. State 1. Expansion. Maximum height about 2meters, stripes at 45 degrees and volume of 3m³. State 0. Compression. 0.3m height and volume of 0.1m³. The joints at 0 degrees. The whole structure is able to reduce 30 times its original shape in less than 1 second. Gravity had an important role helping to reach the state of maximum compression. **Fig. GAD.3** Fei Wang,

Yuxiang Cao, Secil Zontur and Lisa Kinnerud from RC6. Researching the architectural qualities of turbulent flow — Fluid interactions and generation of turbulence by density and viscosity variations. **Fig. GAD.4** Cherry Chen, Lillian Song, Emily Liao from RC3, Shadow Performance Study. A shadow-based interactive installation, which is designed to study people's visual cognitive process. Optical illusions are created on the screen, which are formed from the cast shadows of both participants and the objects they interact with. **Fig. GAD.5 — GAD.6** (Overleaf)Vincenzo D'Auria, Nicolo Friedman, Mark Muscat, Pallavi Sharma from RC1, Variance: Slide.

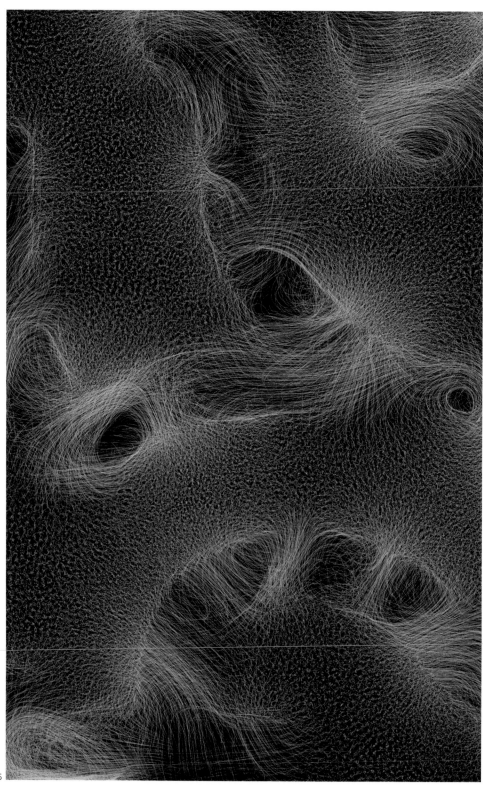

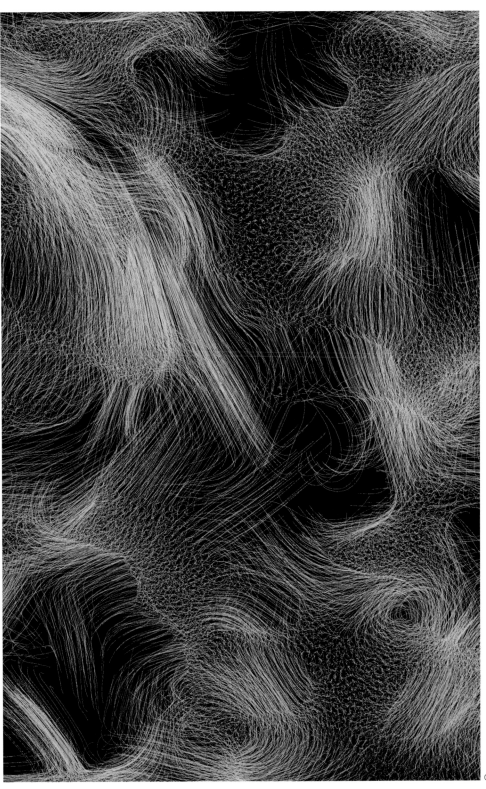

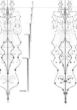

Fig. GAD.6 Maj Plemenitas from RC5, Inherited Redundancy > Resilience_Configurability. **Fig. GAD.7** Maj Plemenitas from RC5, In Progress_#963 > Detail.

GAD.7

GAD.8

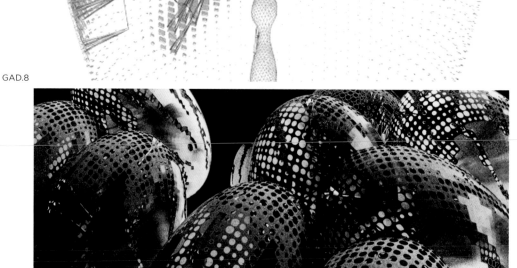

GAD.9

Fig. GAD.8 Hissaan Awaiz from RC2, Algorithmic Exploration v.03: Defining the Core. **Fig. GAD.9** Hissaan Awaiz from RC2, Algorithmic Exploration: Core Render. **Fig. GAD.10** WeiWei Wei, Maria Gavelli & Pinar Calisir from RC6, Structural formation generated through audio inputs.

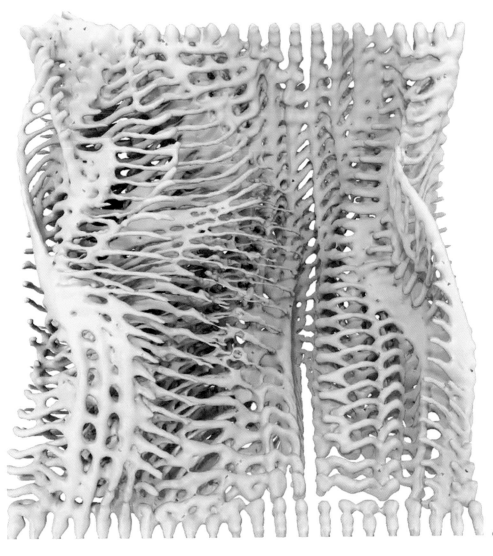

GAD.10

MArch URBAN DESIGN
Colin Fournier

Each year, a different city and a new research agenda are proposed to the MArch UD students. This year, we chose to study Istanbul and to focus the research on social and environmental sustainability. This was not an easy choice, since Istanbul's turbulent history, intricate urban tissue and complex socio-economic structure make it a difficult city to understand, but the students took on the challenge, leading to a rich variety of projects, to which we have given the collective title of "Istanbul stories".

The students were free to choose their own sites and to develop their own briefs. They were encouraged to be experimental, to challenge the status quo, to explore radically new ideas for the city. We stressed the importance of fiction, of setting aside pragmatic considerations and putting forward wild hypotheses for the future of Istanbul, seeking inspiration, perhaps, from the literary and cinematic fictions that have had a profound impact on urbanism: Moore's Utopia, Howard's Garden City, Le Corbusier's Ville Radieuse, Calvino's Invisible Cities, Lang's Metropolis, Gibson's Neuromancer, Scott's Blade Runner, to name but a few. We argued that these imaginary cities act as strange attractors, exerting a profound fascination, lying as objects of desire on the edge of our consciousness, while some real cities also possess this poetic power: Venice, Tokyo, Los Angeles… all of them transgressing the rules of "good" urban design. Istanbul, with its extraordinary history and its myths, its labyrinthine complexity, its sudden mutations, is one of these singularities, inspiring the telling of new stories.

The achievements have been diverse, demonstrating varying degrees of conceptual clarity, political awareness and engagement, social generosity, inventiveness and design resolution. Some areas of research were particularly well developed: the critical political, spatial and social conditions of the so-called "informal settlements", the poor environmental quality of the city's waterfront sites along the Bosphorus and the Golden Horn, the physical disparities and social tensions between adjacent neighbourhoods, the "no-man's land" anomaly of Levant, the disruptions of the urban fabric due to the road infrastructure, the constraints imposed by the difficult topography of many areas, the scarcity of public open space, the clash between the high-rise commercial developments of the CBD and the decaying traditional urban fabric, the threats to cultural heritage, the problems of gentrification, etc…

The students responded to these challenges with imaginative proposals, some of them offering extreme fictions, some highly poetic fantasies, some relatively pragmatic solutions, some embarking on radical design proposals, presenting us with compelling, inventive narratives, providing fresh insights into the spatial and cultural complexity of this chaotic city. Rather than seeking to resolve its riddles, the designs have playfully added new contributions to the already impenetrable and obscure palimpsest of Istanbul's historical layers.

UD.1

UD.3

UD.4

Fig. UD.1 (Previous spread) Daphne Kuo, Story of Haydarpasa. Fig. UD.2 (Previous spread) Hao-Fong Huang, Filling the void between the Grand Bazaar and the Spice Bazaar. Fig. UD.3 — UD.4 Raymond Lee, In-Between Space. Fig. UD.5 — UD.7 Vanessa Nassar, Salvage City.

UD.5

UD.6

UD.7

Fig. UD.8 — UD.14 Ming Deng, Urban Carnival.

UD.8

UD.9

UD.10

UD.11

UD.12

UD.13

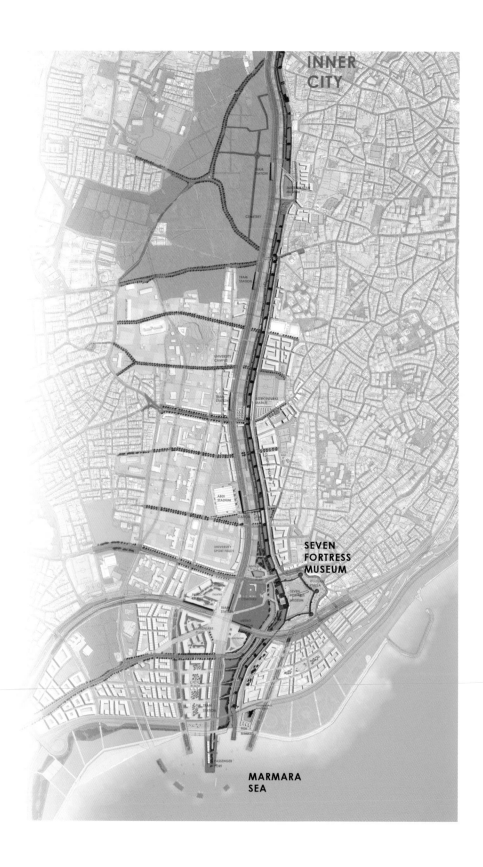

INNER
CITY

SEVEN
FORTRESS
MUSEUM

MARMARA
SEA

Fig. UD.15 Francisco Azagra, Plug-in Theodosian Wall.
Fig. UD.16 — UD.19 Yu Zheng, Living on the edge.

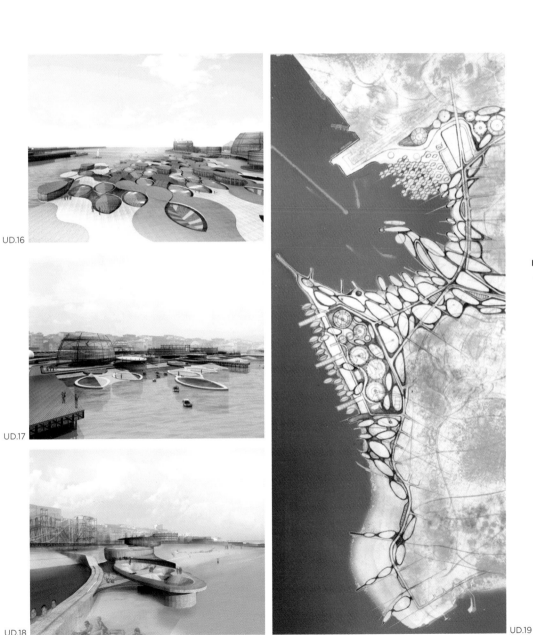

UD.16

UD.17

UD.18

UD.19

MA ARCHITECTURAL HISTORY
Adrian Forty

The specialist programme in architectural history in the Bartlett School of Architecture responds to the fact that architecture consists not just of buildings and projects, but also of the life that takes place within them, and of the ideas and discussions that they give rise to. It is the business of the MA Architectural History to interrogate these discussions, to extend them, and possibly to reframe them in terms of broader debates about culture, history and politics.

We encourage our students to be experimental, to try out ideas from different fields, and to see whether bringing them to bear on architecture changes the way we think about buildings, cities and the life within them. Each one of the projects listed here is a small experiment, in which some particular architectural phenomenon has been put under the microscope and examined in the light of a particular theory or set of ideas, to see whether our view of it might change - or, alternatively, whether a theory might need to be re-assessed.

The one year Master's programme in Architectural History, which has been running for thirty years, is partly a taught programme that prepares people for research, and partly a research programme, in which people undertake a self- selected and self-directed research project - two excerpts are printed here.

2010-11

Antonio Desiderio, 'Branding Surface. An Investigation of Branded Space and Architecture'; Beatrice Galilee, 'The Anxious Space'; John Jervis, 'Prophesying Indeterminacy: John Weeks and the Northwick Park Hospital and Clinical Research Centre'; Dervla Macmanus, 'Staircases: an Exploration of their Symbolic Meaning';Jessica Northend, 'Building Theory: the New Left Review and the treatment of the built environment 1960-2011'; Yeva Sargsyan, 'Past for the Present or Present for the Past? The role of historic architecture in contemporary culture.'; Manuel López Segura, '"There is one difficulty that I see and that is that you think in English". Exchanges between Britain and Italy through the pages of Casabella and the Architectural Review on the occasion of the Neo-liberty debate.'; Nigel Simpkins, 'Performance, representation and the body in dance-architectures of Frederic Flamand'; Elizabeth Sutherland, 'A Trauma Telescoped: Dachau Concentration Camp Memorial Site'; Amy Thomas, '"Mart of the World". An architectural and geographical history of the London Stock Exchange'; Sriwan Tianpongsa, '"Moving Interior", Tracing Meaning and Memory of Panelled Rooms.'

'Plan of the Royal Exchange, Shewing the Merchants' Walks', from *Grose's Antiquities*, 1798.
Copyright City of London, London Metropolitan Archives.

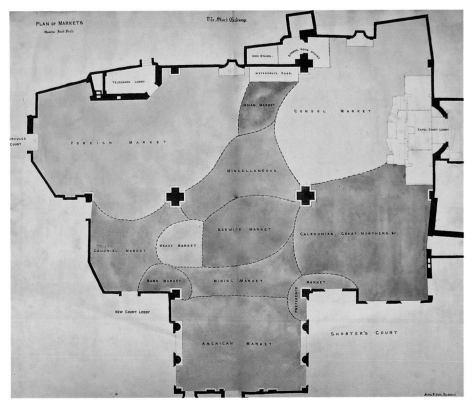

AMY THOMAS

'"Mart of the World", An Architectural and Geographical History of the London Stock Exchange'.

In the following excerpt, Thomas describes some of the shifts in the spatial organisation of the Exchange:

Prior to its formalisation in 1773 in Sweetings Alley, 'social distance' was the only defining characteristic of the stock market. Beginning in a parasitical relationship with other commodity markets in the Royal Exchange and the surrounding alleys, brokers and jobbers existed in a fluid capacity, using the passages to facilitate the distribution of financial information. Paid on commission, the broker was an intermediary man of connections buying and selling on behalf of a client. Moving freely between coffee houses, he would have a detailed knowledge of raw materials, supplies in port and the requirements of manufacturers.1 Working as dealers, buying and selling on their own account, jobbers had a more sinister reputation. Frequently accused of confederating to raise the price of stocks and spreading false information to make the market more favourable, multiple acts were enforced to attempt to quell the nefarious activities of jobbers and ban trading in the alleys, which was often said to be the cause of financial catastrophes, including the South Sea Bubble of 1720.2 The movement of the stock market to Sweetings Alley and later Capel Court was an attempt to contain and regulate an extremely volatile market, which, with the growing National Debt,

Britain's economic stability increasingly rested upon. For reputable brokers, the complex webs of exchange in the dense network of alleys, had come to represent "the clamorous importunity of partial interests" that Adam Smith had warned against; the space became a physical embodiment of the changing state of the economy and the moral attitudes towards the newly industrialised public realm.3 Paradoxically, the way to achieving an efficient, open, free market was via architectural exclusion.

The enclosure of the Capel Court site was enhanced by its diminutive entrances and position in the midst of a dense network of alleys. However, once inside, notions of the free market were encapsulated in the open trading floor where jobbers' pitches were defined only by their distance from the nearest column, wall, or other notable architectural feature. Its basilica form, with peripheral piers and arches forming recesses for the National Debt commissioners around a large central space, continued the tradition of exchange architecture that was prevalent in Europe, with Domien de Waghemakere's building for the Exchange in Antwerp (1531) and Edward Jarman's designs for the nearby Royal Exchange (1669; Dest.1838) setting a precedent.4 The open trading floor permitted mobility that was fitting for the volatile nature of its product, exemplified in an intriguing diagram of the interior of the Royal Exchange from 1798, revealing the zoning of traders according to commodity or its country of origin. Known as 'walks', these sites were unfixed: if the activity of buying and selling depended on the fluctuations of commodity prices, the merchant and broker would need to move about the room to establish such values, whilst affirming the relationships between brokers and the markets they served. As historian Martin Daunton has pointed out, in the early nineteenth century, the network of credit that fuelled Britain's industrialisation was dependent on the web of relationships between industrialists, merchants and brokers, connecting what were essentially local markets.5 The vacuum provided by the trading floor allowed for an informal method of exchange that permitted the circulation of capital between protagonists, in turn dispersing wealth to a mercantile elite. As Daunton puts it, "the whole edifice of business rested upon the shifting sands of credit."6

With the rebuilding and subsequent enlargement of the LSE from the 1850s onwards came the increasing complexity of the floor as a microcosm for imperial trade. An extraordinary diagram by J.J. Cole from 1880 shows the organisation of the trading floor prior to enlargement using colour-coded sections to represent the markets, defined by curved and perforated lines as if to highlight their flux and instability. A subsequent pamphlet written in 1884 "to confer on the arrangements of the Market on the opening of the Eastern addition" uses the drawing as a reference for the proposed reorganisation of the floor in the New House, providing a rare insight into the link between the trading floor and the global marketplace.7 The Sub-Committee's proposal to bring "the Colonial Market into close unity with the Consols Market" (British government bonds) due to their "certain affinity", is telling of the deepened involvement of British government and Crown in the affairs of the colonies following the removal of trade monopolies from joint-stock companies, such as the East India Company, in the mid century. Similarly, the decision to make space "for the American Market to expand" anticipates Britain's increasing role as creditor to the US for its major infrastructural projects and industry. It is also likely that the suggested movement of the Foreign Market to a larger space "under the new dome" and the increased scale of the Colonial Market, would have owed itself to the improved communications within Europe and the Empire following the introduction of the telegraph and first price-sharing system in 1872.8 Technological improvements not only required Cole's attention in the accommodation of new communication facilities, but also in predicting the impact such technology would have on the markets so as to allow the correct spatial provision. These documents reveal an architectural synergy with the markets that went beyond the purely functional; like its members, Cole and the Committee were required to speculate in order to accommodate future fluctuations in market value. Like the global market it represented, markets on the floor were in continuous flux yet relied up on a certain topographical arrangement to assist the processes of exchange. As the imperial distribution of goods and the increasingly international free market was severing the link between market and place that Zukin articulates, its movements were mapped on the floor of the Exchange.9

The design for the floor in the 1970s took on an entirely different, fixed character with freestanding, hexagonal jobbers' booths filling the central space, and brokers' boxes placed on split levels at the Periphery. The booths remained generic without any visible signification of market, presumably in the same spirit of speculation exhibited in Capel Court, yet the social distance that had formerly defined the ordering of markets had been replaced by architectural categorisation. The LSE's unique broker-jobber system, which was soon to be eliminated with the introduction of dual capacity in 1986, had been preserved in the fabric of the building. A broker would go to a 'booth' to receive quotations from a jobber, who was now effectively a wholesaler, before agreeing a price and returning to their 'box' to process the transaction. However, due to the rapidly changing share prices on the new electronic system, brokers were often required to run between booth and box, and as such, the architects were asked to ensure that the distances between jobber and broker were such that no firm had an unfair advantage by virtue of proximity, thereby guaranteeing fair competition.10 This uneasy marriage of the speed of technology and institutional stasis demonstrates the inability of the committee to have predicted the colossal metamorphoses that would take place in finance in the next decade, encapsulated by the rapid redundancy of the trading floor after the Big Bang. As London's growing link with international markets became increasingly reliant upon technology, it became difficult to build flexibly for the future around the LSE's rigid values. Global economic shifts were not alone in shaping its architecture; self-representation, aimed at both its members and the public, was equally influential in the layout and style of all the Exchange's buildings. In fact, in order to spatially understand the LSE's link with the Empire and global capitalism, we must look at its operation as an institution in the context of British Society and the City, and, of course, its architectural expression.

Aerial

flyer flight

ascensorium

stair-dancer

riser dancing step

dancers French flyer

stair-head

going kite winder stair-tree

winder spiral balanced step

stairway stringer

stair turnpike

scale

scala escalier degree

turngrece half-pace

straight cockle-stairs stair-step

quarter-pace pace radial step

Horizon

step handrail newel

slip rest

half-landing

tread flat

stand

stopel

treadle trap landing

sinistral stair box-stair

landing-place

stairwell

stair-foot

resting-place

Terrestrial

DERVLA MACMANUS

'Staircases: an Exploration of their Symbolic Meaning'.

In the following excerpt, MacManus charts
the language of staircases:

Aerial and terrestrial word-images appear frequently in stair language, the aerial words are dynamic, and bring images of movement to mind, where as the terrestrial words are static and imply inertia. Tread and riser are another oxymoronic couplet: tread being the horizontal part of the step where the foot lands and riser, the vertical part, that causes the foot to leave the tread and fly to the next tread or landing. A particularly nice example of an aerial word is kite winder which refers to the middle of three winders in a ninety degree turn. It is word-image which calls to mind a darting, fluttering movement, as a kite dancing in the air. It is an image with something playful and joyful at its core, a celebration of what Bachelard would call the 'joy of ascension'. Further illustrations of the same type of word-images are dancers - slang for stairs, and dancing or balanced step meaning a winder which is only a little narrower towards the centre than at the outer edge. Examples of terrestrial words, have generally to do with landings: landing-place, flat, rest, resting-place, stair-foot, all word-images which bring to mind becoming 'earthed' as if re-establishing the body's connection to the earth. A further less obvious dichotomy is highlighted in the words stairway and stairwell, the former is an aerial word, positive and dynamic (stairway to heaven) where as stairwell is terrestrial, even sub-terrestrial, a vertical tunnel descending to the depths in the same manner as a well dug for water. Box-stair and resting-place have connotations of coffins and burial respectively. Figure 05 is a diagram of stair terminology organised according to their aerial or terrestrial bias.

PhD ARCHITECTURAL DESIGN

Jonathan Hill

Programme Coordinator: **Penelope Haralambidou**, Supervisors: **Dr Camillo Boano, Professor Iain Borden, Dr Victor Buchli, Dr Ben Campkin, Dr Marjan Colletti, Professor Sir Peter Cook, Dr Marcos Cruz, Professor Penny Florence, Professor Colin Fournier, Professor Stephen Gage, Professor Ranulph Glanville, Dr Penelope Haralambidou, Professor Christine Hawley, Dr Neil Heyde, Professor Jonathan Hill, Dr Yeoryia Manolopoulou, Jayne Parker, Dr Barbara Penner, Dr Peg Rawes, Professor Jane Rendell, Bob Sheil, Professor Phil Steadman, Professor Neil Spiller, Professor Phil Tabor.**

Leading to a PhD in Architecture, the MPhil/PhD Architectural Design allows especially able and reflective designers to undertake research within the Bartlett School of Architecture's speculative and experimental ethos. The first to be established in the UK, the Bartlett MPhil/PhD Architectural Design is internationally recognized as one of the most influential doctoral programmes dedicated to architectural design.

The programme draws on the strengths of design teaching and doctoral research at the Bartlett, encouraging the development of architectural research through the interaction of designing and writing. An architectural design doctoral thesis has two inter-related elements of equal importance—a project and a text—that share a research theme and a productive relationship. The project may be drawn, filmed, built, or use whatever media is appropriate.

UCL's multi-disciplinary environment offers a stimulating and varied research culture that connects research by architectural design to developments in other disciplines, such as anthropology, art, digital media, geography and medicine. The programme is intended for graduates of architecture and other disciplines who wish to pursue research by architectural design. More than 40 students from over 20 countries are currently enrolled on the programme.

The Bartlett School of Architecture's two PhD programmes organize a number of annual events for doctoral students. PhD Research Projects, an exhibition and conference with presentations by current practice-based PhD students in UCL, is held in Term 2. Invited critics in 2012 were Professor Philip Beesley, University of Waterloo; Dr Maarten Delbecke, University of Ghent and University of Leiden; Professor Murray Fraser, UCL Bartlett School of Architecture; and Dr Sophia Psarra, UCL Bartlett School of Graduate Studies. Throughout the year, PhD Research Conversations seminars are an opportunity for doctoral candidates to present work in progress.

Seven candidates were awarded the PhD in 2011-2012: Dr Katherine E. Bash, Dr Nat Chard, Dr Sophie Handler, Dr Teresa Hoskyns, Dr Rosalie Kim, Dr William Tozer and Dr Neil Wenman. Their work is on the following pages.

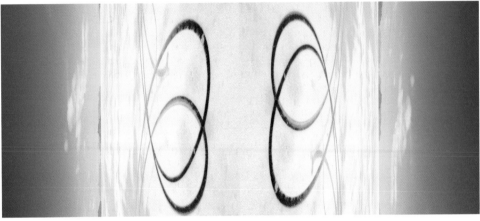

KATHERINE BASH

'Spatial Poetries: Heuristics for Experimental Poiesis'

Primary supervisor: Dr Yeoryia Manolopoulou

Secondary supervisor: Professor Jonathan Hill, Dr Beau Lotto, Professor Graham Harman

The theme of this research is the study of how things take form in experience, consciousness and language. In large part, it explores the identification and the naming of ephemeral event phenomena that are as of yet unnamed, a process of becoming I describe as symmetry-breaking. This exploration is pursued within the framework of a Lived Spatial Inquiry called Experimental Poiesis, a particularly experimental form of making where inquiry is the formal philosophical and poietic tool where the original matrix of the site in question is embedded in what is made. The methods of this inquiry facilitate both the study and the subversion of normal habits of language-focused perception and are called Heuristics— experimental aesthetic practices that are site-adjustable and engaged iteratively, where the results of one experiment become the starting point of the next. Spatial Poetries is the name I have given to the results of these experiments, hybrid in form and prompting shifts in lived experience in the reader.

This thesis pays homage to Observations upon Experimental Philosophy (1666), by the Duchess of Newcastle Margaret Cavendish, as well as The Manual of Scientific Enquiry; Prepared for the Use of Officers in Her Majesty's Navy; And Travellers in General (1859), edited by Sir John F. W. Herschel. In addition, I engage with the work of Gregory Bateson, John Dewey, Ian Hacking, Dalibor Vesely and Roberto Casati, and have found resonance with practices such as medieval monastic rhetoric as presented in the writings of Mary Carruthers, the work of the architecture school Pontificia Universidad Católica de Valparaíso in the Ciudad Abierta (Open City), and the site-based poetic and philosophical works of Ian Hamilton Finlay.

As a hybrid object, the thesis contains a manual for the discovery, analysis and naming of ephemeral phenomena. The Manual is composed of images, text, audio, video, and diagrams. As an assemblage, it both documents a process of inquiry and attempts to provide a taxonomy and rationale for that process and is presented in the form of the Atlas of Experimental Poiesis, a central contribution of this research. This Atlas allows for a process of philosophic reflection that feeds back into and has the capacity to enrich lived spatial-aesthetic experience of readers in general. In specific, it offers a vocabulary and visual structure to undertake the processes of observation, detection and creation of new forms, and the challenge of bringing those experiences to language.

NAT CHARD

'Drawing Indeterminate Architecture, Indeterminate Drawings of Architecture'

Primary supervisor: Professor Sir Peter Cook

Secondary supervisor: Professor Jonathan Hill

Architecture is made to support certain activities. This thesis asks how architecture might also nurture the uncertain. The program and the conventions of architectural drawing encourage ideas of certainty. The architectural drawing is a rehearsal of the architecture it represents. This thesis searches for ways of drawing to rehearse the sorts of engagement we might have with architecture that could nurture an indeterminate condition. This is studied through the invention of seven types of drawing instrument. The early versions represent an indeterminate relationship with architecture while the later instruments nurture an indeterminate engagement through the act of drawing.

Indeterminacy is a condition of uncertainty. At first the instruments concentrate on working with the sublime, an existential uncertainty. In order to understand the spatial potential of picturing there is extended research into the natural history diorama. In parallel to lessons on projective geometry, the dioramas provide a convincing case for the power of the uncanny, an intellectual uncertainty. The lessons from these studies, embodied in Instruments Two and Three, achieved what had been set out in the initial question but also provided new questions, especially about the experience of making the drawing. The later instruments project paint rather than light and provide an engagement with the person who is drawing that is analogous to the condition that is being drawn.

The process of drawing becomes a rehearsal for inhabiting the architecture. The instruments are informed by a number of parallel studies: one that asks questions about ways of appropriating the city (as an indeterminate reception of the world as it is given); another into an opening up of the program, studied through a house, and the discovery of a way to disturb our certainty in the shadow and the invention of an instrument to understand the potential of that discovery.

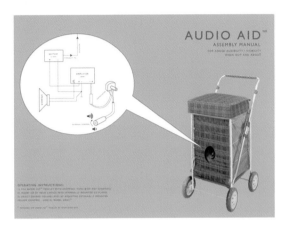

SOPHIE HANDLER

'A Little Bit of TLC: (or the Ludological Curatrix): Developing an Alternative Urban Practice of Elderly Care'

Primary supervisor: Professor Jane Rendell
Secondary supervisor: Dr Penelope Haralambidou

Using a series of temporary urban interventions and a slower paced process of writing and reflection this thesis develops what it terms an 'Alternative Urban Practice of Elderly Care' that actively attends to the neglected relationship between older people and public space. In this way the thesis attempts to open up current limits within spatial practices and academic study that have tended in their instrumental, policy-oriented focus to avoid more creative and playful explorations of how ageing might otherwise affect people's everyday relationship to urban space.

By drawing out the hidden etymological roots of care in curating (from the Latin curare) and borrowing from the theorisations of care-focused feminist ethics [Held], the thesis evolves its own particular methodological temper and personality through the invented persona of the caring 'Curatrix'. Here, the 'Curatrix' builds her own urban practice of elderly care based on the acting 'otherhow' of Doina Petrescu and its related practice of 'urban curating' [Buschonten/Shalk], and through this persona enacts a series of (Ludological) interventions that playfully-critically subvert the standard clinical understanding of intervention (as used in elderly care).

The thesis is structured around three temporary interventions (an event/artifact/a spatial proposition) that explore three age-specific themes in turn (degrees of mobility/sedentary existence/levels of audibility). As these themes are worked through on-the-ground (as temporary interventions acted out with/from/for 'the elderly'), and on the page (through a slower-paced process of critical reflection and alternative writing strategies [Rendell]) the thesis begins to broach the delicate (and hidden) relational/temporal dynamics of a practice engaged, simultaneously, in play, care, fantasy and critique.

In its playfully shifting tone and mode, working not only across disciplinary, practice/theory boundaries or generational (old/young) lines but across boundaries of temper too, this Alternative Urban Practice of Elderly Care advances a model of practice where carefully attending to people's changing relationship to public space in older age involves a dual process of intervention/reflection that shifts deliberately in its inflection between the careful, careless and the carefree.

TERESA HOSKYNS

'The Empty Place: Democracy and Public Space'
Primary supervisor: Professor Jane Rendell
Secondary supervisor: Professor Jonathan Hill

What is the role of physical public space in democracy? This thesis explores this question by examining models of democracy political philosophy and discussing these models through spatial theory — and through three participatory spatial practices — architectural, feminist and political democratic. The research questions whether increasingly representative democratic practice is appropriate for diverse and complex modern cities and examines the effects of representation and participation on public space, exploring possibilities for democratisation.

As a theoretical basis, section 1 examines political philosophy and spatial theory. I explore democracy in ancient Greece and argue that democracy involved diverse spatial practices and public spaces. The assembly at Pnyx, the theatre (agon), the market place (agora) formed a tri-partite model of democracy. However the rise of representative democracy emphasises the assembly as a space of democracy and creates a dislocation of democratic practice from public space. The section investigates contemporary theories for the future of democracy, focusing on the agonistic model advocated by Chantal Mouffe and the civil society model theorised by Jürgen Habermas. I argue that these models can co-exist, are necessarily spatial and require the types of democratic space seen in ancient Athens.

Section 2 provides diverse perspectives on how the role of physical public space is articulated through three modes of participatory spatial practice. The first focuses on issues of participation in architectural practice through a set of projects exploring the 'open spaces' of a postwar housing estate in Euston. The second practice examines the role of space in the construction of democratic identity through the feminist architecture/art collective taking place, producing space through writing, performance and events. The third explores participatory political democratic practice through social forums at world, European and city levels. I discuss different conceptions of democracy practiced within the social forums, expressed in the discussion of the World Social Forum as a space or a movement. I conclude by arguing that participatory democracy requires a conception of public space as the empty place, which allows different models and practices of democracy to co-exist.

ROSALIE HYUN-KYUNG KIM

'The Hyphenation of the Void: From Eastern Ecology to Western Architecture'
Primary supervisor: Professor Jonathan Hill
Secondary supervisor: Dr Yeoryia Manolopoulou

This thesis explores the East-West cultural cross-pollination by discussing the eastern concept of the void through Chinese traditional landscape painting and eastern traditional architecture. This void is not in binary opposition to the full as in western dualism but rather co-exists with the full in a dynamic and complementary manner following the Taoist philosophy. In this perspective, all components of the universe appear interrelated into a continuous whole and this interconnection relentlessly changes following each component's mutation in time. Akin to a floating cloud, the void is thus essentially characterized by its restless movement, its transience.

This interpretation of the void is then converted into architectural design devices by means of 'hyphens'. These are familiar images to western culture that provide a sensible metaphor and/or tangible palpability to the abstract notion of the void. In this research, moss, ruins, English picturesque landscape, Chinese literati garden and Alexander Pope's grotto emerge as conceptual and/ or material hyphens. Their ensuing combination in the architectural practice of the void generates the projects' narratives, provides their biotic substance and affects their visual representations.

The subsequent architecture of the void appears as an organic entity, which grows and decays through its endless interactions with the surrounding environments. This constant 'process of becoming' requires the reassessment of conventional manner of inhabiting space where the user re-evaluates his living pattern according to new criteria. Decay becomes a design incentive by instigating a 'design in reverse' where architecture emerges from the decaying process, prompting the user to cultivate his/her house in-between architecture and landscape, building and ruin, real and whimsical.

The thesis developed a pictorial syntax and visual trope based on Chinese traditional landscape painting to render the contingent environmental fluctuations of the void into engaging imaginary landscapes. The ensuing drawings provide a series of synoptic visions of a complex whole, which they mediate through cropped frames with temporal, spatial and thematic displacements. They offer thereby an inexhaustible amount of perspectives on a project and portray its constant process of becoming, so that the drawings' content and methodology reflect the litheness of the oriental void.

WILLIAM TOZER

'A Theory of Making: Architecture and Art in the Practice of Adolf Loos'
Primary supervisor: Dr Penelope Haralambidou
Secondary supervisor: Professor Jonathan Hill

Adolf Loos repeatedly discusses the role of art in relation to architecture in his essays, but many of his statements appear either repetitive or inconsistent with one another, and are difficult to reconcile with his buildings. Considering Loos's writing and built work together, rather than separately, suggests that instead of being fully formulated as a methodology and then implemented in practice, Loos's argument emerges serially and in a piecemeal fashion with the progressive development of his buildings through practice—a theory of making.

The line of enquiry into the historical and theoretical material is informed by the division of my own design work in practice into sculptural components and furnishings. The research proceeds on the hypothesis that Loos similarly divided each of his buildings into discrete elements that he either understood as art, or considered functional—and that he deployed ornament to signal the latter, rather than the former.

This hypothesis is investigated by tracing the origin and development in his built projects of a number of particular components of the Müller House, in relation to the emergence and revision of specific aspects of Loos's written argument on art and architecture in the essays contemporaneous with these buildings. The investigations are structured by reference to the distinct qualities of each component as identified through the design research, focusing on Composite House.

While the research method is specific to my own design work in practice, the investigation is structured so as to produce autonomous outcomes in relation to Loos and modernism, which are meaningful when decoupled from this field data. Loos has to date been predominantly examined through conceptions of modernism as the expression of function, structure, technology or society; however, it is argued here that modern architecture could conversely be understood, through Loos, as a form of art practice.

NEIL WENMAN

'A Space to House Nothing: Examining the spatial complexities of nothingness, emptiness, zero and void to define the space of nothing, through the adoption of architectural themes and forms of representation in selected conceptual art projects since 1958'
Primary supervisor: Professor Jonathan Hill
Secondary supervisor: Professor Jane Rendell

In reference to Yves-Alain Bois and Rosalind Krauss in Formless: A User's Guide, 1997, which maps out a third area between the traditional dichotomy of form and content in the visual arts as originally suggested by Georges Bataille, this thesis looks at the notion of the Space of Nothing as a third space between form and content through Yves Klein's gallery-emptying Le Vide — The Specialisation of Sensibility in the Raw Material of Stabilized Pictorial Sensibility 1958, the genesis upon which the research is sited.

The thesis demonstrates that artists since the birth of the conceptual art movement in the late 1950s, with specific later reference to the dematerialization of the art object as defined by Lucy R. Lippard in 1967, have continued to explore spatial definition by directly adopting themes and forms of representation taken from architectural practice to describe concept-based and often immaterial, artworks. This lies in a theoretical reading of the spatial within the art of the immaterial. Can the experience of an artwork that is immaterial become corporealized? The titular reference to the verb to house

in A Space to House Nothing is to be understood directly as: to accommodate nothing; to store nothing; to shelter nothing. It does not reference notions of the domestic or the home, nor do gender politics or such readings of the home as a site of gender rules play any role. Can the Space of Nothing be defined as an architectural site?

Analysis is developed through four key terms — nothingness, emptiness, zero and void. These terms are surveyed through mathematics, philosophy and language to create a theoretical model; the Space of Nothing and further explored through a series of specific classifications that catalogue artistic approaches to the Space of Nothing: doing nothing, mapping nothing, framing nothing, occupying nothing and listening to nothing.

NOTHINGNESS, a touring European exhibition of work by 25 international artists, acted as a visual record of enquiry. Galerie Eugen Lendl, Graz, Austria (8 Oct – 27 Nov, 2004) tour Galerija Gregor Podnar, Ljubljana, Slovenia (25 Feb – 2 Apr, 2005) illustrated catalogue distributed by Revolver Books, Frankfurt.

MPhil/PhD
ARCHITECTURAL
HISTORY & THEORY
Barbara Penner

Supervisors: Jan Birksted, Iain Borden, Ben Campkin, Adrian Forty, Murray Fraser, Penelope Haralambidou, Jonathan Hill, Barbara Penner, Peg Rawes, Jane Rendell, Sophia Psarra. Julio Davila (Bartlett Development Planning Unit), Victor Buchli, Ruth Mandel (UCL Anthropology), Stephanie Schwartz (UCL Art History) Graduating Students: Nicholas Beech, Edward Denison, Yi-Chih Huang, Anne Hultzsch, Tat Lam, Jacob Paskins, Léa-Catherine Szacka

Current Students: Wesley Aelbrecht, Ricardo Agarez, Tilo Amhoff, Kalliopi Amygdalou, Sabina Andron, Tal Bar, Eva Branscome, Eray Cayli, Stella Flatten, Nicholas Jewell, Kate Jordan, Irene Kelly, Thomas-Bernard Kenniff, Torsten Lange, Abigail Lockey, Suzanne Macleod, Ivan Margolius, Nathan Moore, Christian Parreno, Dragan Pavlovic, Brent Pilkey, Matthew Poulter, Regner Ramos, Ozayr Saloojee, Maria del Pilar Sanchez Beltran, Pinai Sirikiatikul, Amy Thomas, Nina Vollenbroker, Danielle Willkens

The Bartlett School of Architecture's MPhil/PhD Architectural History & Theory programme allows students to conduct an exhaustive piece of research into an area of their own selection and definition. Great importance is placed on the originality of information uncovered, the creativity of the interpretations made, and the rigour of the methodological procedures adopted.

Approximately 20-30 students from around the world are enrolled at any one time for MPhil/PhD research in this field. The range of research topics undertaken is broad, but most explore the history and theory of architecture and cities from c. 1800 to the present day, with an emphasis on the critical reading of these subjects from cultural, political and experiential viewpoints.

The MPhil/PhD Architectural History & Theory programme draws on the expertise and experience of the Bartlett School of Architecture's team of architectural historians and theorists, who are recognised internationally for their contributions to the field. The programme itself is very dynamic with an active series of talks, seminars, and conferences. In keeping with UCL's multi-disciplinary ethos, connections between architectural research and other fields are encouraged, and there are active collaborations with the Departments of Anthropology, Fine Art and Geography, and UCL Urban Lab.

59 Belvedere Road, South Bank Fellowship Centre for destitute veterans, demolished in 1949 for the Festival of Britain, 1951. Copyright City of London, London Metropolitan Archives.

DR. NICK BEECH

Constructing Everyday Life: An architectural history of the South Bank in production, 1948–1951

Principal Supervisor: Jane Rendell; Secondary: Peg Rawes

This thesis provides a new interpretation of Henri Lefebvre's Critique of Everyday Life (1933–1981), in order to develop a new method of research that locates the critique of the historical objects and practices of construction as 'architecture in production'. To achieve this, the thesis presents a close examination of key concepts in Lefebvre's Critique—'alienation', 'production', and 'critique' itself—and uses these concepts in the investigation of a particular construction process—the production of building sites for London's South Bank, between 1948 and 1951.

The thesis is composed in three parts. Part One argues that a general concept of production is recoverable from Lefebvre's Critique, through the Marxist concept of 'alienation'. This concept is developed by Lefebvre in a series of different spheres—'praxis', 'everyday life', 'space' and 'the state form'. In each case, Lefebvre asks how it is possible to gain critical knowledge of production through its 'alienated expression'. Lefebvre's response to the epistemological and methodological problems raised, are shown to operate in dialogue with select works of Karl Marx and Bertolt Brecht.

Part Two argues that the epistemological and methodological problematics of Lefebvre's Critique remain incomplete until mobilised through an investigation of the particular. Through a critical literature review, the South Bank is shown to provide a unique site for such a mobilisation—an architectural production process expressed in a range of technical literatures and archival sources. A critique and history of the early phases of construction at the South Bank (1948–1951) is developed. Practices of demolishing, stripping out, excavating, and ground exploration, are explored through a careful selection of primary sources and archives—including news items, articles and memoirs, drawings, photographs, contracts and works reports.

Part Three considers these sources as 'alienated expressions', presenting a history of 'architecture in production' through their critique.

Detail of the façade of the Da Hua Theatre (1934), Nanjing, China, designed by Yang Tingbao (1901-1982).

DR. EDWARD DENISON

Architecture and the Landscape of Modernity in China up to 1949

Principal Supervisor: Adrian Forty; Secondary: Iain Borden

This study examines China's encounter with architecture and modernity from c.1900 to 1949. In the context of architecture, it expands current knowledge of the practice in pre-communist China. In terms of the study of modernity, it addresses the uniqueness of China's encounter with modernity through the concept of multiple modernities; a recent theoretical development in social sciences that has yet to be applied to architectural studies. In the context of China studies, it contributes to redressing the current underrepresentation of architecture within studies of the arts.

The methodological approach is inclusive, geographically, temporally and architecturally. It is geographically broad within the bounds of China; temporally, while focusing on the period to 1949, it acknowledges China's incomparably long building traditions and recent urban development; architecturally, it treats contributions of Chinese and Western architects as integral rather than separate.

The central theme of this study is that China's encounter with modernity was mediated multifariously and dominated by contact with Western powers and through contact with an Eastern power, Japan. The heterogeneous origin of modernity in China is what makes its experience unique and its architectural encounters distinctive. These are investigated through a reevaluation of established knowledge of the subject and the inclusion of original archival and photographic material concentrating on Western influence through the Treaty Ports, the emergence of architecture as a profession in China, and Japan's colonial activities in Manchuria.

This study acknowledges the paradox presented by examining China using non-Chinese criteria and considers alternatives to the Westerncentricty that underlies existing approaches to non-Western topics. A multiple modernities approach not only questions the application of conventional theories of modernity or post-colonialism to the Chinese situation, but also offers a more effective way of comprehending the unique complexity of China's encounter with architectural modernity.

DR. YI-CHIH HUANG

Architecture, Space and National Identity: Modern Architecture in Taiwan (1895-2008)

Principal Supervisor: Iain Borden; Secondary: Adrian Forty

The Taiwanese people have suffered severe challenges and several changes to their national imaginations and cultural identifications during the country's period of modernisation since the late 19th century. In particular, following the political liberalisation process in the 1990s, nationalism and national identity has become a rising and controversial issue in Taiwanese society. This thesis explores the relations between architectural production and the formation of national identity in Taiwan's modernisation history. By putting Taiwan and its people as the research subjects, this thesis examines how different political authorities propagandised the imagined communities and promoted national identities to people through architectural production and disciplined spaces.

Influenced by ideas derived from semiotics and postcolonialism, this research sees the formation of national identity as a signification process in creating myths, and as a power struggle between the authority and the people. Architecture, as the symbolic representation of national identity, needs other cultural references and discursive narratives to gain its meanings; and, as the spatial construction of national identity, it also needs functional programmes and social contexts to discipline people's living and activities. By exposing the power structure of the signification process and the spatial administration, this research de-mystifies the authenticity of national identity.

Based on different power authorities that dominated the construction of national identity, this thesis explores four national identities and imaginations which appeared in Taiwan from 1895 to 2008: first is colonial identity under Japanese colonisation; second is Chinese identity under the Chinese Nationalist Party (KMT) administration; third is the prevalence of the American influenced modernist ideology; and fourth is the rise of Taiwanese nationalism. This thesis thus undertakes a comprehensive historical examination of how state powers manipulated national imaginations and constructed national identities through architectural production and people's daily lives.

Pevsner's Buildings of England in the North Porch of Wells Cathedral © CONTACT _Con-3812CA9560D Carolina Rodriguez Grenci

DR. ANNE HULTZSCH

An Archaeology of Perception: Verbal Descriptions of Architecture in Travel Writings

Principal Supervisor: Adrian Forty; Secondary: Iain Borden

This thesis relates two fields, the history of perception and that of language, to each other in order to argue that the ways in which we verbally describe buildings are inherently linked to the way in which we look at and make sense of them. It will show that what we understand when seeing, what we know to have seen, is shaped by the means we find to express and communicate it.

The subject matter of this research is the unfamiliar architectural object as it is perceived, described and imagined while travelling. Contextualising and linking various descriptions of built spaces in travel writings at distinct moments between the seventeenth and twentieth century, perceptual modes of British and German travellers in Italy and England are mapped out. Special emphasis is placed on the context of the seventeenth century, and the birth of Empiricism, which is argued to have led to a new way of perceiving as well as describing the built environment. Texts investigated include travel diaries, letters, guidebooks as well as novels by authors such as John Evelyn, John Bargrave, Daniel Defoe, Tobias Smollett, Johann Wolfgang von Goethe, Jacob Burckhardt, John Ruskin and Nikolaus Pevsner.

Through an archaeology of perception, local and often fragmentary narratives are constructed - 'snapshots' which focus on past moments rather than providing an extensive historical panorama. Processes of rendering, ordering, thinking, looking and reading the perceived are submitted to methods drawn from the following fields: the disciplines of history - the histories of art, sciences and literature - as well as the cognitive sciences, particularly cognitive linguistics, alongside the more specific concerns of architectural history and theory. Modes of perception located and retraced include notions of immediate and detached recording, of fragmented and vectorial structuring, of emotional versus truth-bearing seeing, of a pure and hyperreal looking as well as of itemizing against visual description.

Demolition of the workers' community with Steven Holl's Linked Hybrid in the background. Beijing, China, 2008.

DR. TAT LAM

Linked Hybrid in Beijing: Placing an American Building and its Architectural Concept in its Chinese Context

Principal Supervisor: Jan Birksted; Secondary: Adrian Forty

This thesis takes the American architect Steven Holl's design in Beijing, Linked Hybrid, as a case study to investigate the social, political and cultural context of China's contemporary architecture. The research focuses on the development, in an urban zone in the Dongzhimenwai area of Beijing, of a socialist paper mill community from the late 1980s into the Beijing Linked Hybrid community in 2010. The urban development process was analysed through six emic concepts, which were discovered in the course of ethnographic fieldwork research. These concepts are dayuan (big community or 大院), guanxi (personal connection or 关系), mianzi (face or 面子), shi (trend or 势), mofan (exemplary model or 模范) and shanzhai (fake product or 山寨).

Fieldwork trips were undertaken between 2007 and 2010 to understand how the local community members of the paper mill and Linked Hybrid perceived the changes in their living environment. Key community members and architectural practitioners were traced and interviewed during the period of research. Written documentation from the paper mill's propaganda department archives and the personal archives of an ex-worker about the area before the construction of Linked Hybrid, provided the historical context for the case study.

The Linked Hybrid occupants eventually built a wall to enclose their new residential community, which was specifically designed to be an open community to solve China's problematic urbanism. Thus, the architect's architectural ideals became ineffective when his architecture was situated in the Chinese context that is described in this thesis.

Construction of the boulevard périphérique, échangeur d'Issy-les-Moulineaux, Paris, c. 1964. Photo: Collection Pavillon de l'Arsenal, cliché DUVP.

DR. JACOB PASKINS

The Social Experience of Building Construction Work in and Around Paris During the 1960s
Principal Supervisor: Iain Borden; Secondary: Barbara Penner

My thesis explores the social experience of building construction work in and around Paris during the 1960s. My examination of construction sites shifts the focus of architectural history away from the personality of the architect by considering the wider public discourses of urban development. Building sites became spaces that expressed preoccupations about economic growth, labour immigration and the demolition of working-class districts. Drawing on media archives and rarely examined trade union material, my research reveals voices of publics usually excluded from narratives of the production of the city. My thesis contributes to a history of the experience of urban change.

My first chapter considers building sites from an international perspective, and explores discourses of French national identity with regard to urban transformation. I analyse debates about economic productivity, technology and labour immigration. Chapter Two examines media representation of building sites, and in particular considers how state television helped contribute to a discourse of Gaullist nationalism. Chapter Three explores the living conditions of construction workers. I analyse the existence of bidonvilles on the edge of Paris in the context of modernist architectural and urban theory. I examine how the popular press made an explicit connection between immigrant workers and crime, and I chart the attempts to improve living conditions for construction workers in France. Chapter Four investigates how state urban development overlooked the social impact of construction projects on existing communities. I analyse how local residents protested against the construction of suburban housing estates, roads and airports, and explore how community groups proposed alternative solutions. Finally, in Chapter Five I analyse how the French media and building workers' unions used the phenomenon of construction accidents to push their respective political and social agendas. Interpreted by different parties for differing reasons, construction disasters became the centre of debates about the social implications of modernising Paris.

Teatro del Mondo, 1979. Photo courtesy Paolo Portoghesi.

DR. LÉA-CATHERINE SZACKA

Exhibiting the Postmodern: Three Narratives for a history of the 1980 Venice Architecture Biennale
Principal Supervisor: Adrian Forty; Secondary: Iain Borden

This thesis explores the history of the 1980 Venice Architecture Biennale. Held under the title 'The Presence of the Past', this multi-faceted show displayed international contemporary architecture with an Italo-American twist. After this exhibition, postmodernism became a galvanic term in relation to architecture.

A growing specialist interest both in architectural exhibitions as a 'genre' of cultural manifestation, and in postmodernism as an architectural period or style were the theoretical impetus for this research. Looking at the question of architectural exhibitions in a postmodern context (1968 to 1988), the thesis seeks to unravel three very diverse yet interwoven narratives relating to the 1980 Venice Architecture Biennale. It draws upon recent literature on architectural exhibitions, newly accessible archival material, and original oral history accounts, and looks at exhibition techniques and exhibition spaces, institutional changes, and exhibitions as a site of confrontation between advocates of modern and postmodern architecture. It will serve to demonstrate that the 1980 Venice Architecture Biennale was a hinge in three ways: first, in the development of architectural exhibitions as a 'genre' of cultural manifestations, second, in the history of the Venice Biennale, and third, in the history of postmodernism. Successfully playing on postmodern form and content, the 1980 Biennale also marked a new relation between the worlds of art and architecture, arising from the crisis that had touched Italian cultural institutions in 1968, and the consequent transformation of the architectural product as end object.

Too often seen as an isolated event, the 1980 Venice Architecture Biennale was in reality linked to a series of debates that occurred before, during, and after the exhibition. As the first detailed historical account of the exhibition, this research sheds new light on the history of an event that, despite its transient nature, has continued to remain vividly present in the collective memory.

SUMMER SCHOOL

Bill Hodgson

London's population is currently around 7,500,000 and is growing. It is currently the most populous municipality in the European Union. New housing is required to accommodate the population, airports and railways are needed to move around. Previous attempts to deal with growth have included garden cities, suburban overspill estates and very high density housing projects. In 2012 the Bartlett School of Architecture's annual Summer School will tour the inner city and suburbs of London exploring these areas surroundings recording what they find and developing architectural responses. Proposals may be small interventions or larger projects. Using the Bartlett's excellent workshop and studios and University College London's associated facilities we will stage a practical symposium to survey, speculate and construct.

The Summer School will be held in London from Monday 6th August until Friday 17th August.

Each year we expect to accommodate a group of up to 80 participants of varying ages and differing backgrounds, including prospective university students, international students, secondary school students and those who are simply keen to develop their interest in architecture and the Bartlett School.

For further details to visit:http://www.bartlett.ucl.ac.uk/architecture/programmes/short-courses/summer-school

SUMMER FOUNDATION
Matthew Butcher

Tutors: **Carlos Jimenez Cenamor, Holly Fulton, Anne Ryan, Catrina Stewart**

Eventland

The Bartlett Summer Foundation introduces and prepares students for a future career in architecture and architectural education. Running over the summer, the ten-week programme provides students with a unique creative platform to improve their design communication skills as well as their individual conceptual and critical thinking. Participants are of varying ages and differing backgrounds, including prospective Bartlett students, international students, secondary school students and those who have a career change in mind and want to use it as a test bed to see if they are suited to a university degree in architecture.

As well as critical design skills and conceptual thought processes, students are also introduced to wider design themes and disciplines as a means to expand their understanding of architecture. Supplemental to architectural design classes are workshops on photography, metalwork, pattern cutting, carpentry and filmmaking.

Students this year explored ideas of architecture as a backdrop and architecture as an event, through observation as well as design proposition and construction. These architectural speculations not only housed and framed performance and event, they also performed and became an event. To inform these speculations students were asked to investigate London's transformation as it seeks to host its third Olympic games. As well as the developments in the Olympic park a wide range of temporary architectures, cultural events and infrastructures will convert the city for the duration of the games — creating a city within a city, a city of event.

The program for the course is structured in three parts. The first part, lasting 3 weeks, is about learning skills and approaches to creative problems. In the second part, lasting 4 weeks, students' work is focused around a series of one-week workshops. Each workshop centers on a specific area of architectural design, or one of its related design disciplines, such as theatre design, film or fashion. After completing this stage and for the remaining 3 weeks, students work on a personal project. This final stage is about personal development and realization, as well as learning to be aware of the general architectural context of London. Throughout the ten-week program and running parallel to the main curriculum are a series of visits to several of London's main museums, galleries and cultural events.

Emily Farmer, collage exercise.

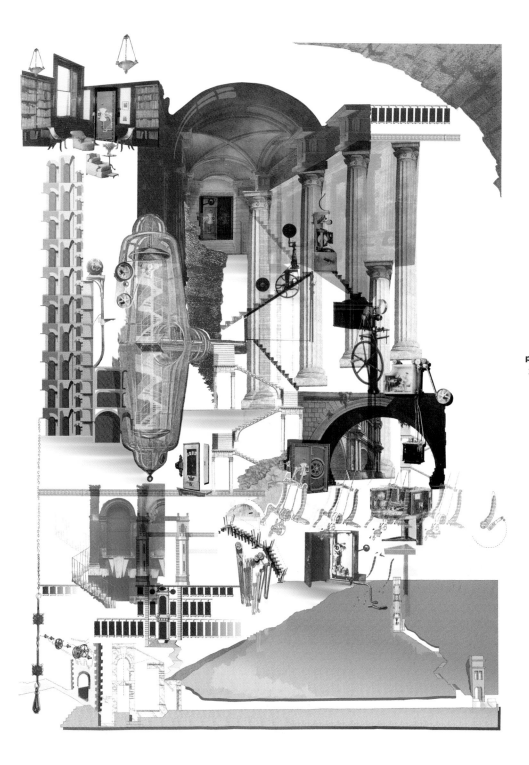

DMC LONDON

London's largest Selective Laser
Sintering (SLS) manufacturing bureau,
at the Bartlett School of Architecture.

SERVICES INCLUDE:

SLS Systems

High resolution. High accuracy models produced in strong, durable nylon plastic with ultra-white finish. Systems capable of producing bespoke or short-run manufactured products/components. Production of excellent master models for downstream processes and applications. Ideal solution for time-critical competition models. Form-fit-function models for pre-production testing and marketing.

Z-Corp 3D Printers

Quick and cost-effective. Early design visualisation and communication. Exploration of multiple design iterations. Models can be used for downstream processes and manufacturing applications.

Artec 3D Scanner

Easy to use, hand-held 3D scanning system for made or found objects. Data can be used for reverse engineering. Integration into new design constructs, animation and renderings.

CNC Routing

205 x 1.5m 3 axis router table for fabrication of large and medium scale parts.

5 Axis milling machine

Complex parts manufacture.

For more information contact Martin Watmough, Director DMC London, on:
Tel: +44 (020) 7679 8565
Fax: +44 (020) 7679 5424
Mobile: +44 (0)77 3979 7248
E-mail: dmc.bartlett@ucl.ac.uk

dmc.bartlett.ucl.ac.uk/architecture/resources/dmc.htm
Image credit: Richard Beckett, Aleksandrina Rizova, Sarat Babu

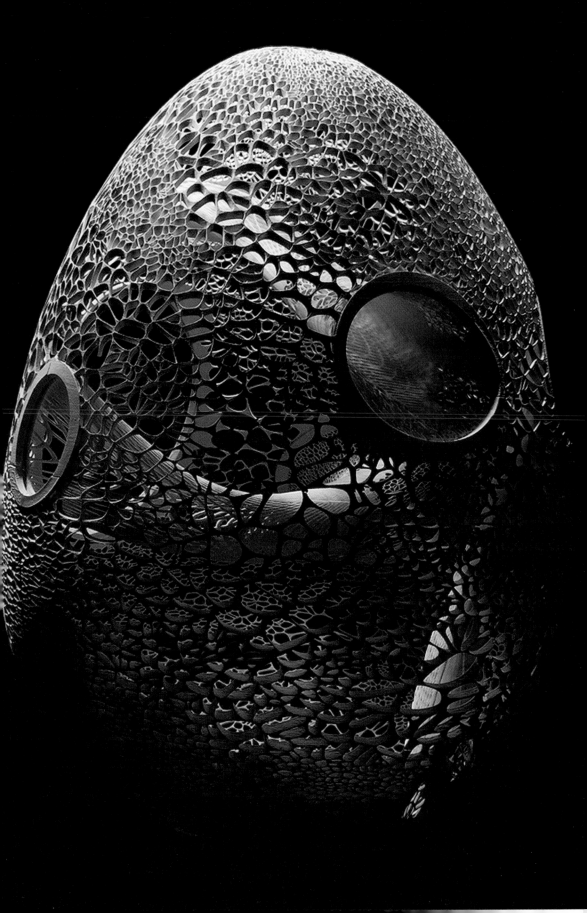

Bartlett Professor of Architecture

Frédéric Migayrou
Chair

Director of School

Dr. Marcos Cruz
Reader in Architecture

Professors & Directors

Professor Peter Bishop
Professor of Urban Design

Professor Iain Borden
Professor of Architecture
& Urban Culture,
Vice-Dean Communications,
Director of History & Theory

Professor Adrian Forty
MA Architectural History,
Programme Director,
Professor of
Architectural History

Professor Colin Fournier
Professor of Architecture
& Urban Planning

Professor Murray Fraser
Professor of Architecture
& Global Culture,
Vice-Dean of Research

Professor Stephen Gage
Professor of Innovative
Technology

Professor Christine Hawley
Professor of
Architectural Studies,
Director of Design

Professor Jonathan Hill
Professor of Architecture
& Visual Theory,
MPhil/PhD by Design,
Programme Director,
Director of Design

Professor CJ Lim
Professor of Architecture
& Cultural Design,
Vice-Dean International
Affairs, Director of
International Affairs

Professor Jane Rendell
Professor of Architecture
& Art

Laura Allen
Senior Lecturer, BSc
Architecture Programme
Director

Julia Backhaus
MArch Architecture
Programme Director

Dr Yeoryia Manolopoulou
Senior Lecturer,
Director of
Architectural Research

Dr Barbara Penner
BSc Architectural Studies
Programme Director,
MPhil/PhD History & Theory
Programme Director

Frosso Pimenides
BSc Architecture
Year 1 Director

Andrew Porter
MArch GAD Deputy
Programme Director

Peg Rawes
Senior Lecturer,
Director of
Architectural Research

Bob Sheil
Senior Lecturer,
Director of Technology
& Computing

Susan Ware
Director of
Professional Studies,
Part 3 Programme Director,
Sub-Dean and Faculty Tutor

Patrick Weber
BSc Architecture
Year 1 Director

Lecturers, Senior Lecturers & Visiting Professors

Alisa Andrasek
Dr Ben Campkin
Dr Marjan Colletti
Dr Penelope Haralambidou
Dirk Krolikowski
Niall McLaughlin
James O'Leary
Dr Peg Rawes
Dr Tania Sengupta
Mark Smout

Teaching Staff & Senior Teaching Fellows

DESIGN

YEAR 1

Timothy Barwell
Margaret Bursa
Johan Hybschmann
Brian O'Reilly
Frosso Pimenides
Sara Shafiei
Matt Springett
Nikolaos Travasaros
Patrick Weber

UNITS 0 — 23

Ben Addy
Laura Allen
Abi Ashton
Julia Backhaus
Paul Bavister
Johan Berglund
Kyle Buchanan
Matthew Butcher
Rhys Cannon
Carlos Jimenez Cenamor
Ming Chung
Marjan Colletti
Marcos Cruz
Pierre D'Avoine
Kate Davies
Ricardo de Ostos
Max Dewdney
Elizabeth Dow

Bernd Felsinger
Pedro Font Alba
Murray Fraser
David Garcia
Penelope Haralambidou
Jonathan Hill
Helen&Hard
Damjan Iliev
Nanette Jackowski
Jan Kattein
Julian Krüger
Chee-Kit Lai
cj Lim
Joerg Majer
Yeoryia Manolopoulou
Niall McLaughlin
Josep Mias
Ana Monrabal-Cook
Izaskun Chinchilla Moreno
James O'Leary
Luke Pearson
Andrew Porter
Bob Sheil
Mark Smout
Sabine Storp
Michiko Sumi
Michael Tite
Nick Tyson
Emmanuel Vercruysse
Paolo Zaide

MARCH URBAN DESIGN
Dragana Antic
Monika Bilska
Nicholas Boyarsky
Krisijan Cebzan
Darryl Chen
Jason Coleman
Ilaria Di Carlo
Robert Dye
Colin Fournier
Daewha Kang
Jonathan Kendall
Graciela Moreno Ternero
Camila Sotomayor

MARCH GRADUATE ARCHITECTURAL DESIGN
Alisa Andrasek
Marjan Colletti
Xavier de Kestelier
Stephen Gage
Ruairi Glynn
Jethro Hon
Guan Lee

Tea Lim
Luke Pearson
Andrew Porter
Jose Sanchez
Daniel Widrig
Fulvio Wirz

HISTORY & THEORY
Tilo Amhoff
Nicholas Beech
Ben Campkin
Megha Chand
Edward Denison
Eva Eylers
Adrian Forty
Christophe Gerard
Jon Goodbun
Yat Ming Loo
Steve Parnell
Jacob Paskins
Barbara Penner
Peg Rawes
Jane Rendell
Tania Sengupta
Brian Stater
Rachel Stevenson
Nina Vollenbroker
Robin Wilson

TECHNOLOGY
Roz Barr
Scott Batty
Stephen Gage
Michael Hadi
James Hampton
Bill Hodgson
Steve Johnson
Tim Lucas
Christian Nold
Luke Olsen
Bob Sheil
Paul Smoothy
Andrew Whiting
Oliver Wilton

PROFESSIONAL STUDIES
Kit Allsop
Sonia Arbaci
Elena Besussi
Elizabete Cidre
Simon Pilling
David Rosenberg
Soo Ware
Katy Wood

RESEARCH ASSOCIATES AND FELLOWS
Dr Jan Birksted
Hilary Powell

DMC LONDON, MEDIA HUB, WORKSHOP, AV, CADCAM
Abi Abdolwahabi
Martin Avery
Richard Beckett
Matt Bowles
Nick Browne
Bim Burton
Justin Goodyer
Richard Grimes
Simon Kennedy
Matthew Shaw
Paul Smoothy
Will Trossell
Emmanuel Vercruysse
Martin Watmough

ADMINISTRATION
GENERAL ADMINISTRATION
Emer Girling
Michelle Bush
Tom Mole
Luis Rego
(research)
Rachael Burnett

COMMUNICATIONS AND WEBSITE
Nadia O'Hare
(communications)
Michelle Lukins
Jean Garrett (website)

FINANCE AND HR
Stoll Michael
Carly Cunningham
Sheetal Saujani

PROFESSIONAL STUDIES
Naz Siddique
Indigo Rohrer
Kim Macneill

FACILITIES
Kevin Jones
John Riley
Matt Wright

www.bartlett.ucl.ac.uk

PUBLISHER: Bartlett School of Architecture, UCL

EDITOR: Marcos Cruz

ART DIRECTION & DESIGN: Johanna Bonnevier, Johan Berglund

EDITORIAL COORDINATION: Nadia O'Hare, Bim Adewunmi

Printed in England by Quadracolor

ISBN 978-0-9568445-7-6

For more information on all the programmes and modules at
the UCL Bartlett Faculty of the Built Environment, please
visit www.bartlett.ucl.ac.uk

Bartlett School of Architecture, UCL
Wates House
22 Gordon Street
London
WC1H 0QB

T. +44 (0)20 7679 7504
F. +44 (0)20 7679 4831

architecture@ucl.ac.uk
www.bartlett.ucl.ac.uk